I0819499

Advance praise for *The Troika*

"In a late-night meeting with Markus Wolf in Berlin, I sized up the old East German spymaster against the backdrop of my professional fascination with his world. In that discussion I saw the contradictions in the man; I saw a man who kept himself faceless as he guarded the secrets, and at the same time I saw a master showman. It was a rewarding glimpse into Wolf's convoluted soul."

—Robert De Niro, actor, director, and film producer

"Markus Wolf was the architect of the most effective intelligence service in the old Warsaw Pact, the one service I considered perhaps my toughest adversary during my years in the CIA's Soviet–East European Division. After Wolf and I had both retired from our spy games, we met in Berlin to reminisce over those years. I found Wolf possessed all the qualities of a master spy: a probing intellect, a sense of charming inquisitiveness, and that most important trait, the hopeless romantic. *The Troika* charts the journey of a scruffy German kid coming of age in Moscow during World War II, to becoming perhaps the boldest spymaster of the Cold War. A remarkable read."

—Milt Bearden, former CIA division chief and coauthor of *The Main Enemy*

"This is the story of a remarkable friendship born in a closed and secretive world of the 1930s, set in the context of rising Nazism, the international Communist movement, and Stalin's purges—a fascinating window on a dark and distant world. Most amazingly, the story is told by one of the most secretive actors of the Cold War, trying to make sense of his own life through the lives of his brother and his friends just as his world crumbles and Germany is about to reunite."

—Svetlana Savranskaya, director of Russia programs, National Security Archive, George Washington University

"Anglophone scholars and students of Germany, especially of East Germany (the GDR) and its secret police operations, will be delighted with the publication and translation of "spymaster" Markus Wolf's 1989 rendition of *The Troika,* his brother Konrad's original film scenario exploring the relationship between three "international" friends, who grew up and went to school in the Soviet Union in the 1930s and met one another in occupied Berlin after the war. Expertly edited by Katharina Friedla and by Christian Ostermann, who also contributes an excellent introduction, the book, which includes scores of interesting documents, reveals much about Wolf's state of mind in 1989 on the eve of the collapse of the Berlin Wall and the end of the GDR. Not unlike his hero Mikhail Gorbachev, Wolf indicates he desperately hoped to save communism by reforming it."

—Norman Naimark, Robert and Florence McDonnell
Professor of East European Studies, Stanford University;
distinguished visiting fellow, Hoover Institution;
and senior fellow, Freeman-Spogli Institute

The Troika

The Troika

A Story of Three Families, Friendship, and the Cold War

Markus Wolf

Edited by
Christian F. Ostermann and Katharina Friedla

Translated by
Sabine Berendse, with Paul Clements

HOOVER INSTITUTION PRESS
STANFORD UNIVERSITY | STANFORD, CALIFORNIA

With its eminent scholars and world-renowned library and archives, the Hoover Institution seeks to improve the human condition by advancing ideas that promote economic opportunity and prosperity while securing and safeguarding peace for America and all mankind. The views expressed in its publications are entirely those of the authors and do not necessarily reflect the views of the staff, officers, or Board of Overseers of the Hoover Institution.

hoover.org

Hoover Institution Press Publication No. 743

Hoover Institution at Leland Stanford Junior University,
Stanford, California 94305-6003

Originally published as *Die Troika* by Markus Wolf, Rowohlt Taschenbuch Verlag, Reinbek bei Hamburg, March 1991

First printing 2026
32 31 30 29 28 27 26 7 6 5 4 3 2 1

Manufactured in the United States of America
Printed on acid-free, archival-quality paper

Library of Congress Cataloging-in-Publication Data
Names: Wolf, Markus, 1923-2006 author | Ostermann, Christian F. editor | Friedla, Katharina editor
Title: The troika : a story of three families, friendship, and the Cold War / Markus Wolf ; edited by Christian F. Ostermann and Katharina Friedla ; translated by Sabine Berendse and Paul Clements.
Other titles: Troika. English | Hoover Institution Press publication 743.
Description: Stanford, California : Hoover Institution Press, 2026. | Series: Hoover Institution Press publication ; no. 743 | Translation of: Die troika. | Includes bibliographical references and index. | Summary: "Three expatriate Communist families in Moscow find their bonds and beliefs tested as they are scattered by World War II and confront the consequential ideologies of the twentieth century"—Provided by publisher.
Identifiers: LCCN 2026002858 (print) | LCCN 2026002859 (ebook) | ISBN 9780817926946 cloth | ISBN 9780817926960 epub | ISBN 9780817926984 pdf
Subjects: LCSH: Wolf, Konrad, 1925-1982 | Wloch, Lothar, 1923-1976 | Fischer, Victor, 1924-2023 | Germans—Russia (Federation)—undefined—Moscow—Biography | Germans—United States—Biography | Communism—Germany—History—20th century—Sources | Germany—Biography
Classification: LCC CT1063 .W6513 2026 (print) | LCC CT1063 (ebook) | DDC 920.043—dc23/eng/20260202
LC record available at https://lccn.loc.gov/2026002858
LC ebook record available at https://lccn.loc.gov/2026002859

Contents

List of Abbreviations

ARD	Arbeitsgemeinschaft der öffentlich-rechtlichen Rundfunkanstalten der Bundesrepublik Deutschland (German public TV station)
CPSU	Communist Party of the Soviet Union
DEFA	Deutsche Film-Aktiengesellschaft (East German film studio)
EKKI	Exekutivkomitee der Kommunistischen Internationale (Executive Committee of the Communist International)
FDJ	Freie Deutsche Jugend (Free German Youth)
FRG	Federal Republic of Germany (the former West Germany)
GDR	German Democratic Republic (the former East Germany)
HVA	Hauptverwaltung A, or Hauptverwaltung Aufklärung (the Main Directorate for Reconnaissance; a department of the MfS)
KJVD	Kommunistischer Jugendverband Deutschlands (Young Communist League of Germany)
KPD	Kommunistische Partei Deutschlands (Communist Party of Germany)
MfS	Ministerium für Staatssicherheit (Ministry for State Security, or the Stasi)
NKVD	Narodny Komissariat Vnutrennikh Del (People's Commissariat for Internal Affairs)
NSDAP	Nationalsozialistische Deutsche Arbeiterpartei (National Socialist German Workers' Party, or the Nazi Party)
RAF	Red Army Faction
SD	Sicherheitsdienst (Security Service)

SED	Sozialistische Einheitspartei Deutschlands (Socialist Unity Party of Germany)
SPD	Sozialdemokratische Partei Deutschlands (Social Democratic Party of Germany)
USPD	Unabhängige Sozialdemokratische Partei Deutschlands (Independent Social Democratic Party of Germany)
USSR	Union of Soviet Socialist Republics
ZDF	Zweites Deutsches Fernsehen (German public TV station)

Foreword to the Translation

Upon the founding of the institution that bears his name, Herbert Hoover articulated a mission that was "from its records, to recall the voice of experience against the making of war, and by the study of these records and their publication, to recall man's endeavors to make and preserve peace." Since its founding in 1919, the Hoover Institution has remained faithful to the vision of its founder.

From its beginning as a small collection of documents on World War I, the Hoover Institution Library & Archives has become a comprehensive research repository on the history of war, revolution, and peace from the beginning of the twentieth century to the present time and is widely recognized as one of the world's great collections. It has earned a reputation as a dedicated steward and custodian of the historical record from sources that might otherwise have disappeared forever. Instead, at the Library & Archives, they are accessible to all.

We are honored to welcome the Markus Wolf collection to the Hoover Institution Library & Archives. For thirty-four years, Wolf, who died in 2006, was chief of the foreign intelligence department of the Ministry for State Security—the Stasi—of the socialist German Democratic Republic. Additionally, the Hoover Institution Press is pleased to present the first publication in English of *Die Troika*, written by the former East German spymaster in 1989. *Die Troika* was Wolf's debut as an author. A collection of narrative and historical materials, the book was among the first in East Germany to break with the taboo against discussing the crimes of Stalin's Great Terror. It became part of a movement that, thanks to the courage of the East German citizens in their peaceful revolution for freedom, led to the toppling of the Berlin Wall and ended Germany's Cold War–era division.

The substantial materials now at Hoover documenting Markus Wolf's life and work are a major source on the workings of the East German foreign intelligence service, which, under Wolf's leadership, was widely credited as being one of the most effective of the Cold War. While the files of the former Ministry for State Security on domestic surveillance and repression have become accessible to the public in Germany over the past thirty years, large parts of the Stasi's foreign intelligence records fell victim to systematic destruction in 1989–90. Wolf's papers therefore provide a unique vantage point into the history of the Cold War's intelligence battles.

As a young scholar of the Soviet Union and Eastern Europe, and even as a National Security Council staff member for George H. W. Bush at the end of the Cold War, I would have given anything to have access to these insights and this material. I am grateful that the collection will be available to future scholars in understanding this crucial period in human history. The acquisition and preservation of the vast Wolf archive will facilitate historical analysis that can inform current policy issues and be an indispensable source for scholars for generations to come.

Condoleezza Rice
Tad and Dianne Taube Director of the Hoover Institution
Sixty-Sixth Secretary of State

Acknowledgments

We would like to express our sincere gratitude to Condoleezza Rice, director of the Hoover Institution, and the Institution's Board of Overseers for their generous support of this book and for facilitating the acquisition of the Markus Wolf papers.

We are grateful to Andrea Wolf for making this publication possible and for entrusting the Hoover Institution with a collection to which she devoted much of her life to preserving and safeguarding.

Katharina Friedla
Christian F. Ostermann

Markus Wolf's *Troika*

An Introduction

Christian F. Ostermann

Shortly before 7 p.m. on March 9, 1989, Markus Wolf (1923–2006), the retired chief of East Germany's foreign intelligence service (known by its German acronym, HVA, for Hauptverwaltung Aufklärung) arrived at the Friedrichsfelde Palace in East Berlin's Tierpark. The neoclassical building that had escaped the widespread destruction of Berlin during World War II was to be the setting for the public launch of Wolf's book *The Troika*. The thunderstorm of flashlights awaiting Wolf was the beginning of a new phase in his career, that of author and public persona, dramatically different from decades of toiling in the shadows of the cloak-and-dagger world of espionage. Earlier that day the West German TV station ARD had taped an hour-long interview with him. Now, in the spotlights of the cameras of the other major TV station, ZDF, he faced "tough questions" by a reporter and then held a public reading of his book. The once-secretive master spy became an overnight celebrity: "It was like in the movie theater," he noted in his diary, with what would become a familiar mixture of conceit and self-effacement, "the arrival of the great star" that felt "somehow entirely unreal."[1]

The publication of Markus Wolf's *Die Troika: Geschichte eines nichtgedrehten Films* ("The story of a film that was not produced") was indeed a small sensation in divided Germany at the time of its release in

1. Markus Wolf, diary entry, March 9, 1989, Markus Wolf Archive, Berlin, Germany (hereafter cited as "MWA"). Wolf noted the next day that the two major West German news shows had reported on the event: "Compliments by everyone that got in touch." Some remarked on his youthful appearance, which, according to the ARD, "had a touch of Paul Newman." Wolf, diary entry, March 10, 1989, MWA. See also Serge Schmemann, "Clamor in the East; Old Master Spy in East Berlin Tells Why He Backs Changes," *New York Times*, November 22, 1989.

March 1989: "the phantom gives a reading," as one prominent West German daily headlined its coverage.[2] As Wolf himself admitted, the public attention was largely due to his reputation as a secretive spymaster. During the Cold War, Wolf had led the foreign intelligence organization for the Ministry for State Security (MfS, colloquially referred to as the "Stasi"). At its peak, this organization fielded some 4,600 full-time operators aided by some ten thousand "unofficial collaborators." Some 1,500 of Wolf's agents had penetrated deeply into the political, economic, and sociocultural fabric of West Germany. Dubbed in the West as "the man without a face," Western intelligence services had failed to obtain a true photo of Wolf until just a decade earlier, almost thirty years after Wolf had first risen to lead one of the most effective, and certainly one of the most notorious, espionage services of the Cold War. West German intelligence had famously leaked the photo to the prominent West German weekly *Der Spiegel*, which in March 1979 splashed it across its cover.[3]

Authored by the East German intelligence establishment's "éminence grise," *The Troika* also stood out for its then-stunning acknowledgment of the horrors of the Stalinist purges and terror of the mid-1930s. However cautious and incomplete this reckoning was, it helped overcome an important taboo upon which the German Democratic Republic (GDR) had been built. The Great Terror of 1937–1938 unleashed by Soviet dictator Joseph V. Stalin had led to the arrest of some 1.5 million people. Hundreds of thousands of Soviet citizens and foreigners were executed or perished in the Gulag's labor camps. In the course of the "German Operation" launched in July 1937 by the People's Commissariat for Internal Affairs of the Soviet Union, or NKVD, some 70 percent of the German section of the Moscow-based Communist International (Comintern) had been arrested. Many were killed; hundreds vanished within the Gulag system. The arrests had touched virtually every family among the German political émigrés that had escaped Nazi persecution by coming to the Soviet Union. It was a deeply traumatic experience—one whose memory those who survived

2. "Das Phantom hält Lesestunde," *Süddeutsche Zeitung*, March 17, 1989; "'Troika': Sensation in Leipzig," *Braunschweiger Zeitung*, March 7, 1989.

3. "DDR-Geheimdienstchef enttarnt: Die Spione des Markus Wolf," *Der Spiegel*, March 5, 1979, https://www.spiegel.de/spiegel/print/index-1979-10.html.

brought with them when they returned to Germany after the end of the war. Yet, until 1989, these émigrés, some of whom rose to leadership positions in the GDR, were forced to abide by a code of silence about what they had experienced. The repression of knowledge and memory of the Great Terror became, as Andreas Petersen has argued, a part of the schizophrenic mental foundation of the new state.[4] In its break with the official taboo in East Germany about Stalin's crimes, *The Troika* was a step in the direction of giving voice to the repressed but never forgotten memory. In that, it also aligned with the glasnost (opening) process taking place in the Soviet Union under Mikhail Gorbachev—a process strenuously resisted by East Germany's hard-line leader Erich Honecker, secretary-general of the Socialist Unity Party of Germany (known by its German acronym, SED).[5] Honecker, like many others in the party-state elite, considered any discussion of the Stalinist crimes detrimental to the cause of socialism, undermining the antifascist foundation of the GDR and delegitimizing SED rule.

The Troika tells the poignant and gripping story of three childhood friends coming of age in Moscow in the mid-1930s. The main protagonists are Markus Wolf's younger brother Konrad, whose family had fled to the Soviet Union to escape Nazi persecution; Lothar Wloch, the son of German communists long involved in Soviet espionage; and Victor Fischer, born to Markoosha and Louis Fischer, the latter a well-known and Soviet-friendly American journalist.[6] The boys formed an inseparable threesome in the streets around Moscow's Old Arbat neighborhood. The older brothers George ("Yura") Fischer and Markus Wolf served as deuteragonists in the story they would eventually come to tell. By the mid-1930s, the lives of the Troika and their families unfolded in the shadow of the Stalinist terror enveloping the country and its community of German émigrés. Lothar's father, Wilhelm Wloch, was arrested in 1937 and eventually perished in a Soviet prison. Konrad's father, the writer and physician

4. Andreas Petersen, *Die Moskauer: Wie das Stalintrauma die DDR prägte* (S. Fischer, 2019).

5. On Gorbachev, see William Taubman, *Gorbachev: His Life and Times* (W. W. Norton, 2017); and Vladislav M. Zubok, *Collapse: The Fall of the Soviet Union* (Yale University Press, 2021).

6. On Victor Fischer, see Victor Fischer and Charles Wohlforth, *To Russia with Love: An Alaskan's Journey* (University of Alaska Press, 2012).

Friedrich Wolf, managed to escape likely arrest in Moscow by volunteering in early 1938 for service in the International Brigades fighting in the Spanish Civil War. Detained on his way to Spain in France, he would not return to Moscow until 1941. For Louis Fischer, the Stalinist show trials and waves of arrests began a process of estrangement from the Soviet Union. As fear and panic gripped every segment of Soviet society, it fell to the troika of mothers, left behind in Moscow, to keep the families together and fight for their survival. With the onset of World War II, the paths of the three *Troika* protagonists diverged: Lothar returned to Nazi Germany and Victor to the United States, leaving Konrad behind. The three fought on different fronts in the war—Lothar serving in the German Luftwaffe, Victor in the US Army, and Konrad in the Red Army. Miraculously, all three survived the war. At war's end, the three found themselves on opposing sides of the emerging Cold War fault lines: Konrad in East Germany, Lothar in what would become West Berlin, and Victor in the US. *The Troika* chronicles the attempts of the three (and the two older brothers), now as adults forged in the crucible of Stalinism and war, to rekindle their deep bonds of friendship across geographical and ideological divisions.

In his foreword to the German paperback edition of *The Troika* (2000), Egon Bahr, the former national security advisor to West German Chancellor Willy Brandt—whose 1970s *Ostpolitik* had allowed for rapprochement with the East and who resigned after one of his closest advisors was exposed as one of Wolf's agents in 1974—recalled being impressed by the politically explosive nature of the book. Bahr immediately recommended it to Brandt, by then one of West Germany's elder statespeople, as an indication that the East German communist state could "collapse overnight like a house of cards."[7] Yet during the tumultuous year of 1989, *The Troika's* publication was just one moment in a torrent of unprecedented and extraordinary events. The media sensation surrounding Wolf's book was soon overshadowed by the worsening crisis in East Germany and the revolutionary changes that would climax in the fall of the Berlin Wall in November 1989.

Still, *The Troika* played a role in the "endgame" of the socialist system in East Germany. In the midst of the revolutionary upheaval engulfing the

7. Egon Bahr, foreword to *Die Troika: Geschichte eines nichtgedrehten Films. Nach einer Idee von Konrad Wolf*, by Markus Wolf (Aufbau Verlag, 2003), 11.

country, the book was among the first public indications that, beyond the growing civil society opposition, there were some among the political elite and state authorities—even within the hated and feared State Security apparatus—that were critical of Honecker's dogmatic course and that sought reforms akin to those launched by Gorbachev after his rise to power in 1985. Wolf's conscious choice of an empathetic narrative style reinforced the book's effect in opening space for discussion of sensitive subjects. With its sympathetic, non-polemical portrayal of the American and West Berlin protagonists that eschewed the class-struggle overtones prevalent in publications by regime insiders, *The Troika* also looked past the friend-foe orthodoxy that undergirded the SED's media and cultural policies. For parts of the communist party membership and the intelligentsia, for the West German and international media, but also in his own mind, *The Troika*'s author became a beacon of hope for reform in East Germany. The leading conservative West German daily, the *Frankfurter Allgemeine Zeitung*, hailed the *Troika* author as a "staunch proponent of openness and reflectiveness, for social and political reforms, for truth and justice."[8] Wolf's often packed book readings and discussions contributed to mobilizing parts of East German civil society in the autumn of 1989.[9] Even within the increasingly organized civic opposition movement, some viewed Wolf as a potential ally. Wolf's embrace of Gorbachev's reforms set him apart from efforts by the East German government to distance itself from the Soviet leader's new course. *The Troika*'s message—that it was possible to forge a mutual understanding of our shared humanity and a sense of common responsibility, even friendship, despite being firmly anchored in starkly different social and political systems—seemed to position its author, especially in the eyes of Western media, as a glasnost-friendly alternative to the Honecker clique.[10]

8. *Frankfurter Allgemeine Zeitung* article quoted in "Ventil geöffnet: Der frühere Geheimdienstchef Markus ('Mischa') Wolf will die DDR auflockern," *Der Spiegel*, June 12, 1989.

9. "Bei Wolfs Lesereise treffen sich die Reformanhänger," *Die Welt*, April 18, 1989.

10. Ilko-Sascha Kowalczuk, *Endspiel: Die Revolution von 1989 in der DDR* (C. H. Beck, 2009), 372; Christoph Links, interview with Christian Ostermann, July 21, 2022. Links was in charge of public relations for *Die Troika* in 1989 as an assistant to Aufbau publishing director Elmar Faber.

Not everyone believed Wolf was truly a reformer. After an extensive interview, *Der Spiegel* reporters concluded that Wolf might be a "brilliant intellectual" but remained an apparatchik who favored a controlled opening of the GDR's political valves that intended not a reform, but a stabilization of the system.[11] Others criticized that in dealing with Stalin's personality cult and monstrous crimes Wolf remained vague, general, well short of an outright and forceful condemnation.[12] For the many victims who had suffered at the hands of East Germany's State Security Service, the "sword and shield" of the ruling communist party, it must have been irritating, even outrageous, to witness a former State Security colonel general, a man from the upper ranks of the party-state, being hailed as a reformist alternative to Honecker.[13] The enchantment of large parts of the Western media with the spy-chief-turned-author seemed especially galling. To hear the former deputy minister for state security argue in the West German weekly *Die Zeit* that *The Troika* demonstrated that "despite different ways of thinking and despite opposing positions on important issues, it is possible to treat each other reasonably, even amicably, if one respects one another," must have struck many, not just within the dissident community, as the height of opportunism and hypocrisy in the face of ongoing and escalating repression in the GDR.[14]

Markus Wolf had headed the HVA from 1952 to 1986, reaching the leadership position at the young age of twenty-nine. Critically important to his rise atop the agency—one that was considered by Moscow to be a most sensitive and significant intelligence and national security asset—had been Wolf's trust relationship with the Soviet Union. As émigrés from Nazi Germany, Wolf's family had found refuge in Moscow in 1934. Spending his teenage years in the Soviet capital, Wolf developed a deep sense of belonging there, joined the communist youth organization as soon as he was of age, and later became a Soviet citizen. He had spent the wartime

11. "Ventil geöffnet."

12. "Ex-Geheimdienstchef der DDR bricht mit Tabus," *Berliner Morgenpost*, August 27, 1989.

13. The MfS was considered part of East Germany's armed forces and used a military nomenclature.

14. Lew Hohmann, "Um die Wahrheit kommt man nicht herum: Ein Gespräch mit Markus Wolf, dem ehemaligen Geheimdienstchef der DDR," *Die Zeit*, March 24, 1989.

training at a special school of the Soviet-controlled Comintern for infiltration missions into Nazi Germany. Later in the war Wolf became instrumental in Soviet psychological warfare as an announcer for the Moscow-based German People's Radio. After the war, he was sent to Berlin and became part of a small team of Moscow-trained German communists to take over the Berliner Rundfunk radio station, which played an important role in Soviet occupation politics in Berlin and throughout the Soviet occupied zone of Germany. He then was dispatched to cover the International Military Tribunal in Nuremberg, set up by the United States, Great Britain, France, and the Soviet Union to try Nazi Germany's leaders. After the establishment of the GDR in 1949, Wolf joined its foreign ministry and was sent to Moscow to assist with the opening of the East German embassy. Two years later he was assigned to the country's foreign intelligence service, then ostensibly part of the foreign ministry. Appointed its leader just a year later, he went on to direct the service for some thirty-four years, serving most of his tenure as a deputy to Minister for State Security Erich Mielke.[15] In that role he occupied a unique vantage point in the German and global Cold War. As it would turn out, the *Troika* project would be critical to Wolf's decision to quit his service as a spy chief.[16]

The Troika had actually been his younger brother Konrad's idea. One of the three *Troika* protagonists himself, Konrad Wolf (1925–1982) became an internationally recognized film director in the GDR and later served as president of the East German Academy of Arts. Throughout his career, Konrad Wolf had grappled with politically sensitive subjects, at times

15. The HVA was integrated into the MfS in 1953.

16. For biographical background about Markus Wolf, see Alexander Reichenbach, *Chef der Spione: Die Markus-Wolf-Story* (Deutsche Verlags Anstalt, 1992); Leslie Colitt, *Spymaster: The Real-Life Karla, His Moles, and the East German Secret Police* (Addison-Wesley, 1995); Karl Wilhelm Fricke, "Markus Wolf (*1923): Drei Jahrzehnte Spionagechef des SED-Staates," in *Konspiration als Beruf: Deutsche Geheimdienstchefs im Kalten Krieg*, ed. Dieter Krüger and Armin Wagner (Ch. Links Verlag, 2003); Nicole Glocke and Peter Jochen Winters, *Im geheimen Krieg der Spionage: Hans-Georg Wieck (BND) und Markus Wolf (MfS)—zwei biografische Porträts* (Mitteldeutscher Verlag, 2014), 231–493; Kristie Macrakis, "Markus Wolf: From the Shadows to the Limelight," in *Spy Chiefs: Intelligence Leaders in Europe, the Middle East, and Asia, Volume 2*, ed. Paul Maddrell, Christopher Moran, Ioanna Iordanu, and Mark Stout (Georgetown University Press, 2018); and Peter Jochen Winters, *Markus Wolf: Ein biografisches Porträt* (Metropol-Verlag, 2021).

deploying autobiographical elements. His 1958 film *Sonnensucher*, which dealt with the controversial topic of Soviet-controlled uranium mining in East Germany, had been censored and not released to movie theaters until 1972. As Academy president, Konrad had found himself at the center of the increasingly tense relationship between a growing number of critical writers and other artists and the hard-line party leadership. The SED politburo's decision to expatriate dissident songwriter Wolfgang Biermann in 1976 had aggravated Konrad's fraught balancing act between parts of the intelligentsia and the regime.[17]

The idea for the *Troika* project had first come to Konrad in the mid-1960s. He revisited the idea at the end of what turned out to be the last reunion of the three Moscow friends in the United States in April 1975. Lothar, the "middle horse" of the threesome, died in the summer of 1976. Since then, Konrad had struggled to make sense of the story and to turn it into a film script. It tormented him in his final years. A short text dated January 6, 1977, outlined the basic idea, but Konrad had failed to go beyond that by the time of his death in March 1982. It spoke to the importance of the project for Konrad that even in his dying days he kept a black leather-bound case with the *Troika* fragments at his bedside.

The *Troika* idea almost died with him. When the question "And what will become of *The Troika*?" arose the day after Konrad's death, Markus Wolf, by his own admission still under the impression of the last feverish conversations about the project at his brother's deathbed, spontaneously replied: "*The Troika* is dead." But toward the end of the conversation with Konrad's closest collaborators, Wolf came back to the subject: "Unless *The Troika* lives on in me." Wolf took the black leather case into his possession, not only because it had been his brother's unfinished "favorite project," but because, as he noted in his diary somewhat vaguely, he might relate it to ideas that had increasingly come to preoccupy him. Thus he declared the material, including the unfinished film narrative, "an absolute taboo for everyone else . . . in order to leave all paths open for the future."[18] His brother's death had deeply shaken Wolf, and perhaps in reminding him of

17. On Konrad Wolf, see Wolfgang Jacobsen and Rolf Aurich, *Der Sonnensucher Konrad Wolf: Biografie* (Aufbau Verlag, 2005).

18. Markus Wolf, letter to Hermann Herlinghaus, n.d. (1985), MWA.

his own mortality, pushed him to pursue ideas that had stirred in him for some time. *The Troika* would become his means of addressing troubling developments in the GDR's socialist reality that had frustrated Wolf for some time.

Just a few weeks after his brother's death, Wolf raised the possibility of resigning as deputy minister with Mielke and Honecker. It is quite clear that his intent to work on the *Troika* project was one of a number of reasons behind his wish to retire at the—young by Communist world standards—age of sixty. But his first foray into a post-MfS career was quickly shut down. According to his successor, Werner Grossmann, Mielke rejected the request, and Honecker was reportedly outraged by Wolf's intention to retire: "A general does not leave his troops." At a time when tensions between the United States and Russia were spiking again in the wake of the Soviet invasion of Afghanistan, the Cold War preoccupied Wolf. His day job left preciously little time to push ahead with the *Troika* project: "Reality is exceedingly holding me captive," he noted in his diary. Still, the project kept drawing him in. Former MfS colleagues claim to have noticed how Wolf increasingly withdrew from the day-to-day business of the spy service, engaging only in the most important planning and control functions. After he had settled on a successor, Wolf finally retired from his leadership positions in the MfS at the end of 1986.[19]

Despite the existence of the black case, there was initially less material for *The Troika* than Wolf had expected: "Some profound expressions of will from Koni [Konrad], but no solutions." Wolf's initial focus was the three protagonists who were anchored in different social systems after 1945, as he captured his thinking in his diary: "Each of the 3 . . . has valid and persuasive reasons for his world view and his way of life. No one has a monopoly on the truth. Life and the environment have shaped each of them. . . . None of the three has completely disconnected from the 'romantic' period of youth in Moscow." Wolf asserted that it was "characteristic" of all three that none of them was "completely content in their area of life, can fully identify with the society in which they live." Each

19. Werner Grossmann, *Bonn im Blick: Die DDR-Aufklärung aus der Sicht ihres letzten Chefs* (Das Neue Berlin, 2007), 100–102; Markus Wolf, diary entry, June 12, 1982, MWA.

would feel at home with the "romantic alternatives" who "simply had enough of the establishment in East and West." A truly authentic portrayal of these different perspectives, Wolf contemplated, would break with the prevailing ideological stereotypes and cultural-political proscriptions. He would take up the project as a way to "raise certain problems of socialism" in East Germany—above all questions of cultural, youth, and media policy, "without being able to answer them all." For the former spy chief, used to managing an organization that provided intelligence findings to the party-state leadership, this was unfamiliar territory. Betraying his image as a self-assured intelligence boss, Wolf approached his new endeavor with some trepidation, unsure if he could master the project.[20]

Wolf's personal archive reflects the immense amount of research that went into producing the *Troika* story. Wolf, for example, listened to the extensive tape recordings that Konrad had made during a 1977 trip to the United States with the other remaining *Troika* protagonist Victor Fischer. Even more important was the research by filmmakers Lew Hohmann and Wolfgang Kohlhaase for a documentary about the life and work of Konrad Wolf, *Die Zeit die bleibt*, which was broadcast in a heavily censored form on GDR television in 1985. The screening of the footage that the film team had shot in the US, especially interviews with Victor Fischer and his older brother George, brought back memories for Wolf: "Suddenly everything is very near again, the Troika story is not only becoming more and more vivid, it is taking on a concrete form," he noted in his diary in November 1984.[21] Starting in February 1983, a series of conversations with Konrad's closest friend and collaborator, the Bulgarian screenwriter Angel Jäcki Wagenstein ("he was like a brother to Koni, perhaps even more"), pulled Wolf ever more deeply into the *Troika* project.[22] Years earlier, Wagenstein had warned Konrad that he, Konrad, might struggle to account for his own intellectual and political evolution honestly—that is, as deeply conflicted as to those of the other *Troika* protagonists. With some relief—or perhaps with the need to reassure himself—Markus Wolf confided to his

20. Markus Wolf, diary entries, June 12, 1982, and March 24, 1983, MWA. For example, depicting life in the United States appeared to him as a "great problem."

21. Markus Wolf, diary entries, January 31, 1984, and November 9, 1984, MWA.

22. Markus Wolf, diary entry, February 27, 1983, MWA.

diary that his views on the *Troika* story aligned with those of Wagenstein. Still, Wagenstein apparently remained skeptical, telling Wolf in June 1986 that he should shelve the project for two years and then publish it as an "authentic documentary."[23]

By 1986 Gorbachev's ambitions to reform the Soviet system through glasnost and perestroika were becoming increasingly apparent. They encouraged Wolf to think that he might accomplish his project without the censorship restrictions that just a year earlier had beset the Hohmann-Kohlhaase film. His hopes rested on "the ally M. Gorbachev." His intent behind *The Troika* and other writing projects that he contemplated, such as a history of the "Red Orchestra," an anti-Nazi resistance organization, was, he recorded in his diary in July 1986, to "address the problems of the struggles of our time with their complicated backgrounds and experiences honestly" and to "seek the truth in the 'process.' After all," he added, "the truth is revolutionary."[24]

Research for the book was well on its way by then. As early as 1983, Wolf had engaged a trusted assistant to help with research and introduced her to the relevant departments in the MfS. His connection with the Stasi continued after this official retirement, which gave him critical access to the ministry's resources for his further projects: For example, ministry employees arranged several meetings with George Fischer in New York. George Fischer readily offered assistance and eventually visited Wolf in East Berlin, spending a sleepless night at Wolf's home providing detailed editorial comments on a draft manuscript. (By contrast, his brother Victor, the surviving *Troika* protagonist, seems to have kept his distance from the project.) Wolf's wife Andrea provided critical help with the completion of the manuscript.[25]

In September 1986, Wolf began drafting a book concept in earnest at his reclusive lakeside dacha in Prenden, a village an hour's drive north of Berlin. By mid-December, he had worked out a structure for *The Troika* as well as the type of narrative style, and shortly afterward he completed

23. Markus Wolf, diary entry, June 26, 1986, MWA.

24. Markus Wolf, diary entries, June 23, 1986, and July 8, 1986, MWA.

25. George Fischer visited Markus Wolf in May 1988. Following two earlier marriages, Wolf married Andrea Stingl in August 1987.

the dictation of an initial book concept.[26] Wolf wanted the chapters to be "uncomplicated and clearly arranged for the reader." The style was to be "interesting and perhaps even tense." Carefully selected photos would not just serve as simple illustrations but "have their own artistic value as documents of contemporary history." A documentary appendix would form "a narrative balanced in rhythm and composition" that was "very precise and authentic" but "did not claim to be scholarly in nature."[27] Konrad's *Troika* thus increasingly became Markus's *Troika*. Framed as his brother's project, it was at least in part an early autobiographical and literary experiment for the recently retired spy chief.

Going beyond his brother's original vision, Wolf decided to add a contemporary epilogue about Konrad's personal and political struggles in the last decade of his life—taking up the challenge that Konrad's friend Wagenstein had posed years earlier. In fact, it was the epilogue that Wolf set out to write first, centered on the crisis created by Biermann's expatriation and Konrad's futile efforts to convince the SED leadership not to marginalize the growing number of disaffected artists and intellectuals. Wolf expected that Gorbachev's rehabilitation of Andrei Sakharov, a Soviet physicist and human rights activist, in December 1986 would make the epilogue resonate at home. The Kremlin leader's actions, he noted in his diary at the end of the month, "are somehow encouraging me to think that the matter could even be made public in two years if it succeeds."[28] Yet with its portrayal of Konrad as conflicted but ultimately committed to the belief that his basic political and artistic concepts could be aligned with the socialist system, *The Troika* also took on elements of an homage to his younger brother.

Wolf wrote the final version of the *Troika* manuscript against the backdrop of the deepening crisis in the GDR in 1987–88. The repressive

26. Markus Wolf, "Concept for the structure of a book about The Troika or the story of a film that was never produced," New Year's Eve 1986/1987, MWA.

27. Wolf, "Concept for the structure of a book about The Troika."

28. D. Scheinhard, memo, November 9, 1987, MWA; "Memo about a meeting with George Fischer on Nov. 16, 1987," December 2, 1987, MWA; "Memo about a meeting with George Fischer on Dec. 19, 1987," n.d., MWA; "Bericht zum Treff Netz am 19. 12. 87," December 20, 1987, MWA; George Fischer, letter to Markus Wolf, January 21, 1988, MWA; Markus Wolf, letter to George Fischer, February 22, 1988, MWA; Markus Wolf, diary entry, December 29, 1986, MWA.

measures of the state; the economic decline and the poor supply situation; a wave of arrests of regime critics at the beginning of 1988; and also the growing distance of the SED leadership from Gorbachev's reform course—underscored by the government's prohibiting the distribution of the popular Soviet magazine *Sputnik* in November 1988—turned more and more people against the system. Small in numbers as it was at the time, the civic opposition began to organize and increasingly networked across the country and even across the Iron Curtain to individuals and groups in the West. No longer could repressive measures alone contain the opposition movement. No less than the MfS warned the SED leadership that "tabooing social problems, tendencies to whitewash in public, and a lack of freedom of expression" complicated the task of effectively dealing with the opposition.[29]

Wolf considered *The Troika* his contribution toward overcoming the crisis and reforming the system. In his close circle of family and friends and in conversations with Soviet officials he criticized the economic situation and the "overbearing regimentation" in the cultural sector. Above all, however, Wolf worried about the relationship with the Soviet Union, the country that had been his personal and political lodestar. He emphatically disagreed with the SED's official line that Soviet-style reforms in East Germany were unnecessary since the problems they sought to address had long been resolved here: It was tragic that "we are making things much more difficult for ourselves than necessary and are not initiating the corrections and fundamental changes in thinking that are still possible here and in fact easier for us to implement." The SED leadership's worsening relations with the Soviet Union convinced Wolf that he had to "take a stand" with *The Troika* "from a firm Party point of view."[30]

This approach bore deep contradictions, but Wolf insisted that he could argue for reforms strongly based on communist party principles. He certainly did not want to join the ranks of the emerging civic opposition with *The Troika*. Wolf, not unlike Gorbachev, was concerned with reforming, not abandoning, the socialist system. The growing protests would, in

29. Kowalczuk, *Endspiel*, 254.

30. Markus Wolf, diary entries, September 29, 1987, October 29, 1987, April 17, 1988, and November 23, 1988, MWA.

his opinion, "hardly bring about any change for the time being, as they put you in a corner from where you can no longer achieve anything." The only thing left to do was to "keep our heads down and wait for this scare to come to an end." How long can the party leadership's self-dismantling last, he wondered. "How long will it still take [for change to come], and how painful will this change be?"[31]

As the crisis deepened, Wolf grew increasingly anxious that *The Troika* might not see the light of day after all. He became nervous about plans for the planned copublication of *The Troika* by a West German publishing house. As he perused the galleys of his book in late 1988, he wondered "how careful I have to be not to wake sleeping dogs." He worried that the party hard-liners would cause the situation in East Germany to deteriorate further, possibly triggering the collapse of the entire system—a situation made all the more dangerous in the larger context of German division. "The hounds," Wolf noted in his diary, "are becoming more and more aggressive and dangerous. They might still manage to put the country in a similar state to that that had developed in the S[oviet]U[nion]. Only . . . it doesn't work that way here and is much more dangerous. Resentment is growing in many directions."[32]

In the fall of 1988, Wolf found out just how tightly the East German government continued to limit any reckoning with the crimes of the Stalin era. He had worked with Lew Hohmann on a documentary film occasioned by the hundredth birthday of his father, Friedrich Wolf (1888–1953), a physician and well-known leftist writer. The film (*Verzeiht, dass ich ein Mensch bin*, which translates to "Forgive me for being a human") explicitly addressed Friedrich Wolf's experiences in Soviet exile during the Great Terror. In fact, it was Markus Wolf who had contributed the controversial passages on the purges to the film. The GDR state television station censored these passages. Wolf and Hohmann objected—Wolf even sent a written complaint to Honecker, but a few days later the SED politburo confirmed the

31. Markus Wolf, diary entry, November 23, 1988, MWA.

32. Markus Wolf, diary entry, November 18, 1988, MWA. The question of how this politically difficult manuscript was able to appear at all remains a desideratum for research. It remains to be clarified who in the HV Verlage gave permission to print it, and whether this was done without consulting the Cultural Department of the Central Committee.

deletion of the passages.[33] The documentary's airing in sanitized form on December 19 only heightened Wolf's sense of urgency: "*The Troika* must come now!" Just under three months later, its time had come.[34]

The handover of the first printed copy of *The Troika* in front of a camera of an ARD team on March 9, 1989, and the subsequent book launch, were just the beginning. Wolf presented his book at the Leipzig Book Fair on March 15, 1989, followed by more than two dozen readings, through which Wolf inserted himself in the discussions around the country in the ensuing weeks and months. Hundreds of people, many of them rank-and-file party members, attended these talks. Large sections of the party base had been unsettled by the silence of the party leadership in the face of the growing crisis in the country, and here was someone who seemed to give a voice to their frustrations. Many party members hoped for a renewal of the socialist system. That in turn had to begin with a more honest reappraisal of history. This was precisely Wolf's concern when he argued for a "rediscovery of the good traditions of the workers' movement of October," for overcoming the "bureaucratic administering" by the government and "rediscovering dialogue with the people." At a time when SED ideologues polemicized against any deviance from party orthodoxies, *The Troika* helped to create space for reassessing and debating the history of the communist movement.[35]

The explosive nature of *The Troika* was also reflected in the initial reaction of the communist party and the state security apparatus. Within the party leadership, there was particular frustration with the fact that Wolf,

33. Markus Wolf to Erich Honecker, October 17, 1988, MWA.

34. Markus Wolf, diary entry, December 19, 1988, and separate insert, "Notation about Lew Hohmann's film about Friedrich Wolf," MWA. The documentary was finally aired in March without any cuts. See "Jetzt ungekürzt: Wolf und das DDR-Fernsehen," *Frankfurter Allgemeine Zeitung*, March 10, 1989.

35. Markus Wolf, diary entry, April 16, 1989, MWA. In May Hanna Wolf (no relation to M.W.), the director of the Karl Marx high school, authored a sharp repudiation of a *Pravda* article critical of Stalin's purges. Hanna Wolf and Wolfgang Schneider, "Zur Geschichte der Komintern," *Neues Deutschland*, May 6/7, 1989 (excerpts reprinted in *Die SED: Geschichte, Organisation, Politik. Ein Handbuch*, ed. Andreas Herbst, Gerd-Rüdiger Stephan, and Jürgen Winkler [Dietz Berlin, 1997], 808–12). For the *Pravda* interview that Hanna Wolf and Schneider were responding to, see Fridrikh Firsov and Kirill Shirinia, "Komintern–Zeit der Prüfungen," *Pravda*, April 4, 1989.

in his first interview with West German TV, had entertained a question about the "*Sputnik* ban," thereby implicitly condoning the widespread criticism of the East German government's actions. Much to the chagrin of party hard-liners, Wolf had also used the interview to give an unequivocal endorsement of Gorbachev. Within hours of the interview, he was told not to accept further interviews with Western media without permission from the top. It is not without some irony that at the same time, West Germany's federal state prosecutor informed Wolf's West German copublisher that a book tour in the Federal Republic was out of question and that the newly minted author would be arrested upon entering West German territory.[36] Wolf saw himself forced to cancel the planned book tour that would have included a visit to his birthplace, Hechingen, in southwestern Germany.[37]

Contrasting with the international media's interest in the former spymaster's literary debut (and not just the media—the US ambassador to the GDR, Richard Barkley, invited Wolf to speak with him about *The Troika*), the publication was initially greeted with stony silence by the East German state media.[38] Then, on April 19, Harald Wessel, deputy editor in chief of the main SED organ *Neues Deutschland*, published a review of *The Troika* that barely concealed a personal admonishment to Wolf to abide by "party discipline."[39] Mielke also reminded Wolf that he was bound by the "discipline of the MfS."[40] In June, Wolf—as an "author"—turned to party chief Honecker and complained about the "reticence of parts of the party apparatus towards book and author" and called for an end to the "restrictive attitude." He did so, he argued, at least in part out of concern over the desire by the West to "maneuver me into a corner where I don't belong."[41]

36. Federal Prosecutor General to ECON Publishing Group, April 12, 1989, MWA.

37. Hechingen, however, was the site of the West German premiere of *Verzeih, dass ich ein Mensch bin*, which was screened there in late May 1989. "Auch in der Zollerstadt wurde gedreht," *Hohenzollernsche Zeitung*, May 27, 1989.

38. Regarding Barkley's invitation, see Richard C. Barkley to Markus Wolf, April 7, 1989, MWA.

39. Markus Wolf, diary entry, April 19, 1989, MWA.

40. Markus Wolf, diary entry, April 26, 1989, MWA.

41. Markus Wolf and Günther Drommer, *Die Kunst der Verstellung* (Schwarzkopf & Schwarzkopf, 1998), 100–114.

Still, at the standing-room-only book events that summer and fall, Wolf received an overwhelmingly positive response, especially for the "new honesty" in the critical treatment of the Stalin era. All of it gave him, as he put it in his diary, a "very strange feeling." He sensed "something like power that is not bound to any function or external insignia. Also, strength and power that are not so easy to shake, something like a mission." He began to feel that he and *The Troika* were representing "others as well as much that is missing, that cannot or may not be articulated." He felt this resonance, too, at the official reception for the fortieth anniversary of the German Democratic Republic in East Berlin's Palace of the Republic. A member of the visiting Soviet delegation headed by Gorbachev, Soviet Germany expert Valentin Falin, shared with him that *The Troika* had come up in his meetings with Social Democrat politicians in West Germany's capital Bonn. "So," Wolf noted under the date of October 7, 1989, "you suddenly find yourself in the middle of the political whirlwind—somehow eerie, strange."[42]

The accolades Wolf had received for *The Troika* contributed to his decision to take part in the large demonstration planned for November 4, 1989, on East Berlin's central Alexanderplatz. In the foreword to his book *Im eigenem Auftrag,* published in 1991, Wolf related, contrary to views expressed earlier, that he had believed he was "on the side of the rebels of these last years." But here the *Troika* author's past, his thirty-year-plus career as a leading State Security officer, caught up with him. In his speech he referred directly to *The Troika* and spoke out "for openly speaking the truth, for civil courage and for dealing with each other in a humane way, even with those who think differently." But he also rejected a general indictment of Ministry for State Security employees, at which point his voice was drowned out by sharp whistling and prolonged jeers. As Wolf stepped down from the flatbed truck that served as a makeshift speaker's platform, someone said to him: "You went from Stasi general to bearer of hope, and now you're going back to being a Stasi general." Wolf retrospectively stated: "The man was probably right."[43]

42. Markus Wolf, diary entry, April 26, 1989, MWA; Markus Wolf, letter to Erich Honecker, n.d., MWA; Markus Wolf, diary entry, October 7, 1989, MWA.

43. Wolf and Drommer, *Die Kunst,* 127–28; Markus Wolf, *In eigenem Auftrag: Bekenntnisse und Einsichten* (Franz Schneekluth Verlag, 1991), 5.

The Troika had been an inflection point in Wolf's life. With his literary debut he stepped out of the shadows into the limelight. He went on to write several other books but arguably none matched *The Troika* in importance and impact. After seeking refuge in the Soviet Union in 1990, he gave himself up for arrest by the authorities of the now-united Germany the following year. In the ensuing decade, he was tried twice for his activities in the service of the MfS. All the while Wolf, through autobiographical writings and frequent appearances on television talk shows, inserted himself into the national debate over the country's divided and communist past. His sober and at times even self-critical, if never fully candid, reflections drew admirers and detractors (and lots of conspiracy theorists). His storied, if incomplete, family past evoked sympathy and critical counternarratives. His principled attitude and his continued commitment to the socialist idea commanded loyalty or respect by some and struck others as hypocritical. His self-assured and urbane manner inspired admiration but also provoked outrage, right up to his death in 2006.

The Troika reflected the controversy that surrounded its author. For some, it was a courageous step by a representative of the SED system in the direction of reckoning more "honestly" with the past than the communist party had hitherto permitted. For others, it was a half-hearted effort to come clean on some of the most tragic chapters in the Party's history—a reservation aggravated by the persona of the messenger whose Stasi background seemed to undercut the message. More than three and a half decades later, this debate has lost little of its fervor. *The Troika* continues to challenge its readers. It is a document of a transformative moment in twentieth-century German and European history that raises important questions for the twenty-first.

I am thankful to Andrea Wolf for the possibility to consult the private papers of Markus Wolf. The papers are to be deposited at the Hoover Institution.

The Troika

Markus Wolf

Preface

The simultaneous publication of *The Troika* in March 1989 in both East and West Germany caused a sensation, as did the first public reading at the Friedrichsfelde Palace at the end of February and the interviews I gave to West German TV stations. At the Leipzig Book Fair the display copy, which was exhibited at the stall of the publisher, Aufbau Verlag, frequently disappeared, and in the GDR [German Democratic Republic, or East Germany] the first edition of *The Troika* hardly made it to the bookstores. The books were so-called stoop products—books that, because of their limited print run, were kept for a certain clientele under the shop counter. Most of the readers in the GDR followed *The Troika* in serial form in the equally popular *Die Wochenpost,* which had a print run of more than a million copies and always sold out.

The greatest interest in the West, speciously, concerned the author himself, who carried the mystique of being a longtime "spymaster" shrouded in mystery. Photographers and cameramen used the sudden opportunity to capture an image of "the man without a face"; the ARD TV station made sure not to miss the chance to interview.

This particular interview was not without consequences. My comments opposing the then–GDR leadership's prohibition of the Soviet magazine *Sputnik* were a bombshell, as this government had tried to suppress the numerous protests against this official ban with harsh responses and penalties. A meeting of the SED [Socialist Unity Party of Germany] politburo that immediately followed the interview deliberated on this wicked deed.[1] To the committee, even more reprehensible than my comments on *Sputnik* appeared to be my statement about the man, Mikhail Gorbachev: "I'm pleased and delighted that he exists!" Because Erich Honecker's unequivocal view was that the course of perestroika and glasnost, which had been adopted by the Soviet Union as of 1985, was extremely dangerous and destructive. He had told me so in person, and in no uncertain terms, in a conversation at the beginning of 1989.

And so, initially, the launch of *The Troika* ended with an internal ruling: The SED media were not allowed to acknowledge the book, and the author was instructed not to give any more interviews to the West. For the lower tiers of the party leadership and the lead editorial offices the announcement of this anathema was introduced with the words, "Not even an accomplished general has the right . . ."

For me a new phase of life began with *The Troika,* one that gave me a different perspective on the realities of the country. Two realities had always existed: the dictatorially imposed mendacity on the one hand and, on the other, the reality of truth, suppressed as it was in a variety of ways yet ever growing in power. This new phase had in fact already begun for me when I began to prepare for my departure from the Ministry for State Security. Under my leadership the intelligence service had had a large degree of autonomy. However, it could effect little with regard to the changes that had become necessary. And so, my departure from the service in 1986, which I had requested some years earlier, coincided with my becoming involved with my brother Konrad's *Troika* ideas and with Mikhail Gorbachev's concept of perestroika starting to take shape.

While writing the book I was aware of the explosiveness of the material. The contents had preoccupied and tormented my brother for many years before his death in March 1982. He had lived with these thoughts ever since the crimes committed under Stalin's leadership became known—and the consequences of what then appeared to be the deformation of

1. Created by a merger of the Communist Party of Germany and the Social Democratic Party in the Soviet occupation zone in April 1946, the SED was the founding and ruling party of the GDR; it held power from its establishment in 1949 until its dissolution following the Peaceful Revolution of 1989.

socialism could no longer be overlooked in the Soviet Union, and in other socialist countries, and in ours as well. He wanted to bring together his thoughts about individual destinies associated with these issues and their causes, and the experiences of his own life, into the art form that was his: film. During his work on the *Troika* material the conflicts in our country had become very acute. They were particularly evident in art and literature for which he, as president of the Academy of Arts of the GDR, felt a singular responsibility. Artists and writers either left our republic in alarming numbers or were expatriated.

These were the same problems and causes that troubled us in the second half of the 1980s, but now the signs of a looming political and economic crisis became much more visible. And so the idea for an epilogue was born, and I started work on the book by writing the epilogue. If the leadership was going to be unable to choose the path of change and openness by the time the book was to be published, the likelihood of a confrontation with its policies was all but a foregone conclusion. With my notorious optimism, I counted on this possibility and told friends to whom I showed the epilogue that with it I would probably be pushing against open doors. Although it would not benefit the book, it would be beneficial for our country. Most of my friends did not share my optimism, and they were proved right. The country's leadership continued with its obstinate opposition to perestroika.

After its publication, and to an extent which I could not have foreseen, *The Troika* became part of the political reality of our country. In numerous public readings before various audiences and from the many letters from readers, I and several other writers were struck by the response we received, which revealed the people's hunger for truth. The way the book dealt with history and Stalin's repressive measures, and the manner in which the problems in our own development were addressed and which the media were forbidden to report—all this was sensational to many. The continued friendship of the protagonists of *The Troika* transcended the decades and all ideological differences; it failed to conform to the official images of the enemy. It was almost seen as a message for a new way of thinking about political and personal relationships among peoples and individuals. "Honesty," "Sincerity," "Courage for Truth," "Tolerance"—those were the words that occurred most frequently. Questions upon questions. Criticism of the conditions at home. Discontent about the prevailing stagnation, about the barely disguised distancing from the changes introduced in the Soviet Union, and about the repressive measures against dissenters; and the rejection of the appalling media policies—all of these subjects preoccupied the meetings and the mostly very open, free exchange of ideas with many thousands of people. It was a new and important experience, which increasingly revealed the growing pressure that was burdening the country. In the absence of change—and I remained hopeful that it would come, and urged members of the government in frequent conversations to bring it about—an explosion was inevitable. I remember there was not a single conversation—no matter whether with large or small circles of people, no matter what station or level of responsibility—that reflected a different view of the situation. The exception was the small circle at the very top that governed inside a bubble.

When the borders with Hungary were opened, the mass exodus of our people—mostly young—began, and the general situation became untenable. Therefore, the role of the author, who was being hailed as "the bearer of hope" during public readings, was over. Something had to happen. But even then, in the summer of 1989, no one could foresee what direction events were taking or how they would fundamentally change the country's—and indeed Europe's—political face.

The 7th of October, 1989, which began with gala celebrations of the fortieth anniversary of the founding of the GDR, was, in my eyes, the beginning of a revolutionary renewal. Mikhail Gorbachev's presence had symbolic significance. At the same time, it provided the impetus to replace the old leadership.[2] After the bloody confrontations on October 7 and 8, a large section of the population no longer expected a change from the top down. Chanting "We are the people," they rose up in a democratic awakening, which the West labeled "the Velvet Revolution [Peaceful

2. On October 18, 1989, Erich Honecker and his closest associates were forced to resign. Egon Krenz assumed the role of secretary-general of the SED.

Revolution]."[3] This awakening indeed took place without violence, an unprecedented occurrence. In my view then, it presented the great opportunity for [establishing] a socialist democracy on German soil, just as we had hoped for.

I believe I have captured in my book some of the ideals for a new and fairer society that had shaped my father's and brother's lifelong ambitions, together with the ambitions of thousands of others, and that had remained with us in our struggle against fascism. The approval by [my] readers, the sympathy of countless people, many of the demands on the streets and in the squares during the first weeks gave hope . . .

But it was just a part of the reality that I knew. This part comprised sections of the intelligentsia, especially the young intelligentsia, who urged change. These were people who were able to articulate their ideas better than others, and who gained some freedom from a government that had become ever more insecure. Insufficient connections were made to other opposition groups—groups who had been exposed to significantly tougher and, yes, more brutal repressive measures from the government apparatus, and who were now increasingly setting the agenda for the demands of the people's movement against all systems and personnel of the old power structure. Too much rejection, and perhaps hatred, had accumulated.

I had a harsh experience with this the first time I appeared before five hundred thousand people on Alexanderplatz at the protest demonstration organized by Berlin artists on November 4, 1989. I accepted the invitation from Berlin artists to speak there on the understanding that I was at one with the protesters, like the other speakers, who in the majority opposed the sinking regime. My speech was accompanied by shrill whistles, and when I got down from the platform truck with a dry mouth, somebody

3. On October 7 and 8, 1989, East Germany was rocked by widespread protests against the communist regime. Demonstrators calling for political reform were met with harsh crackdowns by security forces. These events marked a pivotal moment in what came to be called the Peaceful Revolution, which ultimately led to the fall of the Berlin Wall and the reunification of Germany. Wolf has used the term "Velvet Revolution," which has typically come to refer to the Czechoslovakian nationwide protest movement in November–December 1989 that ended communist rule.

said: "You went from Stasi general to bearer of hope, and now you're going back to being a Stasi general."

Here, I'm interrupting the original preface I wrote in February 1990 in Moscow. At that point in time I couldn't imagine that this man, with his perhaps off-the-cuff remarks on Berlin's Alexanderplatz, should prove to be right. The text that follows was written within a few weeks of the dissolution of the GDR in October 1990. Once more I had withdrawn abroad—this time in the opposite direction—because of impending lawsuits concerning my former job. At the beginning of the year I went to my sister Lena who lived in Moscow in order to achieve detachment, time, and peace for my work on a new book. The loss of a socialist alternative on German soil was apparent and so, after the disappointments and the torment of self-doubt, I saw the book as a potential key for me and my family to secure a place in the reunited Germany. After the elections in March, which left no doubt about an accelerated route toward German unification, I returned to Berlin to stay there, to continue working on the manuscript and to defend myself against allegations that had been made in the meantime concerning my former job at the top of the foreign intelligence service. However, the past caught up with me with such vehemence that there was no peace whatsoever. There wasn't even an hour for talks with friends and acquaintances. There was hardly a moment for a deeper reflection on the great questions of our time, or for any work on the book. Many leading politicians stated that German unification should not stand beneath the banner of retaliation but that of reconciliation; that with the solemnly proclaimed end of the Cold War, its legacies should also be abandoned. One could, therefore, have expected that, with the unification of the two German states, the increasingly malicious attacks would soon be a thing of the past, as would the arrest warrant that the FRG [Federal Republic of Germany, or West Germany] had issued for me in June 1989. Indeed, comments from official sources made me expect this.

What happened was absolutely the opposite.

During those months of continuous pressure and growing slander, all attempts made via political channels and vis-à-vis the public to offer an objective explanation of the role of the foreign intelligence service and its staff failed.[4] Statements by West German politicians and espionage experts alike acknowledging the fact that we acted based on our country's constitution and laws, and that we did nothing different from what was done by the employees of similar services elsewhere—that, just like them, we were integrated into an alliance structure—were ignored. Anticipatory condemnations multiplied. Even the Amnesty Law that the West German government strove to achieve failed to come about prior to [German unification on] October 3. And so, the day of unification threatened all former employees of the GDR's intelligence service, because they were now subject to the FRG criminal law with all its consequences. They practically became outlawed. My own prosecution was even specified in a particular clause of the draft law. This was headline news in the media. Reporters and cameramen were already waiting impatiently for the arrest of the former spymaster on the eve of October 3. Originally meant as a joke in the spring and immediately discarded as too sensationalist, the title of my planned second book suddenly became unexpectedly topical: *Wanted in East and West*.

Reluctantly, I had followed my friends' advice and decided to bypass the spectacle of my arrest in Berlin on October 3. I had written letters to Federal President Richard von Weizsäcker, [former West German Chancellor] Willy Brandt, and [former West German Foreign Minister] Hans-Dietrich Genscher, saying that nothing within me could take me away from Germany: "It is my parents' country. After the long exile they rediscovered their purpose here; their graves are in Berlin, and so is my brother's. For me, this Germany is the place of my work, of my strength, of my love, of my successful as well as my failed and misled efforts." For this reason, a second exile would be out of the question for me. My having been raised to have *Zivilcourage* [civil/moral courage] alone would have been enough to defend myself against what I was accused of—under proper and fair conditions.

In the autumn of 1990, amid this completely confused legal situation and frantic election contests, these conditions did not exist. I wrote to the

4. Wolf here is referring to the HVA (Hauptverwaltung A, or Main Directorate for Reconnaissance) within the GDR's Ministry for State Security (MfS, or the Stasi).

attorney general: "It seems that for me and former members of my Intelligence Service staff who were involved in the Cold War in the same way as employees of similar services, the war seems to continue. Winners and losers are required; retaliation without mercy." I expressed my hope that the plan to punish me and others retrospectively under FRG laws, and for us to face justice for a service accomplished in the GDR, wouldn't be the last word in the matter. And so I found it better to let the situation pass.

Perhaps these months of my diverse life will be a passing episode by the time the reader holds this book in his hands. The idea that Mikhail Gorbachev should be officially greeted and celebrated in Germany as a guest of the state and as a Nobel Peace Prize laureate, while, at the same time, one of his early German supporters and friends is harried and barred from the country, is a paradox.

It is going to be difficult to record and describe one's own emotional landscape and the jumble of contradictory thoughts. In such an unpleasant situation the bitter realization prevails that for many of my compatriots, the end of the GDR means indeed the late victory over the "evil empire." No part of the forty years of the GDR should remain unpunished or even be mentioned. Those thoughts unite me again with all of those who, on November 4, 1989, stood there on Berlin's Alexanderplatz with me on the back of a truck and advocated the peaceful course of the revolution and who still believed, then, in the possibility of a socialist alternative on German soil. Those voices, which had already taken a political stance before October 1989 and then were heard on the platforms and podiums during the demonstrations, have now been almost muted; they have no place in a united fatherland.

I don't believe this muzzling to be permanent. Forty years of the GDR can't be erased; they can't be reduced to the negative legacy of the SED and the Stasi. Whole pages from this part of our country's history can't be torn away, or at least not for long. Those whose voices were heard in October and November 1989 will be present in the future Germany, and will be heard. And so are the young people who respected those voices. We will continually try to identify the causes; what remains are the persistent questions about one's own guilt and responsibility. What had our fathers' generation already neglected, repressed, and done wrong? And what have we done wrong in our efforts to realize the good and noble ideals of our youth in those countries where, just like we did, many people believed in the humane values of socialism? What could we have done more boldly, with greater determination, and earlier to no longer accept the way in which socialism was so terribly and persistently compromised? In this book such questions are raised, but it is only the beginning of a path to understanding that, in the meantime, has moved on considerably. The work on *The Troika,* and also the many readers' letters and later public readings, were steps on this path; they helped me to understand more deeply the reality of life [in the GDR].

Meanwhile, more than a year has gone by during which each month weighs more heavily than many entire previous years. Life experiences, including the bitter ones, were more profoundly reflected on than ever before. Standing before the ruins of an illusory socialism, thoughts about the ideals in which we believed are combined with consideration of the future of this united Germany. If we can find satisfying answers to the major problems that confront mankind, this big country, situated at the heart of Europe, offers both a challenge and, at the same time, an opportunity. Can we rise to this challenge and opportunity under the system within which we are going to live? The way things are at the moment, it's unlikely. We will need old ideals and new utopias. An "-ism" doesn't mean much to people today. Politically engaged young people, in particular, are no longer interested in regimes and the parties that sustain them. The worries of everyday life leave others with little time to look beyond their borders and to think about mankind's wide-ranging problems. But inevitably, they will catch up with us. The number of perceptive and engaged people is growing. My hope lies with such young people whose entire purpose in life does not involve the dance around the golden calf, who will fight for a fairer society in their own and in other countries, and who will also stand up for the protection of our threatened planet. Many of them are doing this because they still believe in the possibility of a humanist democratic socialism. Courage is required in Germany once more.

I also wrote this book to inspire people to *Zivilcourage*. Many readers have been especially captivated by the story of a friendship. The weeks, maybe months, of banishment abroad have once more shown me the importance of true friendship and solidarity. It is the good side of this particular time, another experience that I wouldn't want to have missed.

With that, I come back to the original foreword for this edition [of 1990]:

I presume that for the reader of *The Troika,* the original story of three boys and their families who met in Moscow in the 1930s will be in the foreground: the story of a friendship that lasted an entire lifetime and that withstood many blows, as well as separation by political and geographical borders.

And so I ask myself once again, like so many others of my generation, the question: What is the most important thing in life? Is it the trust of friends and for human beings to create and maintain trust between themselves, regardless of different conditions and circumstances? Certainly. Because, ultimately, each political system is created and sustained by us—the people. The question remains: Are we able to judge whether each of us is going the right way?

Markus Wolf
February/October 1990

To Our Meni

Prologue

"В этом доме с 1934 по 1945 . . ."[5] I read this inscription, carved into black granite. It is strange to see this on our house: a double portrait of father and brother, fashioned in the style of an antique medallion. The severity of the black stone places them back in the past, into history. But for me everything here is still alive, familiar . . .

Every time I visited Moscow after the war, I felt drawn back to the familiar Arbat neighborhood, to this house in Nizhnii Kislovskii Lane. Even now it seems to me as though I could walk into the house, go up five floors taking several stairs at a time, and come across our neighbors the Alpers; or, at any moment, the corpulent Vsevolod Vishnevskii could emerge from his door opposite our apartment. Then, having returned down the back stairs, I would encounter, at the exit to the courtyard, our beady-eyed custodian, Chugunov, who watches the noisy activities of the boys, Koni [Konrad] among them . . .

No, the courtyard scarcely reminds me of "our time." More and more often, since the day Koni's black case came to me, I catch myself thinking that people who have passed away are at my side. The small leather case that he always had close to him during the last weeks of his life and in which he kept what was at the time the most important thing for him—the idea of *The Troika*. The thoughts of making a movie filled the last years of his life: the story of three boys who became friends in Moscow. The contents of the black case, the old photographs, the notes and recordings

5. Russian for "In this house lived from 1934 to 1945 . . ."

from the journeys to the US and his latest visit to Moscow, dominated our last conversations at the hospital.

Now Koni has left me alone with the black case. Its contents started to lead a life of their own. That fills me with unrest, as the idea of *The Troika* contains the attempt to describe the story of our lives, interlinked with the fate of the close friends of our youth, and to discover its meaning with all its turmoil and contradictions. This idea, the *Troika* idea, tries to pick up threads almost lost, to preserve them between the ideals as well as the romance of our youth here in the Arbat, and the experiences and insights of later life.

Looking at the photographs, listening to the voices of Koni, Vitya, and Yura on the tapes, our youth catches up with me; almost-forgotten names once more materialize; questions and thoughts arise that would persist stubbornly in my head and cost me some sleepless nights.

Who should take care of this material now, this material that the brother tormented himself with for so many years, unable to produce something in his favored artistic genre: film? As reality and fantasy started to merge on his sickbed, Koni didn't speak of a film anymore, but of a documentary or a book.

A book?

The eyes of the writer and the film director on the stone relief are directed toward the Arbat and beyond to an indefinite distance. Father and brother can't help me anymore. All I am left with is the attempt to capture the contents of the black case—the story of the Troika—as a document of our lives and our time.

Growing Up in Moscow

Troika means a set of three. The set of three in this story met each other in Moscow in the 1930s.

Different as the backgrounds of the three boys and their families were, they seemed to be bound together inseparably by fate. Germany was in the clutches of fascism. The provocation of the Reichstag Fire on the night of February 27, 1933, was the trigger for terror and reprisals against dissidents. These families would soon feel the effects of this. After hazardous journeys, with short breaks in various parts of the world, the future friends and their parents, brothers, and sisters all eventually found a new home in Moscow. Many of the adults thought that Nazi rule would be short lived and their emigration merely a brief episode. This, as with many other such notions, was wishful thinking.

First, the two "Americans" settled in Moscow. Their parents had met in the United States during the Great War and had married in the early 1920s in Berlin. The father, Louis Fischer, an American journalist, had written several books about the events in Soviet Russia after the October Revolution. He had also published, to great acclaim, many articles in liberal news journals in the US and Europe. The mother came from the Baltic region, then still part of Russia. Her friends called her by her childhood name, Markoosha. She worked as a translator for a Soviet business in Berlin and accompanied Soviet delegations to significant conferences in Genoa and The Hague. In April 1922, in the small town of Rapallo, near Genoa, she witnessed her boss, the Soviet people's commissar, Georgii Chicherin, and the German foreign minister, Walther Rathenau, negotiating and signing the treaty that gave the fledgling Soviet Republic its first international recognition. At the same time, Germany gained more room to maneuver in its negotiations with the Western powers.

From that point on, Markoosha Fischer considered the Soviet Union her *Heimat* [homeland] and became a Soviet citizen. The sons, Yura [George] and Victor, were born in Berlin. They had dual citizenship and arrived in Moscow with their parents when they were small children. But because living and work conditions for foreigners were still difficult at that time, they were sent to Berlin for a while once more, where they were looked after by friends. They lived in the "Rote Wedding" district,[6] went to school there, and joined the Young Pioneers.[7] After the Reichstag Fire they were sent back to Moscow via the Sudetenland.[8] They left in the nick of time, because Paul Massing—their Berliner foster father, and later lifelong friend—was soon arrested.[9] At first he was incarcerated in the infamous Columbia-Haus before being sent to a newly built concentration camp.[10] When he was released at the end of 1933 he wrote one of the first books about the Nazi terror: *Schutzhäftling Nr. 880* [Prisoner number 880].

6. Berlin's Wedding neighborhood, nicknamed Rote (Red) Wedding, was at the time a working-class district that was home to many communists; during the interwar period, the Communist Party of Germany received the highest number of votes in the district for the Reichstag elections.

7. The Pioneers were a Soviet youth group for children ages nine to fourteen. It played a central role in instilling communist ideology and preparing children for later membership in the Komsomol (Young Communist League).

8. The Sudetenland refers to the northern, southern, and western regions of former Czechoslovakia that were primarily inhabited by ethnic Germans, known as Sudeten Germans. These German-speaking communities had been the dominant population in the border areas of Bohemia, Moravia, and Czech Silesia since the Middle Ages. The Sudeten Crisis of 1938 was sparked by Nazi Germany's demands to annex the Sudetenland. These demands culminated in the signing of the Munich Agreement, after which the region was incorporated into the Third Reich.

9. Paul Massing (1902–1979) was a German-American social scientist. In the 1930s, he lived in Moscow, where he became friends with Markus and Konrad Wolf. After emigrating to the United States in 1938, he taught political sociology at Columbia University and later at Rutgers University.

10. The Columbia Concentration Camp, located near Berlin's Tempelhof Airport, was used as a prison by the Nazi Schutzstaffel ("Protective Echelon") starting in 1933. Between 1933 and 1936, thousands of people were imprisoned, tortured, and, in some cases, murdered there. In December 1934, it was formally converted into the Columbia Concentration Camp, and in 1935 it was taken under the direct administration of the Gestapo (Secret State Police).

Meanwhile, Louis and Markoosha Fischer had found an apartment in Moscow in a new block of flats. The Fischer boys very quickly became known as Yura and Vitya through their interactions with the Moscow boys from Sivtsev Vrazhek Lane near the Arbat, a historic area renowned as the home of many writers, artists, and academics past and present.

Our mother arrived in Moscow with Koni and me in April 1934. In Stuttgart, our hometown in Swabia, our father had been a famous communist doctor and author. Immediately following the Reichstag Fire he had to flee abroad. After we'd been threatened many times and had our house searched on several occasions, we followed him to Basel, crossing the border with the help of Swiss comrades. Later we joined him on the small Île-de-Bréhat off the French coast, although we didn't have resident permits. There, Father wrote his play *Professor Mamlock*, which had its German-language premiere at the Zurich Schauspielhaus with Wolfgang Langhoff and Heinrich Greif.[11] In the autumn of 1933, Father was the first to go to Moscow. As a revolutionary author, he was given a one-bedroom apartment with a bathroom and a kitchen in Nizhnii Kislovskii Lane, which, at that time, was unimaginably luxurious. Finally, via Basel, Vienna, and Warsaw, we were able to join him once again. Our apartment, too, was very close to the historic Arbat, only a few minutes' walk from the Kremlin, the very center of Moscow.

Lothar Wloch, together with his parents and his little sister Margot, arrived in Moscow at around the same time as us. He was a blond Berliner and came from a communist working-class family whose name still lives on to this day among old comrades in the southeastern Berlin suburb of Bohnsdorf. There was constant coming and going in the Wloch household. In that turbulent time many young people received support and advice from Wilhelm and Erna. Wilhelm was one of those educated, Marxist-trained workers who understood how to address the people's current needs and problems, and through his work he helped the Communist Party reach an increasing number of people. Wilhelm's visitors also had

11. The play had premiered in Yiddish at the Warsaw Yiddish Art Theater a few months earlier, in January 1934, under the title *Der gelbe Fleck* (The yellow badge).

good conversations with Lothar—he was a "great little chap." They also amused their adopted daughter, Mausi, as Margot was called.

In the spring of 1933, Wilhelm Wloch was already working against the Nazis and was compelled to go underground. During a house search, and in front of her children, Erna was hit so hard with a truncheon that she lost her hearing in one ear. They traveled to the Soviet Union via the Baltic Sea on fake passports. Shortly afterward a Party assignment led the Wlochs abroad again. The children stayed in Denmark until, finally, in 1936, the family ended up on the sixth floor of a hotel for émigrés, the Hotel Lux, on Moscow's Gorky Street.[12] They had two rooms opposite Wilhelm Pieck's apartment.[13] We knew hardly anything about the parents' backgrounds and their activities at that time. There was an air of secrecy about the Wlochs, although this was not uncommon in émigré circles. Certain topics were just never discussed.

The first socialist country became a second home for the families of what would become the Troika, as it did for many émigrés, who sought refuge and support in their fight against fascism.

It was therefore no coincidence that the main characters in this story—Vitya, Koni, and Lothar—met each other at the German Karl Liebknecht School.[14] It was there that the mother of the Fischer boys and Lothar's mother first met each other. Markoosha Fischer, with her instinct for people who needed help, could quickly see that the young boy from Berlin was having difficulty settling into life in the Soviet Union; since Lothar and Vitya were in the same class, it was easy to get them together.

12. The Hotel Lux in Moscow served as a refuge for exiled Communists, especially Germans fleeing the Nazi regime. Many later became key figures in postwar German politics. By the 1930s, Stalin viewed the hotel's international residents with suspicion, leading to intense purges between 1936 and 1938. Fear, denunciations, and nightly arrests gripped the hotel. Many German exiles were interrogated, tortured, and sent to labor camps. Of the 178 leading German communists killed during Stalin's purges, most had lived at the Hotel Lux.

13. Wilhelm Pieck (1876–1960) was a German communist politician who closely aligned with the Soviet Union during and after World War II. He played a key role in establishing East Germany and became its first president in 1949.

14. Karl Liebknecht (1871–1919) was a German Social Democrat—a pivotal group during the Weimar Republic and a driving force behind establishment of the democratic order that was later upended by the Nazis. Alongside Rosa Luxemburg, Liebknecht founded the Spartacus League, a revolutionary group that later became the Communist Party of Germany. He was killed during the failed Spartacist Revolt in January 1919.

At the beginning, Koni and I also had problems with our new surroundings, especially with how to handle the boys on the street who derided us for wearing shorts; even the youngest kids wore long pants. Teasing cries of "*Nemets, perets, kolbasa, kislaia kapusta*"—"German, pepper, sausage, sauerkraut"—echoed in our ears. A strong support system was needed to survive there. Through the mothers' friendship, both for the Wloch kids and for us, the Fischer household provided a bridge to the yet unfamiliar street life of Moscow. To make it easier to get by, Koni was turned into "Kolya" and I became "Mischa." Yura Fischer's invention has stuck with me ever since.

Lothar became the driving force of the triumvirate. He was slightly older than the other two, strong, mostly calm and firm in his behavior. There was no Russian equivalent of his name, so he became "Lotka" to his friends. Vitya resembled his mother in many ways: dark hair, soft facial features, and large, attentive eyes. In contrast to his brother, who was rather plump at the time, and who already betrayed a sense of the restless intellectual he would become, Vitya was energetic, but also calm and levelheaded. He was always in the mood to play outside, to go swimming or ice-skating with the other boys.

Koni, who, like Vitya, was close to his mother, was rather dreamy. Of the three friends he spoke the least. With his deep-set brown eyes and prominent forehead it was hard to figure out his mood. He could keep himself occupied for hours, playing with his thick, dark hair as he did so. He expressed his feelings and his experiences in his drawings. Koni's pictures became a chronicle of that time and of family events. If ever there was a need for a boat to be built during a summer holiday by the water, Lothar would decide the type and size, Vitya would provide the details of construction, and Koni would let his imagination run wild with suggestions for the color design of the model.

The long journey to school from the Arbat to the Sukharev Tower on the Sadovaia [Garden Ring], Moscow's large ring road, seemed to us at the time like a challenging assault course. Being used to Western European traffic conditions and road manners, we had to prove ourselves at charging the totally overcrowded trams, the only means of transport at the time. We had not yet mastered the techniques of sitting on the couplings or hanging off the sides of the carriages. Consequently, our teachers had to accept that our problems adjusting were the reason for our occasional lateness.

There was an international atmosphere at the German school. In the beginning, when the school was located on the Garden Ring, our building also housed a school for Gypsy [Romani] children as well as an English-speaking school. The Karl Liebknecht School was also attended by the children of those many Soviet citizens who had worked in Germany at some time and were interested in mastering the German language. There were also children of Hungarian emigrants and Austrian Schutzbund [Defense League] children—the children of those who had been members of the paramilitary wing of the Austrian Social Democratic Party, and who had taken part in the uprising against the fascist policies of the Dollfuss government in February 1934.[15] These Austrians lived in a boardinghouse just a few steps from our apartment.

In every sense, a "wild bunch" studied at this German school. The ear-shattering sounds of the break times did not always subside into an attentive calm during the lessons. Only the most assertive teachers could manage to be heard. Our poor math teacher, [Sarra] Feinberg, fled the classroom in tears and never came back. Some of that changed with the move into the new school building on Kropotkin Street, one of the first newly constructed school buildings in Moscow.

It was a time of reform and upswing throughout the whole country. "Life has become better and happier," Joseph Stalin had said at the Seventeenth Congress of the All-Union Communist Party.[16] At the time of our arrival there was still rationing and Torgsin shops, where you could buy anything your heart desired as long as you paid in foreign currency. But who had

15. Wolf refers here to events that were part of the Austrian Civil War, which took place from February 12 to 15, 1934. It was a series of violent confrontations in the First Austrian Republic between the Schutzbund and Engelbert Dollfuss's authoritarian government in collusion with right-wing groups; in the wake of which the socialists were defeated, and some were subsequently arrested and/or executed. Ultimately the Social Democratic Party was then banned, and several Schutzbund members fled to the Soviet Union, among other places.

16. However, Stalin apparently said this at a different conference, the First All-Union Conference of Stakhanovites (November 14–17, 1935). The actual quote is "Life has become better, comrades. Life has become more joyous. And whenever life is joyful, work goes better." Quoted in *Pravda*, November 22, 1935.

foreign currency? After food rationing had been abolished, the farmers markets became more appealing. Champions of labor were celebrated and honored. The coal miner Aleksei Stakhanov's name had been given to an elite worker's movement. And the Stakhanovite among the builders, Orlov, had recently made a name for himself during the construction of the Karl Liebknecht School by setting a record for the greatest number of bricks laid in one shift. In 1935, the older pupils; our Pioneer leader, Ahrendt; and some fathers volunteered to work shifts on Saturdays (known as Subbotniks) in order to contribute to the building of the school.[17]

The children of other famous communist authors and officials also attended the school with us. They included: Marianne Weinert;[18] Peter Florin;[19] Moritz Mebel;[20] Gregor Kurella;[21] Marianne Becher; and Till and Ule Lammert, the sons of the sculptor Will Lammert.[22] Dodgeball battles took place in the courtyard leading to Kropotkin Street, but to our annoyance, the team with the tallest and oldest boys, one of whom was Werner

17. "Субботники," derived from the Russian word for Saturday, refers to unpaid, voluntary work, often on weekends. Following the October Revolution, the encouragement of this type of weekend work was part of an initiative to restore the economy.

18. Marianne Lange-Weinert (1921–2005) was a cultural official as well as the author of scholarly works on children's and young adult literature. She fled Berlin with her family in March 1933 due to the communist associations and writings of her father, Erich Weinert. After stays in Switzerland, the Saar region, and Paris, she arrived in the Soviet Union in 1935.

19. Peter Florin (1921–2014) fled Germany with his parents after Adolf Hitler's rise to power and the persecution of Communists. His father Wilhelm Florin was a leading Communist member of the Reichstag. Peter Florin later became an East German politician and diplomat.

20. Moritz Mebel (1923–2021) emigrated to Moscow with his mother and sister in 1932, followed by his father, in 1933. Mebel became a prominent German urologist and a member of the SED. He played a key role in developing the kidney transplant system in the GDR.

21. Gregor (Grisha) Kurella (1925–2016) was a German whose parents sought political asylum in the Soviet Union in 1934 when he was eight years old. Kurella volunteered for the Red Army in 1942, joining the Seventh Administration, where his father Alfred was already engaged in producing leaflets and propaganda materials.

22. Will Lammert (1892–1957) was a German sculptor, posthumously awarded the National Prize of the GDR in 1959. In the early summer of 1933, he was forced to emigrate via the Netherlands to Paris, his Jewish wife Hette and their two sons Till and Ule following on; they eventually settled in the Soviet Union in 1934, but following the 1941 German invasion, he was expelled for being German. His wartime exile turned into a lifelong "Special Exile," and he was only permitted to return to East Germany in 1951. In 1952, he became a full member of the German Academy of Arts. Ule Lammert (1926–2024) became a professor and vice president of the Bauakademie der DDR. Till Lammert became an architect in the GDR.

Eberlein, always had the edge.[23] The game was not known in Moscow, so it attracted a few spectators from the street. We also enjoyed creating a furor with our marching band. Every time we marched on Red Square and drowned out the sound of the big brass orchestras with our high-pitched flutes, we would be greeted over the loudspeakers. The speaker called for solidarity with the German antifascists and with Ernst Thälmann, who had been imprisoned by the fascists.[24]

It was at the school that the bond of friendship between Vitya, Koni, and Lothar, which had first formed in the Fischer apartment, grew stronger. They met on the way to school, made plans to meet under a certain street sign on the Arbat to go to the cinema, and sheltered in the big telegraph office on Gorky Street whenever it suddenly started raining. Like most of the children in their class, all three were Young Pioneers. The collective communal work of the Pioneer group became a regular feature. Almost everyone was assigned a specific job and became accustomed to carrying out their responsibilities within the collective. It was just a beautiful feeling to belong to a community of children, a sensation even more profound than what we remembered from our Pioneer life in Germany. It was like that at the Karl Liebknecht School and it was the same in the school's summer camp near Kaluga, which was named after Ernst Thälmann.

The camp was in a forest, close to the Oka River, not far from where Max Hölz had drowned.[25] Older comrades told us about this legendary figure in the post-1918 revolutionary battles in the Vogtland and in Saxony. We learned the battle songs of that period and sang them enthusiastically

23. Werner Eberlein (1919–2002) was a German politician and senior official in the SED. He rose to prominence as a Russian interpreter for party leader Walter Ulbricht and later served as first secretary of the SED in the district of Magdeburg. In the 1980s, he became a member of the SED Central Committee's politburo.

24. Ernst Thälmann (1886–1944) was a German communist politician and leader of the Communist Party of Germany from 1925 to 1933. He also headed the paramilitary Roter Frontkämpferbund. Arrested by the Gestapo in 1933, he spent eleven years in solitary confinement. Initial efforts by Stalin and Vyacheslav Molotov to secure his release were dropped after the Molotov–Ribbentrop Pact, and appeals were ignored by party rival Walter Ulbricht. In 1944, Thälmann was executed in Buchenwald on Hitler's personal order.

25. Max Hölz (1889–1933) was a German communist who led post–World War I revolutionary unrest in southeastern Germany and later emigrated to the Soviet Union. Independent-minded and outspoken, he grew critical of the Communist Party and died under mysterious circumstances in 1933, possibly at the hands of the Soviet secret police.

around the campfire. The interesting life of a Pioneer—the beautiful woodland walks, filling our large buckets with wild strawberries and raspberries, playing volleyball and swimming in the river—helped some of us to stomach the very simple living conditions: the unfamiliar, bland food (most of the time it was buckwheat kasha and *Milchkissel*) and the frequent sharp bouts of homesickness.[26] Some of us, including Yura and Lothar, were lucky enough to be allowed to travel to Crimea to the large central Pioneer camp called Artek. This was, of course, recorded in articles for the wall newspaper and in the group diaries, which played a large role in our Pioneer lives. Thus this period shaped in each of us the hopes and dreams that would stay with us for the rest of our lives. As much as our future paths would diverge, our sense of belonging to a larger community, knowing that we were not alone and also that we were there for others—those were the principles that would be central to the lives of the *Troika* protagonists. The newspapers, the political news from the *Heimat*, the fight for the release of Ernst Thälmann, and, of course, events in the Soviet Union were part of our everyday life. The word "solidarity" had become an inalienable concept and had a concrete meaning and purpose for us all.

One of our heroes at that time was Georgi Dimitrov, the victor in the Reichstag Fire trial who received a rapturous welcome when he arrived in Moscow. Dimitrov completely upset the self-important autocrat, Hermann Göring, during the trial, when his questions unmasked the web of lies that surrounded the allegations of arson by the communists.[27] Now he was free.

At the same time, Moscow also awaited the arrival of the survivors from the *Chelyuskin*, the ship that had sunk in the Arctic. Their fate sounded like a fairy tale. For weeks they had fought for survival on a drifting ice floe, and there was the story of a mother and her baby who had entered the world on the ice. Our hearts reached out to them. Of course, we children followed with the greatest excitement all the phases of the rescue operation, which various aviators had courageously conducted under the most difficult conditions. The names of the pilots Liapidevskii, Kamanin, and Lewoniewski

26. *Milchkissel*, or milk jelly, was a kind of creamy pudding.

27. A prominent and powerful Nazi leader, Hermann Göring (1893–1946) was the president of the Reichstag and a member of Hitler's cabinet.

were on everyone's lips, and even the appearance of the leader of the expedition, Otto Iul'evich Schmidt, an educated man with a wild beard that reached down to his chest, impressed us all. A few years later, with the first landing of a Soviet Arctic expedition on the North Pole, the expedition's radio operator, Ernst Krenkel, proved once more what these explorers were made of. After the rescue of the people from the *Chelyuskin*, the honorary title "Hero of the Soviet Union" was introduced and awarded for the first time. Yes, they were heroes for us boys. We saw them in Red Square, where the members of the expedition and the pilots had taken up their positions next to the Lenin Mausoleum. We were so excited when we marched past. Of course, the applause was also for Stalin and the other party and government leaders who could be seen on the mausoleum gallery.

It was probably around this time that Lothar, the oldest of the Troika, developed a desire to match the achievements of these heroes and become a pilot. To act selflessly and to risk everything for the good of others, all while fearlessly overcoming dangers—that suited him down to the ground. He had learned that from his father.

A couple of years later there was a similar performance. Valerii Chkalov became the first pilot to fly nonstop over the pole from Moscow to Vancouver. Newspapers and radio stations spoke of a likable, educated, and in many ways exemplary aviator. He had shown intelligence and coolness on difficult test flights. His return to Moscow brought millions of people into the streets, and the confetti parade greeting him turned into a triumphal procession. From then on Lothar, the boy from Bohnsdorf, was nicknamed Chkalov.

In those first years of the Troika, Moscow changed its face. The tramlines were pulled up in "our" old Arbat. While there were fewer and fewer horses and carts, and peasants in bast shoes on the streets, one could hardly keep count of the cars.[28] On our way to school we passed a shaft, like a mine shaft: The Metro was being built. We could marvel at the *Metrostroevtsy*, the Metro builders in their special uniforms who could be seen in the flesh as well as on lots of agitprop posters. Entire streets, beautiful old buildings

28. Bast shoes were shoes often made from tree bark and were usually worn by poor folk in Eastern Europe.

on what used to be Tverskaia Street—now Gorky Street—were shunted aside overnight to make room for imposing new buildings. They remain standing to this day. Moscow was being rebuilt. Of course, those new main streets, multistory blocks, whose design would have curdled the blood of Dessau Bauhaus followers, did not solve the dire housing shortage. They could not even ease the problem, and living conditions were modest. But it was a beginning with new standards, a vision of the future, just like the Metro with its underground stations that looked like palaces. The Mikoian sausages and the ice cream that were eaten on the streets and squares all year round were part of it as well.[29] The public habit of relentlessly spitting out the shells of sunflower seeds, which was still the norm when we first got to know Moscow, gradually disappeared.

The boys of the Troika felt more and more at home in the Moscow of the 1930s. They shared the life of their Russian contemporaries. In the summer, long trousers and a gym shirt (fashionable at that time) were all you needed, and sneakers or sandals for your feet. In the winter, you had a coat, a snazzy Russian fur hat, and felt boots if it got really cold. It was cheap to rent ice skates everywhere in the parks, which had turned into enormous natural ice rinks.

Even though travelers and poets have tried to define it, there are many diverse interpretations of "the Russian soul," and without realizing it, the boys took on some of the traits of the Russian people. Many of these traits appealed both to our parents and to unbiased visitors, as well as to the foreign workers who were involved in large numbers in erecting the first great buildings of socialism. These included a hospitable openness, a readiness to share table and bed—indeed everything one had—with a guest or a neighbor, and a disposition to trust a friend and to do anything for them. Then, too, perhaps some of the locals' excessive insouciance, a certain disdain for order and discipline, and a fondness for company and

29. Mikoian sausages, also known as doctor's sausages, were first produced in 1936 at the Moscow meat processing plant named after Soviet official Anastas Mikoian (1895–1978), an influential Soviet statesman who played a leading role in overseeing foreign and domestic trade under both Joseph Stalin and Nikita Khrushchev. Originally developed as a dietary aid for those weakened by starvation, especially after the Civil War, the sausages became popular in the USSR for their mild taste, low cost, and nutritional value.

liquor-laced celebration also rubbed off on the young Soviet citizens. But definitely among the characteristics of the Russian people are their willingness to make any sacrifice, their ability to develop unimaginable strength, and, when threatened or challenged, to square up for a fight.

In later years, we would argue about the role played by the hard-won collectivization, the socialist transformation of agriculture, and the industrialization pushed through by Stalin as the country faced the grave and imminent ordeal of war, and about their long-term effects on the country. At the time, however, for us, the Young Pioneers and future Komsomol members, Stalin's words were beyond reproach.[30] Everything the Soviet people achieved in those days, whether with the eagerness of a new beginning or with great sacrifice, was inextricably bound up with the name Stalin. Foreign visitors may have snickered at our enthusiasm for the first fruits of socialist construction—and, indeed, in later years, much of what was achieved might not have withstood modern tastes and increased demands. But after so many years of hardship and privation it was a beginning; it launched a vast country's journey out of darkness and economic backwardness into a new era—into socialism. The accelerated development of huge industries and the consequent unremitting loss of many of the comforts of life served as necessary preparation for the ordeals of war. Some of the manifest benefits of socialism are now recognized. Other things, even decisive things, still need to be proven right in today's practice.

Certainly, even then, there already existed "the other"—something profoundly alien to socialist ideals. For many people, including the boys of the Troika, this "other" wasn't clearly identifiable at the time. And even after many years, we were not able to fully comprehend its growth and its pernicious scope.

* * *

On December 1, 1934, in Leningrad, the first secretary of the local Communist Party, Sergei Mironovich Kirov, a prominent official since the revolutionary days, was assassinated by a former party employee,

30. The Komsomol was a Soviet youth organization founded in 1918. It aimed to politically socialize and indoctrinate young people ages fourteen to twenty-eight while promoting community involvement and loyalty to the Communist Party.

Leonid Nikolaev.[31] His murder shook people throughout the country. Kirov was widely known and well loved. At his memorial, and then at the funeral in Moscow at the Kremlin wall behind the Lenin Mausoleum, an enormous crowd gathered while Stalin and all the other leaders honored the dead man. As a result of this murder—the circumstances of which remain shrouded in mystery even today—the word "vigilance" gained a new and ominous connotation.[32] The following years saw an increasing number of arrests and persecutions. Within our families' orbit, the fathers of our Russian classmates who had worked in Germany were the first to disappear; then the fathers of our German classmates and some of our teachers were arrested.

Koni had just turned ten when he got a part in Gustav von Wangenheim's film *Kämpfer* (*The Struggle*). The film tells the story of Georgi Dimitrov's unbreakable spirit during the Reichstag Fire trial, and the significance of his appearance before the Leipzig court for the antifascist struggle in Germany. Some amateurs and many German émigré actors appeared in this film, including Lotte Löbinger,[33] Heinrich Greif,[34] and Bruno Schmidtsdorf.[35] But even a few of these friends and acquaintances got arrested.

At the Hotel Lux more and more relatives of the arrested people moved from the main building into communal apartments in the courtyard. The Wlochs were among the first families so affected.

Portraits of prominent politicians and military men were removed from the walls of offices, factories, and schools. Of the five holders of the

31. The city of St. Petersburg was known as Leningrad from 1924 to 1991.

32. Nikolaev and thirteen alleged accomplices were executed, and Stalin later claimed to uncover a vast anti-Stalinist conspiracy and launched the Great Purge, which included the execution of hundreds in Leningrad and the imprisonment of thousands in labor camps.

33. Lotte Löbinger (1905–1999) was a German actress who began her career in renown stage director Erwin Piscator's ensemble at the Volksbühne (People's Theater) in Berlin. She married the communist leader Herbert Wehner, and emigrated to Poland, then the Soviet Union in December 1933. She returned to Berlin in 1945 to resume her acting career.

34. Heinrich Greif (1907–1946) was a German actor and a member of the Communist Party of Germany. In 1935, he fled to the Soviet Union, returning to Germany in 1945, where he performed at the Deutsches Theater in Berlin.

35. Bruno Schmidtsdorf (1908–1938) was a German actor who went with the Kolonne Links ensemble to the Soviet Union in 1931 and a few years later became a Soviet citizen. He was arrested and executed by Soviet secret police in February 1938.

very recently established military rank of Marshal of the Soviet Union, only the pictures of Voroshilov[36] and Budenny[37] remained. Images of other heroes of the Russian Civil War—Tukhachevskii,[38] Bliukher,[39] and Egorov[40]—had to be removed. It all seemed so mysterious, confusing, and inexplicable . . .

In public hearings celebrated individuals were accused of being "Enemies of the People." A terrible charge . . . As a journalist Louis Fischer was present at the tribunals against these individuals, many of whom he knew personally and whom he had seen fighting alongside Lenin. Grigory Zinov'ev was now on trial.[41] Fischer was friends with the Zinov'ev family, as well as with the families of many other Bolshevik leaders who were subsequently charged. In April 1917, Zinov'ev and Lenin's return to Russia from exile in Switzerland, in a sealed train traveling through Germany and Sweden, was organized by the Swiss comrade Fritz Platten.[42] Platten visited us a few times in our Moscow apartment. He also disappeared one day.

36. Kliment Voroshilov (1881–1969) was a Soviet politician and military leader as well as a close ally of Stalin. He served as the people's commissar for defense (1925–1940), was a member of the State Defense Committee during World War II, and later chaired the Presidium of the Supreme Soviet (1953–1960). He also held key roles during the Russian Civil War.

37. Semyon M. Budenny (1883–1973) was a Soviet military commander, one of the original five Marshals of the Soviet Union. During World War II, he served as commander in chief of the Soviet armed forces confronting German forces in Ukraine. After defeats in the Battle of Uman and the Battle of Kiev, he was relieved of his command. After the war he became deputy minister of agriculture.

38. Mikhail N. Tukhachevskii (1893–1937) was chief of staff for the Red Army and appointed in 1935 to the rank of Marshal of the Soviet Union. He was executed as part of the military purges in June 1937.

39. Vasilii Bliukher (1889–1938) was a Soviet military commander of the Far Eastern Military District and appointed Marshal of the Soviet Union in 1935. He died from his injuries after his arrest by Soviet secret police in October 1938.

40. Aleksandr Egorov (1883–1939) was a Soviet military commander appointed Marshal of the Soviet Union in 1935. He presided over the trial of Tukhachevskii only to be arrested a few months later and executed in February 1939.

41. Grigory Zinov'ev (1883–1936), a close associate of Vladimir Lenin and Lev Kamenev and a member of the Soviet Communist Party's politburo, was accused of treason during the Great Purge, tried, and executed in August 1936.

42. Fritz Platten (1883–1942) was a Swiss communist who lived in Moscow from 1926 onward; he was arrested by Soviet secret police in 1938 and shot in 1942.

The trials led to a change in Louis Fischer's attitude toward the Soviet Union. Since 1922 he, a bourgeois American journalist, had reported on the country with growing fondness, and he had even met Lenin in person. Later, in his autobiography, *Men and Politics,* he wrote about this meeting. It happened during a conference of the All-Russia Central Executive Committee in October of the year when Lenin had his first stroke. It was the first time that his doctors permitted Lenin to appear, and he was allowed to speak in public for only fifteen minutes. The conference delegates asked for a photograph to be taken, and Louis Fischer can be seen alongside Lenin, Kamenev,[43] Zinov'ev, and Kalinin.[44]

Fischer was a friend of the Soviet Union, but never a communist, never a party member. He believed then that, in spite of the repression, the Soviet government had brought a new freedom to the workers, peasants, women, young people, and national minorities, and that, over time, the dictatorship would develop into a genuine new democracy. It was in Fischer's books and articles that many liberal Americans first heard about Lenin's theories and the changes in the Soviet Union after the October Revolution. When word got out about the reprisals of the 1930s, Fischer still hoped that the new 1936 constitution of the Soviet Union would be an important step in the direction of becoming a socialist democracy. That would have been as Lenin would have wanted it. What Fischer witnessed, however, destroyed his faith.

It wasn't until after Stalin's death in March 1953 that it was revealed how the show trials came to happen, and how numerous innocent people—many of them courageous fighters for the revolution and the communist cause—became victims of arbitrary punishment. Among the dead was also Lothar's father, Wilhelm Wloch.

In retrospect, it is difficult to describe how we coped with these events. It is even more difficult, if not impossible, to explain to today's young people what happened back then. It is not as if fear and fright dominated our lives; as if we regarded the Soviet Union as our socialist

43. Lev B. Kamenev (1883–1936) was a Russian revolutionary who served as Soviet deputy prime minister from 1923 to 1926; he was tried in 1935 and 1936 and executed in August 1936.

44. Mikhail Kalinin (1875–1946) was a Russian revolutionary who served as chairman of the Presidium of the Supreme Soviet from 1938 to 1946.

Heimat any less; or as if we experienced our childhood and youth as any less happy.

So many things were contradictory. The situation was not mentioned when we had contact with the affected families. Most people believed that everything was either a huge misunderstanding or the result of malicious denunciations. Some of those who had been arrested were released, including some for whom others had pleaded. Those that had been released seldom spoke about what they had experienced, and even they fed the hope that these were misunderstandings that would soon be corrected.

Wilhelm Wloch believed this, too. Until the very last he believed everything was an aberration or bureaucratic excess. During one of the last meetings he is supposed to have said: "Comrade Stalin doesn't know what's going on." No one doubted Stalin. He remained the embodiment of our cause, our moral and noble cause.

Only later, when Erna and her family sought shelter with us, did we children hear about the arrest of Lotka's father. Before that Erna had asked Markoosha and our mother if we children would still be permitted to be around her family. It was of course not an issue for us. We treated all of our friends as we had before.

When the mother of our half sister Lena, who lived in the Volga German Autonomous Soviet Socialist Republic with many other German émigrés, was arrested, our mother did not hesitate to take her little Lenochka.[45] Our mother, Meni, who many in Moscow affectionately called Elsochka, had become, like Markoosha Fischer, a refuge for many looking for help and consolation. As with so many other things, we only understood much later what they did then and how much courage they had shown. Much was kept from us, of course—partly to protect us, but also because the grown-ups themselves didn't really know what was going on. Even later, when we thought we knew all there was to know, even more would come to light.

45. The Volga German Autonomous Soviet Socialist Republic was an autonomous republic within Soviet Russia that had Engels, on the Volga River, as its capital city. It was dissolved after the German invasion of the Soviet Union in 1941.

We had deeply absorbed into our young consciousness everything we'd learned about communist aims and ideals from our parents, from close friends, from school, and from our beloved films and books about the Revolution. None of this squared with the arbitrariness, injustice, and cruelty. We'd been reading Marx, Engels, and Lenin from a young age. Their ideas were alive for us in this country that we gradually thought of as home. We loved it; its people became and remain our friends. We increasingly mastered and appreciated its language and its great culture. It wasn't its dark shadows that determined our way of life and our thinking.

For us, the threat lay outside the country. The threat of fascism dominated our thoughts. Father's play *Professor Mamlock* was produced with great success, and a film version was being made.

Italy's Mussolini attacked Abyssinia. Newspapers and magazines reported on this and on other preparations for war in Germany. We knew more about the fight against Nazism and the persecution of the opponents of Nazism in our old country than about what was happening on our own doorstep. The children of the many antifascists who were incarcerated and murdered by the Nazis were our friends.

The great experience of solidarity in our youth was the Spanish Civil War. Year after year and day by day we followed the heroic fight of the Republicans against the Franco putschists and their supporters, Hitler and Mussolini. Fathers of our classmates fought in the International Brigades. Louis Fischer was in close contact with the Republican Negrín government, and, through Yura and Vitya Fischer, we met the prime minister's son, Miguel Negrín, in Moscow.[46] Then Louis Fischer traveled to Madrid and devoted himself to the defense of the Republic. When he wrote about Spain, his usually sober journalistic style became passionate. For him, Spain became "the Russia of the Mediterranean." After three months in Spain he went on a lecture tour of the US, raising donations and recruiting volunteers for the International Brigades. Negrín trusted

46. Juan Negrín (1892–1956) was president of the Council of Ministers of the Second Spanish Republic and the head of the Spanish Republican government in exile from 1937 to 1945.

Fischer. On his occasional visits to Moscow, Fischer provided his hosts, Georgi Dimitrov and the foreign minister, Litvinov, with Negrín's personal assessment of the situation.[47] For many years Fischer had been in close personal contact with Litvinov. These visits to Moscow generated a veritable Spain fever in Fischer. The [Soviet] friends deflected questions about internal events in the Soviet Union: Spain is more important, they said. When we win in Spain, we will be happy here too.

We didn't miss a single newsreel in our cinema on the Arbat; Dolores Ibárruri became a symbol of the war in Spain.[48] We followed the fighting anxiously. Spanish posters hung in our small bedrooms. We wore the little berets of the Spanish Republicans proudly as headdresses.

Our father also tried to get to France in order to get into Spain. After his departure, Koni sat down and drew, as he imagined it, an illustrated story about the journey up until Father's return. Those pictures have survived to this day. How important Spain was to us!

Our father failed to reach Spain—it was no longer possible. The West's policy of nonintervention had closed the borders. Ernst Busch, however, was still there, our Ernst! In 1936, the year the Spanish Civil War began, we had sung songs with him, "Das Einheitsfrontlied" ["Song of the United Front"], "Die Moorsoldaten" ["The Peat Bog Soldiers"], and many others, in the Hall of Columns of the union building.[49] Forty-five years later Koni would memorialize this in film.

What a role these songs played in our lives, in the lives of whole generations! The voices of Ernst Busch and Paul Robeson followed us deep into the postwar period. Each phase in a struggle for freedom has its singers and its songs—songs of victory and songs of defeat. These days

47. Maksim Litvinov (1876–1951) was a Russian revolutionary and leading Soviet diplomat who served as the people's commissar for foreign affairs from 1930 to 1939.

48. Dolores Ibárruri (1895–1989) was a Spanish communist who became an icon of the Republican struggle.

49. Wolf here is referring to the House of the Unions, a historic landmark situated in the Tverskoi district, in the heart of Moscow. Originally a noblemen's assembly hall, it was transferred to the Moscow Trade Unions after the October Revolution.

Harry Belafonte,[50] Miriam Makeba,[51] and Isabel Parra[52] stir young people's spirit of solidarity with freedom fighters in America, South Africa, or Asia. Víctor Jara sang in Chile and was immortalized after his cowardly murder.[53] After the fall of the fascist regime in Portugal, how many hopes attached themselves to "Grândola," the song of the carnation? Up until his death, Koni listened over and over again on his hospital bed to the record *Canto General* by his beloved Mikis Theodorakis. It was based on the wonderful poem by Pablo Neruda. Theodorakis himself had presented it to Koni with a personal dedication. In the same way that young people today feel deeply for those who fight for freedom and human dignity, we felt for the courageous Spaniards who attempted to stop fascism with the slogan *¡No Pasarán! ¡No Pasarán!*—"They Shall Not Pass!"

Even after fate had set the Troika on very different paths, none of them could recall the experience of Spain without being deeply moved: the arrival of the little Spanish children; their poignant welcome to the Soviet Union; and the films and songs of those years. In those films and songs resonated so much of what all three had absorbed from the dreams of freedom fighters since the beginning of their conscious thinking. The great ideals and moral principles of the Russian Revolution and its pioneers had left deep and lasting footprints in the hearts and minds of the three boys. The heroes of their favorite films—*Chapaev*, depicted with his swords at the ready in a 1936 drawing made by Koni; *We Are from Kronstadt*; the

50. Harry Belafonte (1927–2023) was an American singer, actor, and civil rights activist who helped bring calypso music to international prominence in the 1950s and 1960s. A close confidant of Martin Luther King Jr., he played a key role in the civil rights movement and later served as a celebrity ambassador for the American Civil Liberties Union, focusing on juvenile justice issues.

51. Zenzile Miriam Makeba (1932–2008), known as Mama Africa, was a South African singer, songwriter, actress, and civil rights activist. Known for her work in Afropop, jazz, and world music, she was a prominent voice in the fight against apartheid and White-minority rule in South Africa.

52. Violeta Isabel Cereceda Parra (born 1939), known as Isabel Parra, is a renowned Chilean singer-songwriter and performer of Latin American folk music. Following the Chilean coup on September 11, 1973, she spent many years in exile in Argentina and France, returning home after the restoration of democracy.

53. Víctor Lidio Jara Martínez (1932–1973) was a Chilean teacher, theater director, poet, singer-songwriter, and committed communist political activist.

Maksim trilogy;[54] or the Lenin films of those years—did not present them with phantoms. These characters were paragons, exemplary in their readiness to utterly commit themselves to the good of the working people. They were prepared to sacrifice everything, even their lives, for the revolutionary cause.

Meanwhile, we were attending Russian schools. Our parents were insistent that we children should immerse ourselves in the country as quickly as possible. It would be our home for the foreseeable future. They didn't want us to isolate ourselves, as some other émigrés had done; instead, we were encouraged to get to know the language and the customs of our peers and participate fully in their everyday lives.

The School Number 110, the Fridtjof Nansen School, which Vitya Fischer and we two Wolf sons attended along with other former Liebknecht pupils, was a former grammar school located on Merzliakovskii Lane. This street was not far from our apartment on the Arbat, in one of Moscow's venerable neighborhoods between Arbat Street, Vorovsky Street, and another street that also led to the city center that was named after the nineteenth-century revolutionary democrat Aleksandr Herzen.[55] Although hardly any descendants of the former elite, members of the nobility and the old intelligentsia, could be found there, the school retained a special atmosphere. It had a fine reputation, and its headmaster, Ivan Kuzmich Novikov, was equally highly regarded, even by the pupils. He personally led the so-called newspaper hour when students were given an opportunity to air their opinions and to discuss current political events on their own. But that was not all. The rich treasures of Russian culture, its music and fine arts, lived with the pupils. The teachers contributed to this. Going to concerts and holding discussions about the paintings in the museums were as natural a part of our daily lives as the old sagas and all the wonderful literature from Pushkin to Yesenin and Mayakovski. But we also devoured Heine, Galsworthy, and Hemingway, and engaged in heated discussions about them. The wall newspapers, which the school's

54. Wolf here refers to a Soviet film trilogy about a factory worker named Maksim, directed by Grigory Kozintsev and Leonid Trauberg, which was produced between 1935 and 1939.

55. Aleksandr Herzen (1812–1870) was a Russian writer, journalist, and political thinker who is widely regarded as the "father of Russian socialism."

classes produced competitively for the frequent anniversaries, were real works of art.

Theater people and writers from all over the world came to our apartment. Vsevolod Vishnevskii, a friend as well as translator of our father's plays, lived directly opposite us. He was a renowned writer, author of *An Optimistic Tragedy*, a play about the Russian Civil War, and the film *We Are from Kronstadt*. After the Revolution he had fought on the front lines in the navy and was a machine gunner in Budenny's cavalry. On public holidays he wore his navy uniform with all his medals, and Koni was proud, of course, when he was allowed to go to the Red Square parades at Vishnevskii's side. He was my guarantor when I joined the Communist Youth League, the Komsomol. We met many authors and their children at camp and in the homes of members of the Union of Soviet Writers.

Members of the intelligentsia were also frequent visitors to the Fischers' place. It was there, mostly on the Fischers' toilet, that Sergei Eisenstein, director of *Battleship Potemkin*, kept himself up to date on world news through American newspapers and magazines. His cameraman, Eduard Tisse, was a friend of the Fischers', as was the journalist Sergei Tret'yakov. Tret'yakov knew our father well. He came to see him in Stuttgart and wrote an article about him. Paul Robeson rubbed shoulders with the Fischers.[56]

Meanwhile, Yura, my classmate, had become a full-fledged member of the Komsomol. His 32nd Lepeshinski Model-School, right next door to the Kremlin, was attended by Mikoian's children as well as those of many other famous people. Because of the staunchly party-line principal there was a distinctive political atmosphere in the school. Stalin's daughter, Svetlana—who, decades later, would cross paths several times with the Fischers in the US—studied at School Number 25, not far away, alongside the children of other German émigrés we knew.

For the Wlochs, everything was very different. They fell on hard times following their move into a tiny room in the stone barracks in the Hotel Lux's courtyard. Contact with similarly affected families there

56. Paul Robeson (1898–1976) was an American actor, bass-baritone singer, professional football player, and activist.

did not make life any easier. Erna Wloch searched in vain for work. Lothar, as was his nature, very quickly tried to take on the role of head of the family and became his mother's caring friend and helpmate. They both did their best to protect Margot, the baby of the family, from their everyday anxieties. For a long time she was told that Daddy had written from abroad, that he sent her his love, and that he hoped she would study hard at school. In fact, Margot and Lothar were good students. Margot quickly learned to speak Russian like a native Muscovite. She had Russian girlfriends who called her Margochka, and she felt completely at ease with them. But it wasn't possible to hide the truth from her for long. She saw her mother sell her beautiful kimonos, her silk blouses, her fur coat, and the ivory Chinese mah-jongg set so that she could pay for the necessities of life. Then she experienced Erna queuing up at the different detention centers, waiting until her letter was called to deposit money. If this was happening, it was clear that Daddy was alive, and in there.

Life got easier for her when our mother suggested to the Wlochs that they move in with us. The apartment was very overcrowded, but in the summer there was Peredelkino.

Peredelkino! This small, picturesque suburb of Moscow was barely an hour by train from Kievskii Station and had been selected by the writers as a retreat. With the growing success of his plays, our father had the opportunity—and a little money—to rent and develop a parcel of land that was thick with birch trees. From the property, at the edge of the settlement, we could see, beyond a meadow, the stream that meandered into the village pond, a hill with a small cemetery, and the old Orthodox church.

A friend of the Wlochs' had a good idea. From a newspaper publishing company—and for free—he got hold of the cores around which newsprint was wound, a cheap building material. This friend designed a semi-detached house. For the Wolfs' half he conceived an extensive wooden veranda, the ceiling of which would become the balcony. The other half was taken by good friends of our father, Asja Lācis and Bernhard Reich, a married couple who were deeply involved in the development of German theater. Born in Latvia, Asja was a revolutionary who ran a Latvian theater company in Moscow where our father's plays were performed. Bernhard

Reich was one of Bertolt Brecht's closest friends and collaborators.[57] He had already moved to Moscow as a theater scholar in the early 1930s. Asja's daughter Dagmar, called Daga, was one of us.

Soon there was a simple and beautiful summerhouse that everyone loved. For the Troika it was paradise. Hardworking Lothar, focused and ever helpful, led the troops with the groundwork and later with the care of Meni's lovingly planted herb and vegetable garden. The Fischers too put in their shift. On one occasion, they brought Paul Massing with them. He, the Berliner foster father of the Fischer boys, was a remarkable man. He was in his late thirties, calm and reserved on the surface, and with an athletic build; he was handsome. We had read his book about the tortures he'd suffered under the Nazis. He was a hero to us for that reason alone. An agronomist by profession, he had been, like many young Marxists, a supporter of the Soviet Union since the 1920s. He'd joined the staff of an academic newspaper published by the Moscow Agricultural Institute. That is how he came to be in Moscow, where he got to know the Fischers. In 1931 in Germany, together with Dr. Arvid Harnack, he founded the Working Group for the Study of the Soviet Planned Economy (ARPLAN). I've only recently discovered this, now, as I write these lines. Today I realize that when we got to know Paul Massing, Arvid Harnack had already become involved in the hazardous intelligence battle at the heart of Hitler's preparations for war. Harnack fought alongside Harro Schulze-Boysen in the antifascist resistance organization that would later be named after the two of them.[58] He was executed along with his comrades at Berlin-Plötzensee on December 22, 1942. The strands of fate would intertwine, as they so often did, on this very spot.

57. Bernhard Reich (1894–1972) was an Austrian Jewish director and drama theorist and is regarded as a key figure in German theater of the 1920s. He collaborated with leading directors including Max Reinhardt and, notably, German theater practitioner, playwright, and poet Bertolt Brecht (1898–1956). After surviving Stalinist repression, Reich spent the final two decades of his life in Latvia.

58. Harro Schulze-Boysen (1909–1942) was a German journalist, a lieutenant in the Luftwaffe, and a leading member of the Rote Kapelle (Red Orchestra) resistance group. A staunch opponent of National Socialism, he sought to expose the crimes of the Nazi regime and was executed in 1942.

That summer in Peredelkino, none of us had a clue about the conspiratorial work that Paul Massing was doing on behalf of the Soviet Union. Nobody knew that every day in Moscow he anticipated his own arrest. Thanks, presumably, to the American passports held by him and his wife, he eluded it. Back then, Paul was our buddy. He knew interesting ways to keep us entertained and occupied. There was fantastic food he treated us to in his hotel, courtesy of his vouchers. We could play cops and robbers in the corridors. But he never let any of us beat him at chess.

At the same time, the sons of the Lammert family joined the ever-growing Wolf colony in Peredelkino. The German sculptor Will Lammert, who'd emigrated to Moscow, had no work or any commissions. He didn't even have his own apartment; his wife Hete worked as a doctor in the Schutzbund children's home. That's why their sons, Till and Ule, boarded with the Austrian children there. The Lammerts took up the offer of lodging in the Wolfs' dacha. They winterized the lower floor. Consequently the younger son, Ule, became something of a horse running alongside the Troika. Later he was to become a faithful friend of our family.

In the next, particularly beautiful summer, with our father in France and Asja Lācis arrested, Peredelkino once more became a meeting place for many friends of the family. Hans Rodenberg[59] and Alfred Kurella[60] with his son Grisha were frequent guests. Eva Siao and her newborn son, Lion, lived in our dacha for the whole summer.[61] Eva was of German-Jewish descent and, since 1930, had lived with her brother in Sweden. During a tourist visit to the Soviet Union, she met the Moscow-based Chinese writer and communist Emi Siao by the Black Sea. It was love at first sight, followed by a lifelong union of adventure and challenging times.

59. Hans Rodenberg (1895–1978) was a German theater director, translator, and film producer who held key roles in the GDR's Academy of Arts. He emigrated to the Soviet Union in 1932 and became deputy director of Mezhrabpomfil'm (a German-Russian film studio) in Moscow in 1935. Until returning to Berlin in 1948, he worked in the USSR as a writer, scenarist, and broadcaster.

60. Alfred Kurella (1895–1975) was a German writer and cultural official in East Germany's SED. He moved to Moscow in 1934, wrote for the *Deutsche Zentral-Zeitung,* and became a Soviet citizen in 1937. In 1943, he joined the anti-Nazi National Committee for a Free Germany. His brother Heinrich, also in Soviet exile, was executed during the Great Purge. Kurella returned to East Germany in 1954.

61. Eva Siao (1911–2001) was a German-born photographer who lived and worked in China.

The baby was named Lion because Eva specially revered the writer Lion Feuchtwanger and because the name had a Chinese ring to it. When the baby cried in his carriage in the meadow, Ule Lammert called up to us: "Little Feuchtwanger is screaming!" Eva, who was also a photographer, provided us with the very first photograph of the Troika and many other mementos of that summer in Peredelkino.

Two four-legged friends, Troll and Dosor, were also part of dacha life. Troll was a beautiful, gentle Saint Bernard. The Wloch family carried her through their times of need, sacrifice, and austerity. When she caught distemper, she was cosseted by the whole commune and eventually nursed back to health. Dosor, on the other hand, was a real wolfhound, although he was more of a playmate than a guard dog.

We young Germans were soon very welcome guests throughout the entire writers' colony, especially among the young women. There were the daughters of Konstantin Fedin and Il'ia Selvinskii, Nina and Zilya, who taught us boys our first dance steps to the music of an old gramophone.[62] Fierce volleyball games took place on the property of dramatist Afinogenov, also an acquaintance of the Fischers'.[63] Even the poet Boris Pasternak allowed himself to be distracted from his work and came over from his house next door to watch, with a smile and with his hands in his pockets, how his wife, Zinaida Nikolaevna, tried to keep up with the young people's game with a cigarette between her lips.

Boris Pasternak, one of the greats of Russian literature, and also a sensitive translator of the German classics, was among the writers who were defamed and denounced shortly after the war. He was buried in the quiet little cemetery in Peredelkino in 1960. It was not until years after his death that he was given the justice he deserved.

In spite of everything that was going on, Peredelkino was like an idyll to us—the carefree games, swimming in the pond, the mushroom hunts,

62. Konstantin Fedin (1892–1977) was a Soviet and Russian novelist and literary official, best known for his early works that explore the struggles of intellectuals in Soviet Russia.

63. Aleksandr Afinogenov (1904–1941) was a notable Russian and Soviet playwright and dramatist whose works examined various aspects of Soviet life, focusing on issues such as labor struggles, the Communist ideal, and the complexities of a transforming social order.

the nightly dances, the first young loves with kisses under the full moon, skiing on New Year's Eve . . .

None of us were really aware that the intensity of first love was blossoming between Lothar and Zilya, whose affection everyone was trying to win. While the Troika boys were already engaging in deep conversations about the meaning of life, this young pair were discussing it, and other things, with even greater seriousness. They dreamed about the future, made plans for their lives, and couldn't imagine ever being apart. This is how Peredelkino remained in the memories of the Troika: romantic, peaceful, full of summer warmth or pure white snow and glimmering clear winter air.

But clouds were forming, and they were becoming increasingly threatening . . .

The flames of war began to spread all over Europe. On August 23, 1939, the Union of Soviet Socialist Republics and Germany signed a nonaggression pact. There were fierce debates about it among the émigrés in Moscow. It was in fact extremely difficult for them to stomach the pictures on the front pages of *Pravda* showing Stalin standing alongside the Nazi foreign minister Ribbentrop.[64] On the reciprocal visit to Berlin, Molotov stood beside Hitler.[65] It was equally difficult to accept some of the rationale for the pact offered to the public. Too stark was its contradiction to the way that Hitler-style fascism had, until very recently, been characterized.

The émigrés who were trapped alongside our father in France, and those members of the International Brigades coming from Spain after Franco's victory, rationalized this pact as an understandable attempt by the Soviet leadership not to be exposed on its own to Hitler's drive eastward, and to buy time for the country to defend itself. Before the pact, the Soviet Union had tried for months, in vain, to achieve a policy of collective security in Europe and to reach an agreement with the Western

64. Joachim von Ribbentrop (1893–1946) was a German Nazi official and diplomat who served as the minister of foreign affairs in Nazi Germany from 1938 to 1945.

65. Vyacheslav Molotov (1890–1986) was a Soviet politician, diplomat, and revolutionary who played a central role in the Soviet government from the 1920s through the 1950s and was one of Joseph Stalin's most trusted associates.

powers to counter Hitler's aggressive expansionist plans. The antifascists who lived in the West could see all around them the evidence of how the British and French governments' policy of nonintervention in the Spanish Civil War only encouraged Hitler's continued belligerence. After the German army had marched into Austria, this policy led, in the autumn of 1938, to the Munich Agreement, a betrayal of the Czechoslovak republic. The names of the British prime minister [Neville] Chamberlain and the French prime minister [Édouard] Daladier became bywords for the fatal policy of "appeasement."

Louis Fischer renounced the Soviet Union once and for all after the signing of the nonaggression pact, and, in his autobiography published a few years later, aptly illustrated the disastrous consequences for European peace of the Chamberlain/Daladier policy. He described how, before the Munich Agreement, the Soviet Union attempted to combine efforts with the Western powers in order to protect Czechoslovakia, to which it provided military aircraft at short notice, and how the foreign minister Litvinov again and again called on the League of Nations to cooperate. Fischer elucidated the Soviet Union's attempts to prevent a world war. Although he had begun to break with the Soviet Union over the Moscow Trials, he refrained from any public criticism. Instead, he explained himself in his book *Men and Politics*: "Why, instead of holding my tongue, did I not come out in 1937 or 1938 as a critic of the Soviet regime? It is not so easy to throw away the vision to which one has been attached for fifteen years. Moreover, in 1938, the Soviet government's foreign policy was still effectively anti-appeasement and anti-Fascist, much more so than England's or France's or America's. It helped China with arms to fight Japanese aggression. It helped Spain with arms to fight the Nazis and Mussolini. It encouraged Czechoslovakia to stand firm against Hitler. I did not know how long it would last. But as long as it lasted, I hesitated to throw stones in public. Even now I think I was right. In private, if asked, I made it clear that I had cooled toward Soviet domestic policy. My friends can confirm that and so, if they will, can some of my ex-friends."

Only after the nonaggression pact was signed did he give up on this restraint and start to publicly compare Stalin with Hitler. In spite of everything, however, our father still believed that the Soviet Union was the fundamental bastion against fascism. Therefore, while in France, a serious dispute arose between him and Fischer, causing an end to their friendship.

The Troika boys knew very little of all this. For them, the goings-on were difficult to understand, and in 1939 there was a lot for everyone to think about. Events came thick and fast. We were interested in many things. We did not understand everything. Like most of the adults, we trusted the leadership, but we also shared the feelings of aversion to anything which in any way appeared to be sidling up to the hated Nazi regime.

On September 1, 1939, Germany unleashed World War II.

The fathers of the three boys were far from their families.

There was hardly any news from Wilhelm Wloch. Lothar, Margot, and their mother moved permanently into our city apartment. Meni and Erna slept in the beds, Margot slept on a folding bed, Lothar slept in the kitchen, and Koni and I shared our small walk-through room. Sister Lenochka also stayed with us from time to time. At night, one of us always got a visit from Troll, the Saint Bernard. In the summer, in Peredelkino, we could use the loft; life was a lot easier there.

Lotka hardly ever talked about his father's fate or about his own problems that came with that. He was becoming his mother's precocious helpmate. She discussed everything with him.

Louis Fischer continued to concern himself with the Spanish Republic, and also with the American Lincoln Battalion. He traveled between the US and France. He was seen as a traitor by many in the International Brigades. At the same time the French secret service suspected that he was spying for the Soviet Union. In order to be reunited with his family, he applied to the Soviet embassy in Paris in May 1938 for a temporary visa for his loved ones to leave the Soviet Union. As there was no response, he turned directly to Eleanor Roosevelt, the wife of the US president. Fischer later reported that Mrs. Roosevelt, after having a conversation with him, personally approached the Soviet ambassador in Washington on his behalf.

Shortly after the outbreak of the war, our father was detained in Paris and sent to Le Vernet, a camp in the foothills of the Pyrenees. By a variety of methods, we got letters and messages from there. They show that the inmates were treated as if they were in a concentration camp. Members of the International Brigades from Spain, including leading communists such as Franz Dahlem,[66] Heinrich Rau,[67] and Paul Merker,[68] continued the struggle among the diverse inmates with their differing political standpoints, and they called the shots. The spirit of solidarity among the friends and comrades at Le Vernet created the conditions that enabled Friedrich Wolf to write in the camp barracks. Thus there came into being thrilling stories about life in the camp, and the play *Beaumarchais*, about the poet who wrote [*The Marriage of*] *Figaro* around the time of the French Revolution of 1789.

In Moscow, with the support of our friend Vsevolod Vishnevskii, Mother fought to obtain Soviet citizenship for our father. Others searched for different paths to freedom; many did not succeed. For our father, a return to the Soviet Union was the only option. In those days that was not a matter of course, and it certainly was not easy. It took many nerve-wracking months.

After his daring journey on a passport with somebody else's name, Father's and our day finally arrived in March 1941, which Koni remembered like this: "It was, I think, a Sunday. And it was at Kievskii Station. It was there that we experienced our father as a real person. For me, it was unforgettable. It was an experience that involved the profound tension and the intensity of an entire life, of his character, of his personality, and for both of us it was larger and more powerful than the period of separation. As we drove to Kievskii Station with Vishnevskii, we knew nothing. Nothing yet. There were only a handful of people on the platform. And us. Vishnevskii said: 'Your father will arrive in a quarter of an hour.'

"Everything was empty. A train was coming. It stopped. And out of the train came people, members of the International Brigades. They were in tattered rags, scarred. And they had a flag. They unfurled it—the flag of

66. Franz Dahlem (1892–1981) was a leading figure in the German Communist Party. Following the Nazi rise to power in 1933, he fled to France, later participating in the Spanish Civil War. In 1939, he was interned by the French authorities and, in 1942, handed over to the Gestapo. He was subsequently imprisoned in Mauthausen concentration camp. After the war, Dahlem settled in Berlin.

67. Heinrich Rau (1899–1961) was a communist politician. After World War II, he was a member of the politburo of the Central Committee of the SED and chairman of the State Planning Commission in the GDR.

68. Paul Merker (1894–1969) was a German politician and prominent functionary of both the Communist Party of Germany and, later, the SED.

the Spanish Republican Army. A few words: *Pasaremos*. And with this flag, among these people, was our father."

By the time our family was finally reunited, the Fischers and the Wlochs had already left Moscow.

For the Fischers, the family reunion was a reverse image of ours. Vitya was the only one Markoosha spoke to about the plan to leave the Soviet Union for good. Yura had become such a committed [Komsomol member] that the parental plans would have overwhelmed him. How was he supposed to make a home in America when he had never even seen it? The Fischers were granted their exit visa in 1939. It was a quiet, understated parting. Our mother was their only friend who saw them off from the station.

Then we received messages from Finland. We got one or two letters from New York. With the Nazi invasion of the Soviet Union in 1941, we lost contact . . . until one day Yura, wearing an American uniform, appeared at the doorstep of our Moscow apartment. But by then the war was almost over . . .

The Wlochs were beset by the cruelest fate. Shortly after the Fischers' departure, Lothar heard, more by chance, of his father's death.[69] Erna battled to have it confirmed. Eventually it was.

Wilhelm Wloch, a German communist, was a true friend of the Soviet Union. He was among those who stood at the side of the first workers-and-peasants state out of deep conviction. He did underground work at the invisible front. As with Richard Sorge, orders took him to China.[70] Innumerable international activists such as Arvid Harnack and Harro Schulze-Boysen gave their lives in the fight against fascism and war. They did all they could to protect the first socialist country against the approaching danger and to issue warnings before it was too late.

69. Wloch became a victim of Stalin's purges. The People's Commissariat for Internal Affairs (usually referred to by its Russian initials, NKVD) arrested him in July 1937, and in April 1939, he was sentenced to twenty years in a labor camp. According to Soviet records, he died of heart failure in October 1939 while being transferred to another gulag.

70. Richard Sorge (1895–1944) was a German-Russian journalist and Soviet military intelligence agent who operated in China and Japan before and during World War II. A member of the Communist International (or Comintern), he used the code name "Ramsay" while spying in Japan. In 1941, he informed Moscow of the exact date of Germany's planned invasion of the Soviet Union and later confirmed that Japan had no intention of attacking the USSR.

Wilhelm Wloch, believing in the Soviet Union and its goals and ideals until the end, became, like others, a victim of arbitrary, unsubstantiated allegations. Those among his fellow victims who survived continued undeterred in the fight against fascism, in order to liberate their fatherland and, afterward, to build socialism. If Wilhelm Wloch had survived, he would have been among them and with us. I am sure of it.

For seventeen-year-old Lothar, the death of his father would be an incurable and lifelong pain. He never recovered from the shock. He became even more serious, more reticent. Even with his sweetheart, Zilya, he hardly ever spoke about his pain and his feelings. When she talked to him about her problems and worries, he looked at her seriously and said: "When you get to know life and people better, you will discover your own worth."

Lothar had high standards for himself. He believed that now that he was an adult, he had to carry full responsibility for the family.

Thus, it was entirely understandable when he supported his mother's decision to take advantage of the nonaggression pact with Germany to return there. Erna Wloch had her siblings in Berlin, and she had lost all hope for a future in Moscow. In September 1940, she submitted her application to leave the country. On December 16 the time came to go. In the afternoon, Lothar visited Zilya one last time in her apartment near the Tretyakov Gallery museum. In order not to endanger her, he traveled by a circuitous route using various forms of transport. "What will become of you, when I am gone? Promise me you will look after yourself. Do it for me." He put out his cigarette and took his leave with: "See you again!" From the station, he phoned Zilya one last time but didn't reach her. Shortly before nine o'clock that night, the train carrying the Wlochs left Moscow—destination Nazi Germany . . . Unbelievable!

With Lothar ("Lotka," "Chkalov") gone, it was as though the heart of the inseparables was gone. The Troika had come apart. The third member was left alone in Moscow. At first he was sad, but he was only fifteen; there were still other friends. And then, very soon, came June 22, 1941.

All the experiences of childhood and of youth culminated in this decisive turning point, the trial of war.

Childhood was over.

The Berlin Reunion

No one could remember exactly how or when the photo of the Troika in postwar Berlin came to be taken. Was it in 1945, or not until the following year? The photo that, thirty years later, would spark the idea for a film.

In the American sector of the divided city, Lothar was in the process of moving from a basement apartment into somewhere fit for human habitation. Captain George Fischer was helping him.

Yura, who had been Americanized and went by the name of George, came to Germany with the US Army and had tracked down the Wlochs in Berlin-Wedding. Not much of this working-class neighborhood, where he had lived before 1933, remained. It had been devastated by the war. It was only natural that George took his brother Vitya's place in the postwar Troika.

Koni, a lieutenant in the Soviet army, had bypassed Berlin in his movements with the troops in May 1945. He landed in Potsdam for a short time, via Bernau, Sachsenhausen, Spandau, and Brandenburg. With his long journey behind him, the war ended for him in the city of Premnitz on May 9. He was now working for the Soviet Military Administration in Halle, although nearly every weekend he visited his parents in Berlin-Pankow or me in Charlottenburg in western Berlin.

When the three met up again at Lothar's after five years away from each other, they picked up where they had left off. Their families had been forced worlds apart, the whole earth had almost been torn to pieces, and yet it seemed as if it was only yesterday that they'd last been together. The three were happy to have survived this murderous war and to have found each other again. They felt at ease, as only old friends could. That Troika photo was taken at that time.

Later, none of the three could recollect just what they had told each other about their war experiences, how they reflected on their time together in Moscow and the politics of those years, and which memories they still shared. Their relationship with each other was very personal. Nothing could come between them or prevent them from picking up the old friendship and taking it forward. And yet there were so many stories to tell and to argue about.

Lothar, the "Chkalov," had not served with the Red Air Force, as he had once dreamed, but instead with Hermann Göring's Luftwaffe. Although, as he often said, he had not flown fighter planes, he had nevertheless worn the swastika-bearing eagle on his uniform. He had therefore entered the country in which he had once lived, where he had left many friends and his one great love, as an enemy. On one occasion, in one of his letters from the Eastern Front, he declared that he was now somewhere he had been before, in 1937: the Crimean Peninsula where Artek, the Pioneer camp, had been situated. Not far from there, on the Caucasian coast of the Black Sea, Koni, the seventeen-year-old Soviet Army volunteer, began the long journey back to the country of his birth. It was there, in the village of Kabardinka, that he had his first experience of an air raid and saw his first dead body; a Soviet soldier blown to pieces by a bomb. Later, on the advance from the Caucasus into Germany, he witnessed firsthand the scorched-earth policy practiced by the Nazi Wehrmacht between the Don and the Dnieper—the ruins of Warsaw and the mountains of corpses in Majdanek and Sachsenhausen. George Fischer had spent the last year of the war as an American officer, also in the Soviet Union. He was a liaison officer on an American air base near the city of Poltava in Ukraine. In February 1945, during the Yalta Conference that was attended by Stalin, Roosevelt, and Churchill, he was working at Saky, the Crimean air base prepared for the conference.

Incredible as it was, not even Lothar's harsh denunciation at the Berlin reunion of both the Soviet Union and its staunch allies, the German Communists, could disrupt the harmony of their meeting. Lothar, the middle horse of the triumvirate, gaunt, rescued from destitution, and lovingly supported by the two victors, struggled under the almost unendurable weight of his experiences.

When the Wlochs crossed the border into Germany, shortly before midnight on a December evening in 1940, they were taken from the train in Tilsit and arrested.[71] In the town jail they were kept apart. Erna and Margot were locked up in a cell with prostitutes and thieves. Old mattresses for them to sleep on were spread all over the floor. Lothar was put with the men. The next morning they were allowed to stay together in an ice-cold laundry room. Around noon a police officer removed the two children and they were taken off to foster parents. It looked like it would be a long time before they would see their mother again. But then, however, some duty station decided otherwise, and the children were allowed to travel on to Berlin with their mother.

Waiting at the station evening after evening was the kindly Lis Gebauer, an old friend from Bohnsdorf. She had been given advance notice from Moscow of their imminent arrival. The three reached Berlin on the day after Erna's forty-fourth birthday. They had to report to the immigration office in Tegel and were interned in the Tegel Palace manor house. Margot began to learn German, a language that at the time she could neither read nor write. Lothar didn't want to join the Reich Labor Service, so he volunteered for the air force, even though he was not yet eighteen.[72] Someone had told him that by signing up he would also be helping to support his mother. He was called up at the beginning of 1941. He was assigned to ground duties at first due to suspicions about his political background.

Erna Wloch had no claim to an apartment, and so she shuttled back and forth in Berlin between Lis, who at the time lived in Neukölln; her sister in Heiligensee; and her husband's aunt in Moabit. She earned a living by writing advertisements for the business directory. At the same time, she was repeatedly called to Gestapo headquarters in Prinz Albrecht Street for questioning. She made an effort not to endanger any of her friends; she

71. Tilsit is a former German and East Prussian town nowadays known as Sovetsk, in Kaliningrad Oblast, part of the Russian Federation.

72. The Reich Labor Service was a major paramilitary organization in Nazi Germany, created to combat unemployment, militarize the workforce, and instill Nazi ideology. As the official state labor service, it was divided into separate divisions for men and women.

never concealed her past and never attempted to ingratiate herself with the Nazis by highlighting her ordeals in the Soviet Union.

Even among her friends she remained tight lipped. One of the few people with whom she formed a stronger relationship was Rudi Greulich, a friend and comrade from the Bohnsdorf days. With him she could speak freely and discuss political matters. Rudi Greulich, who had just been released from prison, later spoke of how hard he had been hit by the news of Willi Wloch's death. Erna had said very little about it and still believed that her husband's fate had been the result of a grievous error. They were both very happy to have found each other. They supported each other through their friendship and shared the same political convictions. All they longed for was the end of the war and of Nazi rule. But Rudi Greulich was soon to be conscripted into the 999th, a Wehrmacht unit into which the Nazis conscripted so-called untrustworthy elements to mount a last-ditch effort to fight. Many of the antifascists who were recruited into this "suicide squad," including Rudi Greulich, used the earliest opportunity they could to defect. The happy reunion was therefore brief for both of them.

Meanwhile, Lothar had been called up from ground personnel into the active air force. When he wrote that letter home in 1943 detailing the location of his deployment on the Eastern Front, he could not have known where the war had driven his beloved Zilya. He could not have known that during this time, the name Wloch was appearing in a theater program in Chistopol on the Kama River, east of the Volga. By taking Lothar's family name as her stage name, Zilya, an aspiring actress in the area to which she had been evacuated, tried to keep their childhood dream alive across the gulf of their sudden separation. This is how life surpasses the imagination of the poet!

Lothar continued to fly his missions over Ukraine. He served in France, Italy, and Poland. Eventually he even attended pilot training school. He was in the West when the war ended, and it was there that the British captured him. In order to achieve an earlier release, he gave as his home address the address of our aunt Grete Dreibholz, our mother's sister, who lived in Essen in the British occupied zone. Because she had stood by us throughout the whole Nazi period, she had had to endure a certain level of harassment. Meni had given the Wlochs her sister's address when they were still in Moscow. In summer 1945, after three months in a POW camp, Lothar battled his way through to Berlin and resumed his role as head of the family. Erna, weakened by the typhus epidemic, was reduced to skin and bone.

Without a high school degree or vocational training, Lothar had to look for work. He applied to train as a bricklayer for a construction company. He worked hard and helped his mother wherever possible. He hauled stump wood from Heiligensee to Wedding so that they could have at least a little heat in the house during the unusually severe winter of 1945–46. In Berlin people fought to survive.

By the end of 1945, Margot was home again as well. In 1941, she had been sent from Tegel to a home for ethnic German children living abroad in Hohenelse near Rheinsberg. Children of expatriate Germans from former African colonies, South America, and elsewhere were housed there. In the large dormitory, every child was given a small locker with their native flag on the door. Strangely, nobody found it offensive that the red flag of the Soviet Union was on Margot's locker door. She didn't suffer any discrimination. However, since leaving the Soviet Union and throughout her schooldays, she hadn't made a single friend. She often thought about her old girlfriends who had remained in Moscow.

When she required a so-called Certificate of Aryan Descent, Margot also discovered that she was not the Wlochs' natural-born child. It was then that she met the parents of her biological mother, who had been only sixteen years old when she had Margot. The mother's parents had opposed the child's adoption by the Wlochs. After the children's home in Hohenelse, Margot returned to Berlin. She lived with her mother Erna, always in other people's homes; went to various schools; and then was evacuated with her class because of the increasing number of air raids—first to the Baltic Sea, later to Zakopane in Poland, and finally to Czechoslovakia. She witnessed the Americans marching into Landau on the Isar River. She trudged from Bavaria with a few other pupils over the green border into the Soviet occupation zone. She encountered the young Russian soldiers on the border without any fear. They were no strangers to her. Her knowledge of Russian certainly played a part in her eventual safe passage to Berlin where she found Lothar and her mother in her grandparents' tiny apartment in Wedding. The grandparents had been killed in an air raid.

It was at this time that George appeared at the Wlochs'. He got hold of staggering quantities of inconceivably hard-to-get American canned food and attempted to find them all a better apartment in the American sector.

* * *

And so, finally, life for the Wlochs began to return to normal. Erna felt better day by day. Lothar was able to commit to the idea of becoming a construction engineer, and Margot attended the Händel School in Frankfurter Allee in the eastern part of the city.

When Koni turned up and all of them met at Lothar's in Schlachtensee,[73] or at George's in Dahlem, the "family" was together again, almost like the old days in Moscow. Once again George was called Yura, and Lothar became Lotka again. There was no shortage of reasons to celebrate. Vodka or whiskey was drunk in the usual quantities for the time, and conversation inevitably turned to the other members of our families. Yura's parents were in the US; our mother still lived in Moscow, with her suitcases packed; our father had moved in with me and my family in Charlottenburg and occupied himself with his various tasks. I myself was working as a special correspondent for the Berlin broadcasting station, Berliner Rundfunk, and the newspaper *Berliner Zeitung* at the International Military Tribunal war-crimes trials in Nuremberg. Vitya was also supposed to come to Germany. Like his brother, he was in the US Army. George had last seen him in France.

Apart from that, everyday life, which was very different for each member of the new Troika, was filled with all manner of duties and responsibilities. The two Allied officers did their best for their friend's family, to ease some of the burdens involved in the struggle for existence in postwar Berlin. The two officers could siphon off a little from their American PX rations or Soviet *payek* without any trouble. Cigarettes and alcohol were

73. Schlachtensee is located in the Steglitz-Zehlendorf district in southwestern Berlin. After World War II, the area was part of the American occupation zone and later belonged to the Western sector of divided Berlin.

in demand on the black market and could easily be exchanged for essential items. To do so, one didn't necessarily have to join the crowd of thousands of soldiers and civilians trading, buying, and selling in front of the burned-out Reichstag.

Koni, meanwhile, had his own problems. He was an officer in the Red Army and felt himself to be a Soviet citizen. At the same time, however, as the son of a German communist and writer, he was expected to see his future in the country where he was born and where his parents lived. Twenty-two years later, in one of his most successful films, *Ich war neunzehn* [*I Was Nineteen*], Koni captured this turmoil, this jumble of conflicting feelings and impressions within the young German-born Soviet officer. Drawing on his scribbled diary notes in Russian, he wrote the screenplay with [the Berlin screenwriter and film director] Wolfgang Kohlhaase.[74] He gave the hero of the film the name Gregor, probably after his friend from Moscow's Karl Liebknecht School, Gregor Kurella, whom we called Grisha and whose life took almost the same path as ours. The audience experiences the last weeks of the war through the hero's eyes, and shares the Soviet officer's mistrust of the Germans when they rushed to hang out white flags at the eleventh hour, without a clue about exactly what had happened or why. And these same Germans eyed the nineteen-year-old Gregor/Koni with the same mistrust that was reflected sometimes in fear and submissiveness, sometimes in arrogance, and even in hatred. There were, of course, the German antifascists, who were released from the prisons and concentration camps, and immediately started doing what had to be done. Koni felt close to these Germans, and thus the meeting between Soviet officers and those antifascists, just like the one Koni actually experienced at a May 1945 celebration in Sanssouci Palace, became one of the most powerful scenes in the film.[75] Those impressions of the last days of the war continued to affect him in Halle. Koni had the task of cooperating with German artists, intellectuals, and students. Before his lecture on what the future would hold for German youth, "Traitor to the Fatherland"

74. Konrad Wolf's war diary was later published as part of *Aber ich sah ja selbst, das war der Krieg: Kriegstagebuch und Briefe 1942–1945* (Edition "Die Möwe," 2015).

75. Sanssouci Palace, in Potsdam, just outside Berlin, was erected by the Prussian king Frederick the Great.

was written on the board in the University of Halle auditorium. How difficult it was for him to connect with people who were not yet ready to face up to their guilt or complicity in war crimes! Now, it seemed, everyone denied having any knowledge of the atrocities that had taken place in the occupied countries. This rejection of personal responsibility preoccupied us greatly at that time. The question of guilt, the question that many people didn't want to hear answered, preoccupied our father as well. The founding manifest of the Central Committee of our party, the KPD [the Communist Party of Germany], on June 11, 1945, contained clear and courageous words that we supported wholeheartedly.

Depressing thoughts, however, were not uppermost in our minds in these early days. There was also a new momentum and an enthusiasm for starting afresh. We threw ourselves into our work, literally up to our eyeballs. There was no time for lamentation. Everyone was needed. Soon, many young people, engaged by antifascist elements, followed the mostly old opponents of the Nazis. They were searching for a new purpose in life. The term "Zero Hour" stood for the immediate tasks of providing the population with water and essential items, and getting the initial transport systems up and running. This was achieved very quickly. Antifascists worked hand in hand with the officers of the occupying powers, clearing away not only the rubble in the streets and squares but also the mental rubble in people's minds.

Among the German communists with whom Koni had dealings was Peter Florin. He had been in the same class as me in Moscow. Peter now worked as an editor for the newspaper *Volkszeitung* in Halle. Bernard Koenen, one of my teachers at the Comintern School, was first secretary of the KPD, and then of the SED, of Saxony-Anhalt.[76] He was, as was Peter's father, Wilhelm Florin, one of Ernst Thälmann's closest comrades. Bernard Koenen had told us a lot about his meetings with Lenin and Thälmann. Koni felt a strong connection with these Germans, however,

76. Wolf is referring here to the Party School of the Executive Committee of the Comintern, which was responsible for training cadres and preparing elite revolutionary leaders for communist parties worldwide. The school was evacuated in 1941 from Moscow to Kushnarenkovo in the Ural foothills.

for now a long journey back to his homeland lay ahead of him. At that time Koni's future plans were focused still almost entirely on Moscow.

It was Koni's good fortune that in Halle, in the military administration led by General Kotikov, the future city commandant of Berlin, Volodya Gall, an older comrade in arms, now remained as his direct superior. Gall was a scholar of German and a connoisseur and admirer of German culture. He loved the work of Heinrich Heine and quoted from Schiller's *Die Räuber* [*The Robbers*] and Goethe's *Faust.* He was a friend of the "other Germany" and was proud to have seen Ernst Thälmann speak when he visited the Soviet Union prior to 1933. To be sure, there were other superiors as well, narrow-minded bureaucrats who had often made Koni angry during the war and about whom he had often written in many a despairing letter. In the department of the Soviet Military Administration in Germany, however, which was responsible for working together with the Germans, there were mostly intelligent, educated, and far-sighted officers; men like Colonel Sergei Tiul'panov, the literary scholar Aleksandr Dymshits, and many others. These officers, who in civilian life were university lecturers or party functionaries, took Stalin's words very seriously: "Hitlers will come and go; the German people, the German State, remains." This quotation could be seen everywhere in the early postwar period. To breathe life into it required a strategy with stamina. Political and cultural life developed rapidly and with such breadth and in such variety that the question of guilt did not remain an abstract idea for long. The development of this [Soviet-occupied] part of Germany was due in no small part to the vigilance of those officers who protected against certain sectarian mistakes, mistakes that old comrades were frequently prone to making after all they had been through.[77] In other countries liberated by the Soviet Union, these very mistakes had serious consequences. The Nazis and war criminals in what was, at the time, the Soviet occupation zone had their possessions expropriated and were held accountable—unless they had run away to the West. All other citizens

77. Under Soviet orders, those German communists who returned from exile in Moscow to support the Soviet occupation government sought to prevent radical measures proposed by many communists and others on the German left who had stayed underground during the war and who now saw a chance for a radical transformation of Germany.

were required to cooperate. For Koni and all of us, these years became a school for a policy of broad alliance.

This path was, nevertheless, constantly strewn with obstacles. It was still only a minority of people that consciously committed themselves to this journey. The economy seemed to founder hopelessly at rock bottom. The poison of anti-Bolshevism, left over from the Nazi era, was still potent, and many newly created media in the West made sure that the events of the last weeks of the war did not fade from memory. In order to create new reservations [against the Soviet Union], newspapers and radio stations criticized relentlessly the dismantling of undamaged machinery and industrial facilities as reparations for damage done in the Soviet Union, the lack of information about the prisoners of war, or the recognition of the new border along the Oder and Neisse Rivers.[78] The Cold War slipped into gear. And even back then, our newspapers and broadcasts were already ignoring delicate, uncomfortable, and complex problems, which gave our enemies the upper hand. With little direction from above, we had to make up our own arguments to stand our ground in the political debates.

When the Troika met, therefore, its get-togethers did not take place on a remote island. The American sector of Berlin was located at a hot spot for the mounting tension. Captain George Fischer was on the staff of the American commander in chief, General Eisenhower, the future president. Afterward, and for quite a considerable time, he served in the Berlin headquarters. Since this was in the political sphere, he was not far from the events of the looming Cold War. Even at those early meetings between American and Soviet representatives near the end of the war, he had seen signs of a growing mistrust among the Allies. Now the tensions were increasing, and they could not but affect our relationships as well.

When George visited me during the war crimes trials and stayed with me—the Americans housed the international press at the castle owned by the pencil manufacturer Faber, in Stein, near Nuremberg—the victorious powers still seemed to be united. Indeed, the judges and prosecutors

78. Wolf here is referring to the just-made border between Germany and Poland, which subsumed some of Germany's eastern territories under Polish administration.

maintained the agreement made about the International Military Tribunal. It resulted in joint condemnation of the crimes of the Third Reich and of almost all defendants via the guilty verdict delivered in the fall of 1946. It was an enormously significant verdict, but one that even then could no longer be taken for granted. The first effects of the Cold War were beginning to appear. In the major Western European and American newspapers, my fellow journalists' reports of the trials were relegated further and further to the back pages. They became shorter and poorer in content, and eventually disappeared altogether. Instead, headlines piled up about the "suppression of freedom" in countries that were now described as belonging to the Soviet bloc. We later found out that Göring and others among the accused closely registered these signals. They hoped that an open conflict would break out between the Western powers and the Russians, and reckoned that it might save their skins.

Even as the Tribunal was continuing and the whole of Europe was suffering from its war wounds, a discernible shift in tone became apparent in speeches given by the British premier, Churchill, in Fulton,[79] and by the US secretary of state, Byrnes, in Stuttgart.[80] The Cold War against the former ally was publicly promoted as the new political doctrine. The confrontation played out not only at the various international conferences, but also in our day-to-day politics. The Troika, and everyone else, were all in the middle of it; not between the fronts, but on the particular spot where fate had placed us, with all its contradictions and struggles.

79. On March 5, 1946, at Westminster College in Fulton, Missouri, Winston Churchill—invited by President Harry S. Truman—delivered his famous address, "The Sinews of Peace," known also as the "Iron Curtain" speech. Speaking as a private citizen after his 1945 electoral defeat, Churchill warned of Soviet expansion and the deepening divide in Europe, declaring that an "iron curtain" had descended across the continent. He urged a strong Anglo-American alliance to safeguard peace and freedom. The speech is considered a defining moment in the early Cold War, shaping Western perceptions of the Soviet threat.

80. James Byrnes (1882–1972) a veteran politician from South Carolina, was appointed US secretary of state by President Harry S. Truman in July 1945 and served until January 1947. He played a pivotal role in guiding US foreign policy during the transition from World War II to the Cold War. In his "Restatement of Policy on Germany" speech, or "Speech of Hope," delivered in Stuttgart, Germany, on September 6, 1946, Secretary of State Byrnes signaled a shift in US postwar policy, emphasizing economic reconstruction and a more hopeful future for Germany.

George Fischer retained his emotional ties to the Russian people and their culture, but politically he had become an American from head to toe. The growing friction between the onetime allies deepened his critical attitude toward the Soviet Union. In Berlin he cultivated close relationships with committed anti-Soviet, anticommunist Social Democrats as well as former communists.[81] After a factional split from the SPD,[82] Franz Neumann, the then-chairperson of the party in Berlin, was often a guest at the villa where George lived in Berlin. His friends, American trade union officials, were working for the military government. The umbrella organizations of the big US unions were deploying enormous resources both to influence the development of European trade unions to their advantage, and to support opposition groups in the Soviet zone in Germany as well as in the people's democracies.[83] George Silver, the experienced American union leader, led this work in West Berlin.[84] Under his direction sackfuls of food packages were brought in. George then passed them on to the Social Democrats and Communists who had absconded to the West in order to organize "independent unions." George Fischer's life was divided: On the one hand, he lived with these people in a villa, spoke about socialism, and felt different shades of red; on the other hand, he worked for a traditional military service. American officials did not take note of this group of people yet. It was not until later that they recognized that those anticommunist unionists and intellectuals could be useful to them. Anyway, George sympathized with them.

They were the same sort of people we were having a difficult time with on our side, the ones who refused to join the unification of the two workers' parties and who fought against it tooth and nail. Koni experienced

81. The Social Democrats here refer to the Sozialdemokratische Partei Deutschlands (SPD), or the Social Democratic Party of Germany, originally founded in 1875.

82. Wolf here is referring to the Social Democrats who did not join the merger of the KPD and the SPD in 1946.

83. "People's democracies" here refers to the Soviet-controlled communist systems in Eastern Europe.

84. George Silver was an employee of the labor affairs branch of the American military government in Germany. Formerly with the Congress of Industrial Organizations in the United States, he managed the distribution of CARE packages to pro-Western trade unionists in Germany.

these conflicts in Halle. While working, temporarily, as a translator for the Soviet delegation, he also had the opportunity to observe how, at the Allied Kommandatura in Berlin, negotiations increasingly degenerated into fruitless debates between the former allies. Held in quick succession, conferences between the foreign ministers of the victorious powers, which were supposed to breathe life into the Potsdam Agreement and prepare the peace treaties, became platforms for unproductive recriminations.[85] The Soviet Union's proposals for peace treaties and the establishment of conditions for a reunified Germany were countered by US Secretary of State Byrnes's demands for elections on the American model.

Throughout all this, Koni traveled regularly to Berlin. Often at a late hour, his motorbike had to decide whether to go East or West, to his parents' apartment in the East or mine in the city's West. He still stopped in at Lothar's or George's as well; he liked being there with his friends. The rather unconscious avoidance of burning political questions during these meetings might have been the reason that the friends felt comfortable in each other's company. It seemed as if nothing had changed between them. But was this really true? Each of the three had a profoundly different view of the world; they each had their own deeply held convictions; each was deeply committed to them; each was embedded in his beliefs. Their varied political positions reflected the very different developments in the Soviet occupied zone and the Western occupation zones.

In 1946, difficult domestic problems arose within the Wloch family. Erna's health deteriorated, and she applied to emigrate with the children to Switzerland, where her favorite brother's wife still lived. She believed that the family would be able to rebuild their lives more easily there than in Berlin, where they were continually haunted by the past. But Lothar had a new girlfriend, and he didn't want to leave without her. A serious conflict developed, and the argument was loud and intense. A few months later Erna died. Our father, a doctor, tried to help her, but there was nothing he could do. Her life's battles and the deprivation of the past years had damaged her health, and so her heart simply gave up. Her death shook

85. The Potsdam Agreement, signed at the Potsdam Conference, held from July 17 to August 2, 1945, in Potsdam, Germany, brought together the three main Allied powers—the United States, the Soviet Union, and Great Britain—to determine the postwar order for Germany.

everyone who knew her. For Lothar it was another blow; he blamed the same people who he thought of as responsible for his father's death.

Before Lothar met the girl who later became his wife, his feelings for his first love, Zilya, flared up once more. In 1946, probably through the involvement of my mother, a short but very intense correspondence developed between Lothar and Zilya in Moscow. With these letters, a part of Peredelkino and something of the happiness found there was briefly re-created.

To hold these letters in my hand after so many years evoked a strange and poignant feeling. Written in a Russian that reveals the writer's German origins—with grammatical errors, and in a naive style—they exposed an intense and pure love. None of his friends would have believed that Lothar would be able to open his heart to another person in this way: "In those years I have often thought about you. Our time together always seemed like a long-lost dream. More than once I longed for a person like you by my side. When I heard that you are alive, I instantly thought that I had to come and see you and speak to you."

In these letters he described his workday: "Get up at five in the morning, at work on the building site by six, heavy-duty physical work until five in the afternoon; from 5:30 p.m. to 8 p.m. evening school for construction engineers, 8:30 home, dinner, homework, and then sleep. Sundays: essential domestic duties; organizing wood for heating, and so on." He maintained again and again that it was not his forte to describe his feelings. In his life, rationality always had to come first, feelings second. And yet, those dozen letters exuded so much warmth that one could imagine how profoundly this powerful first love colored his future life: "When Yura brought your fifth and seventh letters today, he said: 'Well, Lotka, it is Sunday for you today!' He was right. Whenever one of your letters arrives, it's like Sunday for me . . . In the beginning I was a bit scared of the strength of your feelings for me. To be honest, I couldn't imagine that such a feeling could exist at all. Isn't it greater than love? In all these five years you were my ideal and continue to be even more now. I have often looked for a woman like you and never found her. It's obvious, there is only one Zilya and that is quite all right!" How could it have been possible for him to banish all his feelings for a country that he knows is loved above everything by the person he's writing to? Every letter speaks of the yearning for a reunion. Both fought for such a meeting—but to no avail.

What would have happened if . . . ?

In each of Lothar's letters he mentions Koni and Yura; he describes meetings, but above all two initials frequently occur: E.O., Elsa Ottovna, our mother's first name and patronymic in customary Russian usage. Unlike her sons, Meni herself was a very reliable and enthusiastic letter writer. Immediately after the end of the war and in the years to come, she herself corresponded with Zilya. Their letters are an eloquent chronicle of the time, of the Troika, and of her environment. In these letters you can see her love for and anxieties about the fate of the Wloch family, and the deep blow of Erna's death in August 1946: "Lothar called on the 17th. He was hardly able to speak. Erna has died . . . I went to Lothar. He is in a dreadful state, but very brave as only people like he and Erna can be. He tried to be brave. Erna looked as if she was asleep and could open her mouth any minute and start speaking. It is unimaginable that she won't be here anymore. I'll go there once more and take the flowers that she loved so much. Lothar refuses any help. He wants to do everything for her by himself. I understand him. He cried a lot and said that she shouldn't have died so prematurely. How many plans they still had! We all knew that she was very sick, but we never thought that she would die so soon. Lothar got the news of her death on the 16th at 10:30 a.m., which is the very day and hour when, exactly six years ago, he was told his father had died. Both Lothar and Margochka are of course very independent, they will go on exactly in the same way as when they lived together with Erna. I will support them, of course, but can't replace Erna. There is too much sorrow at this time."

Meni writes again and again about her closeness to Lothar and his life. The letters are very touching and, here again, in spite of all the mistakes, the Russian sounds beautiful, because every line is shot through with honest feeling. Meni regards Lothar and Margot as her own, shares their worries, and tries to understand both of them while respecting their individual natures. The letters provide an inkling of the role the mothers played in the lives of the heroes of this story. The fathers certainly had an influence on the development of the boys. Each of the fathers was a personality, someone deeply committed to his own principles. Many of these qualities were passed on to the children. But the fathers, Louis Fischer and Friedrich Wolf, were seldom home. They often traveled, and there were other women in their lives. The mothers, by contrast, were always there for their sons, each of them in her special way a remarkable woman. Markoosha—even from her looks the true Jewish mother—was soft, cosmopolitan in her thinking, naturally open minded toward everyone, and highly educated. She was fluent in five languages and a very good pianist. Erna, by contrast, was a typical working-class Berliner woman—intelligent, plain-speaking, with her heart in the right place, willing to do any work or make any sacrifices in order to help someone. Her facial features were severe, but most of the time there was a smile in her eyes; she was always ready to laugh her infectious laugh, if there was anything left to laugh about.

It's not at all surprising that our Meni felt close to both of these women. The children felt the influence of their mothers every day: perhaps not as pronounced as their fathers' influence, but no less strong. For the Troika, the mothers were crucial. They gave each of their sons a place to grow; they raised each to be independent and to behave responsibly, but also to show tolerance toward other people. Tolerance, along with calmness and balance, was certainly the characteristic that others most valued in our mother. This was also true of her relationship with our father. She certainly didn't have an easy time with him; inner strength was needed. Even when, temporarily, he had feelings for other women, she was always his indispensable partner in political conviction, in work, and in life. This same tolerance is clear in her letters to Zilya, when she, with cautious happiness, speaks about the blossoming love between Margot and Koni, about their very different personalities, and about the problems that consequently arose.

Following his mother's death, with Lothar's future wife having moved in with him, Margot no longer felt comfortable there. The two young women didn't get along. In this situation, when she felt lonely and isolated, her friendship with Koni developed into something deeper. Koni visited our dad on his fifty-eighth birthday on December 23, 1946. Afterward he took Margot with him to Halle until the New Year.

It was good for Margot to have a friend who was patient and didn't ask difficult questions. He simply belonged to the greater family, to the circle of friends. For Koni, too, this was a good relationship. He was not confident with girls. Once, in a letter to his parents from the front, he speculated that what fate had in store for him was almost certainly the life of an eternal bachelor. He had known Margot since they were children. And politically they were on the same wavelength. This closeness made many things easier, and also softened the pain of growing distant from Lothar. On the other hand, this personal closeness was one of the reasons for the friends' estrangement. Lothar obviously expected Koni to have an influence on his sister, which Koni had neither the wish nor the ability to bring to bear. Margot's decision to put distance between herself and her brother was her own.

For a time she worked as an assistant at the Kaiser Wilhelm Institute in the American sector. She wanted to study biology and was supposed to enroll in the Freie Universität [Free University] established on the site of the Institute. But she decided to study at the Humboldt University in the east of the city. She also felt politically at home there. Just like Koni, it was as if she had just arrived straight from Moscow and had never made the detour via the Hitler Reich and West Berlin. Unlike Lothar, she, like many other victims of injustice, still believed in the country where she had spent her childhood, and in the socialism that had taken root there and that her parents had been committed to. The break with Lothar was not, therefore, solely attributable to her poor relationship with his wife. Her conscious decision to live in East Berlin provided a solid foundation for her love for Koni.

The political struggle could be felt firsthand at Humboldt University. The faculty and students were split down the middle. The tone was increasingly set by the new professors and students who had come from the Arbeiter-und-Bauern-Fakultät.[86] Even in clashes in West Berlin they raised the flag of their convictions. Against a background of growing anticommunist hysteria, this often took a great deal of courage. Margot was on their side and thus on Koni's side as well; he felt increasingly close to this new German youth and thus overcame his own reservations.

86. The Arbeiter-und-Bauern-Fakultät (Workers' and Peasants' Faculty) was an institution that trained workers and peasants for their university entrance exams.

Koni, who held the rank of first lieutenant, was released from the military in Halle in the middle of December 1946 and arrived in Berlin a little later. He now worked as a civilian employee at the House of Soviet Culture at Kastanienwäldchen Square.[87] Like the rest of the old center of Berlin, the avenue Unter den Linden was in ruins. Rauch's statue of Frederick II on horseback was still encased in its bombproof shell, but it would soon be moved to Sanssouci Park. Huge rallies and demonstrations took place on anniversaries and holidays in front of the castle ruins at Lustgarten. I had to report on these in my capacity as a radio journalist.

The House of Soviet Culture quickly became a political and intellectual hub for all Berlin. Koni and his colleagues regularly worked very late at their tireless task of fighting anti-Soviet sentiment, both old and new. Koni sensed that his efforts were resonating. Many people came to the house at Kastanienwäldchen Square. When he attended presentations, either as speaker or interpreter, he felt a growing popular interest in the country that was, until recently, the embodiment of evil. Soviet choral and dance ensembles that performed at the radio station's large broadcasting studio in Masurenallee—one of the few Berlin halls left undamaged—were enthusiastically embraced by the German audience. There was a discernible change in the relationship between the people of the two countries that had shared so much mutual suffering. While this was encouraging, it was only the beginning. The Nazi past was far from being overcome. Rejection and mistrust remained conspicuous and could be found everywhere.

Our father devoted himself obsessively to his cultural-political tasks. He was totally preoccupied by the Germans' responsibility for what had happened. His plays *Professor Mamlock* and *Was der Mensch säet* [What man sows], written during the emigration, were being staged, and were intended to help his fellow Germans come to terms with the past. But at the same time there was more at stake: Everything had to be done to prevent a repeat of the recent past—to avoid a new war. Increasing signs of this in the West were a cause for concern; our parents' trip to Stuttgart, our old *Heimat*, confirmed this.

87. The House of Soviet Culture building is known today as the Palais am Festungsgraben.

My Nuremberg trials reports and new material revealed during the trials of the mighty leaders of the IG Farben companies gave my father the idea for the film script, *Der Rat der Götter* [*The Council of the Gods*]. The members of the IG Farben board had given themselves this title. Using firsthand reports and fragments of documentaries, the film revealed the secrets of how the Nazis rose to power and exposed those to whom war meant good business. The film was directed by Kurt Maetzig, with marvelous actors like Paul Bildt, Willy A. Kleinau, and Fritz Tillmann in the cast.

The film was one of the first great successes of the DEFA, one of whose founding members was our father.[88] It's not quite clear how much this film influenced Koni's decision to apply to study directing at the VGIK film school in Moscow. He completed his high school graduation at a Soviet evening school for military personnel in Berlin-Karlshorst and applied to Moscow. And lo and behold, he was accepted. And with that, once again Berlin receded, and Margot stayed behind.

They had three years together in Berlin. Gradually, the relationship, which grew out of a shared childhood, developed into real love. This love was occasionally tense and not without its challenges; the circumstances of the time did not help. Koni was an officer and civilian employee for the Soviet Military Administration and had solid plans for the future as a Soviet citizen. Margot was German. It seemed as if insurmountable official obstacles were getting in the way of their marriage plans. Neither of them had an easy personality; they were both stubborn. Another reason they couldn't resolve their disagreements and problems was that when things became difficult, Koni retreated into his shell and didn't say a word. Already, in those days, one of his most conspicuous characteristics was his tendency to brood in silence. And this was why from time to time in their relationship, one or the other wanted to break up. Finally, Koni was about to begin studying in Moscow, and with that came their separation.

Margot met her future husband and father of her children, Kurt Goldstein, in 1950 during the *Deutschlandtreffen* [Whitsun gathering of

88. The DEFA (Deutsche Film AG) was the state-owned film company of the GDR. Founded in 1946, it produced around seven hundred feature films, 750 animated films, and more than two thousand documentaries before its dissolution following the fall of the Berlin Wall.

German youth], in Berlin.[89] And, again, one of those twists of fate cropped up. When Kurt was a young man, he had been interned in the same French camp, Le Vernet, as our father, and they knew each other well. Koni and Kurt, so different in age, tried to sort out this triangular relationship with grace. Koni could not accept the separation from Margot. With a flood of letters, phone calls, and telegrams, he desperately tried to get her to change her mind about the finality of her decision. It was to become one of his unhappy dramas with women. In Moscow, Zilya witnessed her friend's emotional torment. He could cry on her shoulder and tell her everything.

For Ule Lammert as well, Zilya became a port of call. He and his family got stuck in Kazan' on the Volga and, try as he might, they couldn't get an exit permit to return home. He had begun to study architecture in Tatarstan. And Zilya became his confidante as well, someone to whom he could pour out his heart. When the Lammert family finally got the necessary travel papers, they traveled to Berlin via Moscow, where Koni, Ule, and Zilya were reunited. They celebrated at the fashionable Georgian restaurant, Aragwi, which was very close to the former hotel for emigrants, Hotel Lux, on Gorky Street. Zilya and Lothar had lost contact. She got married but did not find happiness. The two young German lads were for her a memory of her adolescent dreams in Peredelkino.

For three more years, his studies at film school tied Koni to Moscow; they fascinated and completely absorbed him. In 1951, during the Third World Youth Festival in Berlin, he completed an internship with Joris Ivens; by 1953 he worked as Kurt Maetzig's assistant on a film about Ernst Thälmann. By now a citizen of the GDR, he finally became a director in his own right with his 1954 thesis film, *Einmal ist keinmal* [*Once Is Never*]. Another step in the long journey was completed.

But let's return to our story about the "new" Troika, to the year 1946, which is drawing to a close. At the beginning of 1947, Lothar completed his masonry apprenticeship and got married. The wedding, which brought us all together again, was a cheerful and lighthearted celebration

89. The Whitsun Gathering of German Youth 1950 (Pfingsttreffen der FDJ 1950) was a major event organized by the Free German Youth, or FDJ, in East Berlin during the early Cold War. It functioned as a key propaganda effort by the SED to promote a vision of German unity aligned with communist ideology.

with hundreds of flowers and lots of wine. Even so, it became some kind of turning point. The paths that had crossed once more in Berlin began yet again to divide. Each had his own family and his own work and ambitions. The get-togethers became less frequent.

With financial support from George and help from his working wife, Lothar was able to study for a degree. He graduated as a construction engineer in 1949 and, with his characteristic tenacity and energy, started his own business in the West Berlin construction market. Through his business he believed he had found his own way of connecting his father's ideals to his own ideas about social justice. He had turned his back on communism. Between us, this was not an issue: He knew of our abiding commitment to this ideology, to our second *Heimat.* He knew that in this part of Germany, which was then the Soviet zone, we poured all our energy into a path of progress that was heading in an exactly opposite direction from that of the West. He knew that Koni did not shed his beliefs when he took off his Soviet officer's uniform. Still, Koni remained his friend. When talking with other people, with old comrades, Lothar blamed the communists for his fate. Like so many, he was sucked into the wake of the confrontation that was increasingly determining the mindset of people in the "Front Line City," West Berlin. He supported the then-mayor of West Berlin, Ernst Reuter, and the SPD under Franz Neumann.[90]

George changed too, but in a different way. He was now back in the US, studying at Harvard University, where he began a career as anticommunist expert on the Soviet Union. His transformative years from Soviet to American citizen were far behind him. After his arrival in New York in 1939, he coped with the kaleidoscopic and contradictory impressions of this vast and completely new world with a different kind of emigrant life. He had dealings with the Massings and other former German comrades, as well as other Europeans and émigré Russian Mensheviks, including Markoosha's older sister. In high school he was still known as an active leftist, but now he began to metamorphose more and more into an anticommunist social democrat. His parents' influence, their stories about

90. Franz Neumann (1904–1974) was chairman of the Berlin SPD and a member of the Bundestag.

the actual background of what they had experienced in the Soviet Union, and Stalin's elimination of those he perceived as enemies played a role in his transformation.

As a student at the University of Wisconsin, and later as a US Army volunteer, he became acquainted with Middle America—young "ordinary Joes." He discovered the contrasts within this incredible, multifaceted, and eccentric American life: the isolation of intelligent and politically active American communists; the contradictions between democratic traditions and the often unfair, sometimes infantile—even almost inhuman—living conditions. His favorite authors were Thomas Wolfe and William Faulkner.

These years, with his wartime and postwar experiences, had a formative impact on George's professional pursuits. His knowledge of life in the Soviet Union and his education there appeared to predestine him for this line of work. Harvard was where the US elite were educated. It was home to a major research center for Soviet studies. George Fischer rapidly advanced to become a well-known expert on Russia. He described himself as centrist. Initially, he researched the Union of Liberation during the period prior to the Russian Revolution of 1905. He was interested in how—to use Western terminology—a centrist-constitutional movement was able to persevere in czarist Russia. Henry Kissinger and Zbigniew Brzezinski, who were his contemporaries at Harvard, became his colleagues and friends.[91] The affections of the former Komsomol member for the country of his childhood and early adolescence, which were still present during and after the war, began to fade, as did the memories of good friends in faraway Moscow and the room in Sivtsev Vrazhek Lane to which he once vowed to return. Although he was against the McCarthyite anticommunist witch hunt, which turned into a kind of medieval inquisition, his conservative liberalism increasingly took on an American and anti-Soviet character. He had a lot of contact with the Vlasov people. Those people were former Soviet citizens who collaborated with the Nazi armies to fight against their own country. Their wartime leader was the

91. Zbigniew Brzezinski (1928–2017) was a Polish-American political scientist and statesman. He served as national security advisor to President Jimmy Carter from 1977 to 1981.

former Soviet Army General Vlasov who had turned traitor while imprisoned in a German POW camp. After the war, with Vlasov executed, many of his followers stayed in the American occupied zone, where they drew the attention of those who were interested in their further use.[92] George began to study the motives and modes of thinking of these collaborators, and he later published a book about them. Over a period of five years he made frequent trips to Munich to visit the Russians living there and used the occasions to visit Berlin to meet up with Lothar.

Since Lothar was now doing well, he no longer needed financial support. But the meetings with George responded to a different need: a way of balancing things out. They drank a lot and laughed about the fact that the fat, rich American who came to visit an affluent German family preferred to order lard and headcheese in simple pubs. And they philosophized for hours on end. Victor [as Vitya called himself in the United States], who was studying for a technical degree in the US, traveled to Berlin much later and also met up with Lothar.

There was no longer a Troika. A get-together with Koni did not happen. The Troika of their childhood was already long gone, and all those friendly gatherings of the immediate postwar years gradually fizzled out as time went by. In a certain way, however, Lothar remained the middle man. Occasionally he met up with Koni, and less frequently with George. He had a great need to talk with people from different backgrounds who had nothing to do with business. Lothar and the two Fischers talked for hours about capitalism and socialism and about politics in the East and the West. All three of them shared a rejection of the Soviet model of socialism; they also agreed that things in the Soviet occupied zone and later in the GDR seemed to be developing along similar lines. Lothar understood that Koni could not engage in that kind of debate and avoided it for the sake of their enduring relationship. Lothar still continued to search for a political *Heimat*—without success.

Every now and then he and the Fischers talked about his relocating to the US. Initially, he thought about studying at the Massachusetts Institute

92. Andrei Vlasov (1900–1946) was captured in 1945 and later repatriated by the Americans to the Soviet Union, where he was executed.

of Technology alongside Vitya. Once Lothar had become the wealthy head of a construction company, they would discuss a new, unconstrained life in Alaska. That was where Victor Fischer was living, fulfilling his dreams. He had always been more inclined to be a practical person, at one with nature and the natural sciences. He did not ruminate about life's questions as did George, the intellectual; he was much more calm, at ease, and realistic. That was probably why he felt close to Paul Massing, his soulmate.

For Vitya, the transition from young Soviet citizen to the American way of life was emotionally different from George's. In 1939, he sailed alone and ahead of the others on that huge ocean liner, the *Queen Mary*, to meet the Massings in New York. Without speaking a word of English, he attended school there; he went to the cinema and watched Western movies, which were easy to follow. He did not like New York at all, but Wisconsin, in the Upper Midwest of the US, where he lived in a communal house with many other students, was better. Still, for many years to come, he would continue to feel lonely. He had no friends; others around him remained strangers. He spent the turn of the year, from 1941 to 1942, in Wisconsin. His still had a vivid memory of the final New Year's Eve in Peredelkino with all his friends. What would it be like there now, after the winter battle of Moscow?

In these difficult years, when Vitya often thought of the friends left behind, Paul Massing was exactly the right support for the boy. Paul was in the process of becoming a sociology professor not far from New York City. He filled Vitya with enthusiasm for the western United States, and they made plans. The events of the 1930s in the Soviet Union had caused Paul Massing to drift away from the country where he believed his political ambitions and ideals could be realized. Unlike his wife, though, he never openly criticized the Soviet Union; never even wrote one critical line that, during the wave of anti-Soviet sentiment in America, would certainly have been to his advantage. A little later, he and his wife separated. Paul loved village life and the countryside. He lived in rural surroundings, at times very close to Markoosha Fischer. The Fischer boys enjoyed being with him more than with their father. And so, in those years of transition, Vitya had a trusted, paternal friend to help him quietly to settle into a completely new environment and to preserve the moral values learned in his childhood. Even in later years, after George and Victor were on their own and each had built his own life, they maintained a close relationship with Paul. His personality and his calm and profound manner of thinking continued to exert enormous influence on them. His students, who were mostly of a leftist persuasion, respected and loved him for those qualities, because, despite his own experiences, he never spoke negatively about the history of the political left. After his retirement, Paul Massing returned to his native Rhineland where he died in 1978 in Grumbach, his birthplace.

All his life Paul Massing remained a fatherly friend to the Fischer boys. By contrast, their biological father increasingly took himself off into the realm of the famous journalist and writer. In the postwar years, Louis Fischer made frequent and extended trips to India. He met Mahatma Gandhi and held lengthy discussions with the spiritual leader of the Indian people. He was fascinated by Gandhi's personality and recognized the huge influence of his teachings on India's struggle for independence. Fischer wrote notable books about this, which formed the basis of Richard Attenborough's Oscar-winning film *Gandhi*. Gandhi's ideas can possibly be seen as a paradigm or foundation for future movements that produced men like Martin Luther King in the US; Nelson Mandela in South Africa; Salvador Allende in Chile; and ever-new martyrs—courageous fighters in the battles for their people's freedom and independence. Fischer's books certainly influenced his sons, but both of them wanted to free themselves from the burden of their father's fame and make their own way. In doing so, they chose different paths.

Vitya's ideas on life were, in many ways, similar to Lothar's, and that's why he repeatedly encouraged the successful but unhappy West Berliner to cash out, leave everything behind, and go to Alaska. Such suggestions remained unfulfilled dreams because of changes within Lothar himself. He had become a businessman—a small one, but a well-to-do one. In the middle of the 1950s, Lothar launched out on his own. His first personal project was the house of the famous film director, Wolfgang Staudte.[93] The connection was probably Karl Schneider, who grew up in the Wloch

93. Wolfgang Staudte (1906–1984) was one of the most important German directors of the postwar period.

family before 1933 and who worked as a film architect for the DEFA after the war. He also worked on Koni's films. Hence, Lothar got to know the film producer Artur Brauner, for whom he built the CCC Studios and who arranged commissions for Lothar in the social housing industry. Lothar's business effectively became Brauner's architectural office. Brauner owned land and received tax benefits for building subsidized social housing. Lothar said that he could have worked on bigger and more interesting jobs if he had had the "right party book" and the connections—the type of connections that were later exposed in the West Berlin construction scandals. But he refused to go down that path. The SPD no longer had his trust; the ideals of his youth would not allow him to become involved in corruption. He wanted to stay clean and he wanted to be independent. For that he worked extremely hard and exercised great self-discipline. You had to work hard if you worked for Lothar. But above all he drove himself relentlessly and, eventually, exhausted himself. Lothar felt great responsibility for his staff. Even when the economic situation seemed to demand it, no one was ever fired. Consequently, he couldn't leave West Berlin. This city wasn't merely the seat of his success and the place where his family lived the good life; he also felt the obligation to stay and not to give up. For a while he even entertained the idea of founding his own party, but in the end, he found constructing social housing was his way of putting his ideals into action. Paradoxically, he made his money by means of contracts with the wealthy in this bizarre creation that was West Berlin. Still, he could never completely detach himself from the ideals of his days in Moscow—ideals to which his father had devoted his entire life.

Even though Lothar was informed after the Twentieth Congress of the Communist Party of the Soviet Union [CPSU] that Wilhelm Wloch had been rehabilitated, he did not retreat from his anticommunist position.[94] Later, however, with his two sons, and with others, he did enjoy reflecting on his time in the Soviet Union, his Moscow schooldays, and his friends

94. The Twentieth Congress of the CPSU, held in February 1956, is best known for Nikita Khrushchev's "Secret Speech," in which he condemned Joseph Stalin's cult of personality and repressive rule. Titled "On the Cult of Personality and Its Consequences," the speech launched the process of de-Stalinization and had far-reaching effects both within the USSR and internationally.

at that time. It led to an inescapable conflict within himself—one that he suffered from and could not cope with. His father had been a practitioner of the political struggle and in that remained his role model. Lothar recognized in George an intellectual, a professor whose life and interests laid, like those of Louis Fischer, in the sphere of theory. He was well able to see that in the East many of his father's ideas were being fulfilled, that difficult things had been accomplished. Indeed, he was willing to acknowledge such accomplishments. He did so too when he would come into East Berlin to attend the premieres of Koni's films. But in philosophical discussions with the Fischers he lamented the fact that the West watched from afar as the East succeeded in bringing up its young people to support the new government, and in shaping them into active contributors. In the East they knew exactly what they wanted to achieve. Perhaps that was also the root of his growing pessimism for the future of his city.

Who could have known, or even guessed at, the tortuous path along which this city, this divided country, and this badly scarred continent would develop? At the time, on both sides of the divide you still had congresses and conferences taking place under the banner of German unity. But in the summer of 1948 a new currency was introduced in western Germany, which triggered the West Berlin blockade, and the situation worsened dramatically. Throughout Europe and the whole world the political atmosphere approached a deep freeze.

In February 1948, a change in the power balance took place in Czechoslovakia. Waves of fear and shock gripped the West, but there was unrest as well in our neighboring country. In my role as a radio journalist in Prague in May of that year, I saw how quickly, in tense situations, tempers can flare up on the streets. In June 1953, under different circumstances, we experienced something similar in our own country.[95]

All signs pointed toward confrontation: the outcome of the civil war in Greece, facilitated by the Truman Doctrine, proclaimed by the US

95. The 1953 Uprising in East Germany, also known as the June 17 Uprising, was a wave of strikes and protests in East Berlin against the GDR and Soviet domination. Sparked by mounting work quotas and food prices, it rapidly grew into a mass movement calling for political reform and greater freedom. The revolt was violently crushed by Soviet and East German forces, leaving many dead or imprisoned.

president and bearing his name; the founding of the state of Israel, which became another breeding ground for the permanent conflict in the Middle East; the resumption of the colonial war in Vietnam; and the looming danger of a war gathering like menacing clouds on the horizon above Korea. And it was a time when the US still thought it had a monopoly on atomic weapons.

World peace was under terrible threat, a bad time for friendships across the political fronts. Our family lost its connection with the Fischers; only via Lothar did we receive a rare message. But the relationship with Lothar was loosening too. Each member of the Troika lived his life in the world in which he was placed.

Once again, their story seemed to have come to an end.

The Get-Together in New York

Nearly thirty years passed, half a lifetime, and everything was normal—as it should be, according to the indisputable rules of this world. Everyone just lived his life in familiar surroundings among people he knew. The emotional bonds between the Troika frayed even though the two Berliners met regularly, more often in the East and less frequently in the West. Through their meetings they continued to sustain not only the fading friendship, but also the friendship's growing disagreements and contradictions. And the Troika no longer existed anyway. Our third man, the "Yank," was far away, and not only geographically. How could it have been otherwise? It was simply the way things were!

And then came the meeting. Actually, that was very normal, too. It was only for one day, on a return flight from Moscow to New York—a stopover at Berlin's Schönefeld airport; a day with "the Russian" in East Berlin; the middle man of the Troika joining, then taking the American with him to West Berlin; and finally, a flight out of Tempelhof the next day, back to New York. Really, it was nothing out of the ordinary.

But then came the invitation to travel to the US—an official invitation, of course, from his university. There were complications, but the West Berliner took matters into his own hands. He was determined, and applied himself as if his life depended on it. And it worked! The adventure was on again—dynamic, tangible, and ready to be experienced. The West and East Berliners flew together from Schönefeld, via Amsterdam, to New York. They spent ten days there and the memories flooded back: the years in Moscow, the postwar years in Berlin. It was all there, but it was also so far away; further away than ever . . .

That was how, two years later, Koni described the events leading to the 1975 meeting in the US, during which the final Troika photograph was taken.

Later, the two travelers gave very different accounts of the flight. They agreed, however, that in order to calm their nerves, a bottle of Stolichnaya was drained during the transatlantic journey. According to George's report of meeting them at Kennedy Airport, both friends were soused when they got off the plane. He said that Lothar's description of Koni's excitement at taking his first journey into the land of infinite opportunity was rather dramatic, while Koni, conversely, thought that Lothar's agitation was due to his anxiety about the outcome of this reunion of the hostile brothers.

The first day in New York was as unexceptional as the border controls, and the drive into Manhattan made much less of an impression on Koni than he had expected. After some strolling around the city, the friends were invited for a meal at Markoosha Fischer's place on Fifth Avenue. There, Lothar, the self-appointed chief organizer, decided that Yura would be in charge for a day. The Troika, in its Berlin version, then took the subway to a friend of George's who owned an old Leica camera. They wanted to restage the postwar Berlin photograph.

Susan Heuman, who was meant to be just the photographer, witnessed the reunion, which was to culminate in a dramatic finale. Susan's own story is remarkable. Her Jewish-German parents immigrated to the US via France in the 1930s. They had to endure the American version of anti-semitism and to work incredibly hard as well. Eventually, Susan was able to go to college. She also attended lectures by Paul Massing, who helped her to deepen her instinctive left-wing sympathies with concrete knowledge. It was there that she met George. Because of her political convictions she eventually had to leave the university.

For the New York photograph, the three men in their fifties tried to adopt the same poses they had had in the photograph taken in the ruins of Berlin thirty years earlier. In it, the chubby American has turned into a contemplative-looking, bearded professor. Compared to the others, his jacket hangs loosely on his body. On the right-hand side is the former lieutenant, also tubby and with a full beard, who smiles into the camera. And the man in the middle no longer shows the signs of his postwar emaciation. His heft and general demeanor bear witness to the assurance of a self-made man.

At this meeting, Lothar's dream of reviving this friendship that had been separated by borders, oceans, and tumultuous times, and to become once more the linchpin and the mediator, seemed to be coming true.

So, George/Yura was in charge for the day. He took his friends to his favorite place, Greenwich Village, the idiosyncratic area lying beyond the hullabaloo of the city, with its assortment of nineteenth-century houses. It's a neighborhood where intellectuals and bohemians used to live. This is where Yura felt at home. Certain parts of it even reminded him of the atmosphere of Moscow's Arbat. His mother used to live in Greenwich Village when she met Louis during World War I. Now she lived in a nearby hotel. Here, not far from the Hudson River, and usually in small, ground-floor premises, were many restaurants, pubs, and bars, frequented by people that enjoyed alternative lifestyles and a kaleidoscope of political opinions: homosexuals, feminists, and people of all races. First, they went to Yura's favorite restaurant, Mother Courage—a place for feminists and their friends. They ate and drank their fill, moved on to other bars, and finally, hours later, ended up in the snug back room of a tavern called the White Horse where they could talk without being interrupted.

So far, everything was almost as it used to be. They talked about God and the state of the world; about their families and friends; about politics and culture; about the fate of the entire world; and their individual lives. Koni and George had met only very briefly in Berlin so there was lots of catching up to do.

George, somewhat abruptly, had left his well-paid job as a distinguished Sovietologist after twenty years of active involvement in the Cold War. He held left-wing political views. With a dramatic, life-changing transformation behind him, he now worked at the City University of New York. This transformation began at the onset of the 1960s, when he started to revisit the Soviet Union more often and rekindled his contacts with old acquaintances and Soviet friends. Among these were people who observed the reality of the Soviet Union with a critical eye but who didn't identify with militant anti-Sovietism. He began to read a lot of novels and highly regarded books by Vera Panova,[96] Tendriakov,[97] Granin,[98] and Paustovskii.[99] These works eased his acclimatization into Moscow's cultural life and served as a basis for discussions with friends old and new. Aleksandr Tvardovskii, the author and editor of the renowned literary journal *Novy Mir*, embodied more than just George's hope for change. George saw in this intelligent and visionary poet—creator of the legend of the literary hero Vasilii Terkin—someone fighting for the de-Stalinization of culture and a "sympathetic, suffering and compassionate member of the Central Committee with peasant origins." He met Koni's teacher from the Institute of Cinematography, the director Sergei Gerasimov, and got to know some younger sociologists and philosophers whom he instantly liked.[100] He also renewed his contacts with some of the families he had known before. A few times in Peredelkino he visited Kornei Chukovskii, a senior figure in Soviet literature.[101] His house was quite near the dacha where the Wolfs used to live. And so the Moscow of his childhood once more became familiar; friends called him Yura again, and he became increasingly less interested in that Cold War discipline called Sovietology.

At the same time a new movement was emerging among American students—and in Europe, too. It was a blend of Marxist thought and anarchic views, hippie culture and antiestablishment attitudes. It was influenced by rock music, drugs, sexual freedom, radical culture, and other ways of liberated living—whatever anyone understood by this term. This movement had a great effect on George, and he felt he was a part of it. It was, therefore, logical that he supported a student strike at Columbia University, a cornerstone of the American establishment, where he taught and lectured on Marx. The university authorities found this behavior in

96. Vera Panova (1905–1973) was a Soviet novelist, short story writer, and dramatist who rose to fame in the mid-1940s and became one of the USSR's most beloved writers.

97. Vladimir Tendriakov (1923–1984) was a Soviet short story writer and novelist.

98. Daniil Granin (1919–2017) was a Soviet and Russian author.

99. Konstantin Paustovskii (1892–1968) was a Soviet writer nominated for the Nobel Prize in Literature.

100. Sergei Gerasimov (1906–1985) was a distinguished film director and screenwriter from the Soviet era, renowned for his impactful contributions to both cinema and film education.

101. Kornei Chukovskii (1882–1969) was a Soviet poet, translator, literary critic, and the author of numerous children's books.

one of its professors entirely unacceptable. He was not granted tenure, and George had to go.

The public City University of New York offered him a position that, even though it was at a less prestigious institution, nevertheless provided him with the opportunity to extend his studies in sociology and to develop his own ideas on the possibilities for social change. Along with other like-minded people, he believed that this was where communal and social protest would bring about, step-by-step, democratic self-government in New York City. The rejection of any top-down power, any government bureaucracy, and the achievement of self-government from below—this was his political credo as he tried to explain it to his friends.

George saw this dramatic change in his life as a huge liberation. A house in the countryside that he had acquired seemed to facilitate his new lease on life. It removed him from the pressures of the everyday and gave him time to think about the world and his own place within it. Such luxury was unimaginable for the two Germans.

Everything Koni heard from George, and what he overheard from conversations at the neighboring tables, aroused his curiosity. He had always been most interested in the individual human being and his fate. Now he experienced firsthand the phenomenon of a movement that he had previously only heard and read about. He had only to look around to see these odd-looking men and women who would create an uproar at home in the GDR simply through their appearance. What kind of people were they? What kind of ideology made so many of them, who mostly came from bourgeois backgrounds, leave everything behind, and, with flowers in their hair and their songs, stand up against the armed omnipotence of the State?

Ten years earlier, in West Berlin, around the time of George's transformation, the student Benno Ohnesorg had been shot dead during a demonstration against the visit of the Shah of Iran. It was an event that propelled the youth protest movement in a new direction.[102] Similar

102. Benno Ohnesorg (1940–1967) was a German student who was fatally shot during a protest in West Berlin against the state visit of Mohammad Reza Shah Pahlavi. His death at the age of twenty-six fueled the growth and radicalization of the West German student movement in the late 1960s. The police officer who shot him, Karl-Heinz Kurras, was working as a secret agent for the East German secret police.

things happened in Paris and elsewhere around the world. Large groups of young people took militant action. The idol for some was Che Guevara, Fidel Castro's comrade in arms in the fight against the fascist Batista regime in Cuba. Koni, like many of us, had a wonderful photograph of Che in his apartment; he had read his diary. For a long time Koni, along with Wolfgang Kohlhaase, had the idea of making a film about Tamara Bunke, a German who grew up in South America. As a member of the Free German Youth [FDJ] organization, she went to Cuba. She became a supporter of Che and worked undercover with him. Later, as a guerrilla, she went into the Bolivian bush, where she and Che perished in 1967. Tamara had chosen "Tania" as her pseudonym after the Moscow schoolgirl, Zoya Kosmodem'ianskaia. In the winter of 1941, this young partisan was captured by the Nazis, tortured in the cruelest way, and then hanged. Zoya was our age when we left the besieged Moscow to travel east. Under her cover name of "Tania," she became the most respected hero for Soviet youth. Twenty-five years later she became Tamara Bunke's idol. We shared these two women's beliefs and motivations. It was even possible to comprehend the utter desperation of children from decent middle-class families that caused someone like Ulrike Meinhof to oppose the authority of a hated social order, through the naked violence of an individual act of terrorism.[103]

In Greenwich Village, the friends were in agreement in their rejection of such a path, but their views on the people at the neighboring tables differed. Lothar did not conceal his aversion. The mere thought that his two adolescent sons could get mixed up with this group of idle, drug-addicted hippies was an abomination to him. When he and his family had visited George in the US a few years before this trip, he had even taken offense at George's long hair and beard and told him he was an aging bohemian.

Koni was more interested in these people's motives. He asked George, and particularly Susan, detailed questions. He knew about Black Power. He retained the image of the Black US Americans on the medal podium

103. Ulrike Meinhof (1934–1976) was a German journalist, left-wing militant, and cofounder of the Red Army Faction (RAF), often called the Baader–Meinhof Gang in the media. The RAF, a far-left militant group established in 1970 and active until 1998, was regarded as a terrorist organization by the West German government.

during the Olympic Games in Mexico, when they raised their arms, clenching their black-gloved fists, during the American national anthem. Koni knew of the boxing idol Cassius Clay's conversion to Islam and his refusal to serve in the Vietnam War. He sacrificed sleep for many a night watching this great boxer's fights on TV. He was fascinated by the rousing sermons of Martin Luther King, who, with his nonviolent approach, had become the leader of the civil rights movement in the US—a true political force that challenged the ruling class. As different as their motives and methods of fighting were, there was an essential logic to the fact that both Martin Luther King and Che Guevara were killed at almost the same time by bullets of the same origin.

At the time of the Troika's reunion in the US, many young Americans were distressed by the events in Chile. In September 1973, the socialist president Salvador Allende had become the victim of a military coup d'état that was instigated by the CIA and supported by the US. To his dying breath he and his colleagues withstood the onslaught of the insurgent generals at the presidential La Moneda Palace and thus left the Chilean people his legacy. Once again, the US had assumed the role of the world's policeman, preferring the terror of a military dictatorship to a freely elected government that it defamed as being pro-Soviet. Many young people found this no longer tolerable.

But why did those people, who rejected the injustice of the imperialist system and fight against it, not follow our way—since after all ours was the right and proper path? Everything that Marx and Lenin said was proven and logical, and validated by everyday life. How could we stand up against this misanthropic system, except with a movement that has the support of the masses and is led by an organizing force? And why did the communists in the US and West Germany constitute such a dwindling minority—among them such marvelous and clever people as Henry Winston,[104] Angela Davis,[105] and Paul Robeson? These people sacrificed themselves, they performed heroic deeds, and yet . . . On the other hand, some other alternative

104. Henry M. Winston (1911–1986) was an African American political leader and Marxist civil rights activist.

105. Angela Davis (born 1944) is an American Marxist and feminist political activist, philosopher, academic, and author.

movements, with all their diverse and contradictory philosophies, were able spontaneously to activate masses of people and win astounding numbers of electoral votes, like in West Germany. Why?

George's theorizing was not convincing. He himself doubted whether, in the foreseeable future, the model of self-government he imagined could be realized in the US in the foreseeable future; in those few countries where such attempts had been made, they had been only tentative. His responses to Koni's and Lothar's questions were contradictory and unsubstantiated.

Naturally, during the course of this long evening, they talked about more than just George and his notions of building a better world. Since Koni seemed to be the one who had achieved the most, he was asked similar questions, too. He embarked on this trip as a celebrated film director and president of the Academy of Arts of the GDR. For the scheduled screenings in New York and Alaska he had in his luggage his first internationally successful film, *Sterne* [*Stars*], which won an award at Cannes. He was eager to see how his most autobiographical film, *Ich war neunzehn*, would be received. The film reflected his agony at being torn between the two countries that he both called *Heimat*. And his film *Goya*, coproduced with Angel Wagenstein after the book by Lion Feuchtwanger, would inspire very different reactions. Answering his friends' many questions during this New York session, he time and again returned to his films and the work associated with them—work that put everything in his private life on the back burner. He was convinced that in his own way, he was reaching the people, his audience, through his work, imparting important things, things they were not aware of, and thus could have an impact. After all, what he was most concerned with in his art was to address basic societal issues and the individual's response in moments of conflict and challenge.

He did not evade his friends' penetrating questions and doubts, nor did he conceal personal conflicts—and there were many. One film that meant a lot to him, *Sonnensucher* [*Sun Seekers*], was denied release and was rehabilitated, so to speak, only many years later.[106] Just as his father

106. *Sonnensucher*, from 1958, tells the story of two young East Germans who are forced to work in a uranium mine in the USSR. The film was banned, by demand from the Soviet embassy in Berlin, until the year 1972.

had in 1937 when his play *Die Matrosen von Cattaro* [*The Sailors of Cattaro*] was withdrawn from the repertoire in Leningrad, he had to fight for it to be shown. This was the same kind of *Zivilcourage* [civil/moral courage] that our father had repeatedly demonstrated in the field of art and politics. Wasn't the film version of *Goya, oder der arge Weg der Erkenntnis* [*Goya, or the Hard Way to Enlightenment*], about the Spanish painter, a reflection of the problems and challenges faced by artists amid our present struggles? Wasn't having a firm perspective on life and politics the most important thing for an artist, as for any human being engaged in the world? Koni was convinced that an artist—indeed, every committed person—had to identify his own position and then fight for it regardless of the consequences. During the discussion that evening he used the term "*Zivilcourage*," which is what his father had asked of him in a letter he wrote to Koni when he was at the front on his nineteenth birthday. And whether at home or during these strange arguments in the hippie pub in New York, this was Koni's principle.

Lothar had mixed views on Koni's films, which he somehow thought were also his films. In Berlin he never missed a premiere. Lothar was angry when Koni told him about a premiere at the last minute. In his business he could not rearrange everything at the drop of a hat, but he attended anyway. He saw the premieres as important family events; he thought highly of the films and enjoyed their success. In New York he refuted Koni's belief that his films would be able to bring about change. They talked about internal political measures in the socialist countries. Lothar mentioned the events in 1968 in Czechoslovakia.

George was also deeply upset by the events of 1968, and about the Soviet Union he still spoke with sorrow. That country continued to be where, for him, the greatest revolution ever had taken place. The smell of a certain subway station in New York made him homesick because it reminded him of the Moscow Metro. He felt that the revolution's aims and its great potential were either fading or lost. Everywhere he looked, he could see only stagnation. He sympathized with the progress in Chile under Allende and he approved of some of the social achievements in Sweden and Israel. He agreed with much of what Nikita Khrushchev had addressed in his time and the goals he had proclaimed; and developments in art and literature had fostered hope. On this, he concurred with Koni. George listened intently to Koni's thoughts about the issues facing young people in the GDR. He thought he could sense Koni's doubts about whether his own and older comrades' traditions of antifascism and their ideals concerning the intellectual aims of socialism were correctly understood and adopted by the younger generation. Despite their great differences, George and Koni understood each other; they listened attentively and repeatedly asked questions.

Lothar was less open minded. He was impatient and harsh in his judgments. At the very beginning of the evening he had surprised his friends by telling them that he had not only read Chingiz Aitmatov's book *The White Ship*, but that he had also committed its contents in all its detail to memory.[107] He spoke with affection about this wonderful book and its author. Now, at the mere mention of politics in the Soviet Union, he got angry. Koni, George, and Susan did not notice how, during this long conversation that was repeatedly punctuated with eating and drinking, a wall had appeared between them and Lothar. Lothar's intention in organizing this get-together had been to build a bridge between the communist German and the anti-communist American. Now, after only a couple of days, and in spite of their different opinions, the two bearded intellectuals understood each other better than Lothar understood either of them. Furthermore, Susan openly sympathized with their points of view. Lothar was surprised to find himself apparently sidelined and isolated. He was no longer the self-assured boss, the leading central figure from the photograph that had just been taken. He had returned to the condition of the defeated German of the postwar photograph, helplessly looking for an anchor between the two allies. And there it was again, as if intensified by a magnifying glass: the pain of his entire fragmented life, the fate of his family, his city, and the whole world.

The trigger for Lothar's outburst was the subject of Vietnam, which featured on and off throughout the evening. The US was in the process of withdrawing from the south of this long-suffering country. Finally! When you consider the cost of this dirty war in lives, in international reputation,

107. *The White Ship* is a novella by Kyrgyz author Chingiz Aitmatov, first published in 1970, that paints a grim portrait of Soviet life in Kyrgyzstan. A film adaptation of the story was released in 1976 under the same title.

and in destruction! A deep rift divided American society and the nation was split apart. People spoke of "Vietnam syndrome."

George said that, after much torment, he had come to acknowledge that it was not the worst thing for a country to become communist if its people wanted it. And the Vietnamese were ready to fight to the end for this—to sacrifice everything in order to withstand the military and technical superiority of foreign intruders. It was the conviction of the Vietnamese people that finally ejected the superpower, the US, from their country. It was not easy for George nor for many Americans to recognize this. Susan talked about her meetings with American soldiers who refused to take part in this war. Koni reported examples of solidarity with embattled Vietnam in the GDR, mostly among young people.

This was the point at which Lothar snapped. He raised his voice and shouted something about the treacherous Americans who have left the Vietnamese to their own devices: "Why doesn't America act? Why do the Americans let this happen? Why do the Americans just stand idly by?" Angrily, he rejected George's attempts to calm him down: "You have to act immediately! Stop with the nonsense! You, Professor, are just like your father—a theoretician who'll never achieve anything! You just lecture from on high and know nothing about life!" And to Koni: "You are a fence-sitter. You shut your eyes because you're afraid of the truth, because you're a passive parasite who just wants to keep his position!" Lothar had become purple in the face. Susan feared for his life and tried to calm him down. Tears poured down his cheeks; he was drenched. Responding from here on only to Susan, he lamented the fate of the Vietnamese who had been left to their own devices. Humanity had been betrayed by Moscow and Washington. It wasn't worth living any longer in this world. Again and again he broke out into aggressive shouting. He compared both Americans and Russians with the fascists, and included his friends in that. When Lothar said he was in favor of dropping a nuclear bomb on North Vietnam, Susan couldn't believe her ears. He was like a sick fanatic. George explained to Susan that behind this outburst there was a little more than just the fractiousness of a drunken man.

On the way home, after Koni got out of the taxi, Susan was afraid to travel alone with Lothar. While she had sympathy for him—she could see that he was going to pieces inside, and in need of help—she was also scared, because he had behaved like an ultra-right-wing American. She did not want to be by herself with him, so they too got out of the taxi and walked the streets for a long time. During this walk, close by the United Nations building, Lothar told her why he had gone back to Germany before the war and that his father had been killed in the Soviet Union. Susan had this strange feeling that he wanted to die, that he would kill himself. Lothar was still upset and crying. She thought Lothar's tears were like the enraged tears of a little lonely boy who has lost an argument. Eventually, they took the bus to Susan's apartment and said goodbye in front of her house.

After all the conflicting facts and opinions she had heard throughout the evening, Susan struggled for a long time to get a clear image of the three men who had come to her to have their photograph taken. She felt a connection with two of them. While each of them in their own way had aroused her sympathy, she felt closest to Koni. She felt the pain in all three, and thought she understood that none of them truly had a home. Each of them had his own personal history and each of them carried their own individual burden.

The flight to Alaska pushed the events of that evening in New York into the background. Koni had heard that Lothar was having these outbursts more and more often. When he visited, Lothar was usually accompanied by his wife, and he frequently became aggressive toward the people he was talking to—including his wife. It always began after a few drinks. Koni and Lothar's previous arguments had habitually been conducted in a teasing tone, but there had never before been such an outburst of aggression, hatred, blind arrogance, and despair. During this get-together of the friends, which Lothar himself had organized, everything he had repressed in his past burst out of him, and with such unsuspected force. And with it came the recognition of the impotence of a man who stood between two fronts. Lothar saw himself as the sole fighter for justice and humanity.

The incident was not mentioned again. Koni enjoyed Alaska and discovered the country for himself. The enormity of the landscape; the blending of the natural world with islands of modern architecture and technology; the ability of the Americans to not just make money but also create something worthwhile—all those things greatly impressed him. Approvingly, he wrote in his travel journal several times: "*Vot svolochi amerikantsy*" ["Those Americans—those bastards!"].

In Fairbanks, Victor greeted them like old friends. The original, the Moscow Troika, was once more reunited. Vitya now sported a beard as well; he had not had one during their prior short meeting in Berlin. He was now called Vic and was a grand host who was happy in this country, where he felt at home. Despite his many responsibilities and commitments, he freely disposed of his schedule and generously makes time for his friends.

He had lived and worked here, in this largest of the States, for twenty-five years, living his dream and fulfilling the promises of their shared youth.

At the airport Vitya's wife and children also gave the guests a very friendly welcome. They drove to the house in three cars. On the way, on a hill on the outskirts of the city, Koni saw the modern university where he'd be showing his films and delivering his paper. The idea for this visit had been born a year ago, when Vitya had stopped over in Berlin on his flight back from the Soviet Union, and where they had all met for the first time in thirty-five years. Vic told the president of the University of Alaska that his friend was a renowned filmmaker and winner of many international prizes. This was how, alongside the invitation to the City University of New York, the official invitation to Alaska came about. The foreign ministries and embassies of both countries were engaged, and now the president of the Academy of Arts of the GDR was in Alaska. It was something like an adolescent prank, but on a much higher level!

Vic's house sat in a forest of birch, beech, and alder trees. He had designed it himself, and everything in it was practical. Immediately, it seemed as if all was as it used to be: The boys from Moscow were reunited. They remembered that back in their youth they had plans for journeys up to the far north, although at that time it would certainly have been Siberia. They seemed to remember, however, that they had also talked about Alaska.

Throughout the next day Koni and Lothar made pelmeni. Koni was in his element and in all modesty called himself the world's greatest pelmeni expert, sharing this distinction (but only just) with his teacher and colleague, the Soviet film director Sergei Gerasimov. Lothar told Victor's family about the great scene in Koni's film, *Ich war neunzehn,* where the Soviet officers prepared for the victory celebrations with a true pelmeni-fest in Sanssouci Palace. Once Vitya had seen the film, he understood the significance in Koni's life of these little pockets of dough filled with meatballs. The film moved him deeply. He saw the nineteen-year-old in the uniform of a Soviet lieutenant and visualized himself in Soviet uniform—if he hadn't left for the US in 1939 . . . He could identify with the people in the film, and he wondered whether he would have survived; so many more people died in the East than they did in the American army. It seemed a miracle that the Moscow Troika had survived, and that now, at a party in Fairbanks, Alaska, its members were eating the Russian traditional meal. Russian was also the common language among the friends. Vitya had almost completely forgotten his German. Only when difficult subjects came up did Vitya use English, Lothar German, and Koni either Russian or German. Vitya's wife, Gloria, and the other people present often did not understand a word, but the Troika had no trouble understanding each other.

Victor wanted to show them as much as possible of his Alaska, and his line of work. On the first day they flew in a little charter plane to Prudhoe Bay, where the pipeline began and where BP [British Petroleum] was sitting on the source of the black gold. Koni felt like a character in a science fiction film: an icy, glistening snow desert, only 1,500 miles from the North Pole, and, in the middle of it, the strange technical building of the BP Center.[108] There was also an Arctic Hilton hotel equipped with all technological wonders, and every imaginable level of modern comfort. Although Koni was surprised by the application of knowledge originally derived from space exploration—the hotel was designed and built by the [Johnson] Space Center in Houston—he was more impressed by the vastness of the natural environment and the industriousness of the people.

Victor explained that through his work he was ensuring that the country wasn't recklessly exploited, but that the economy contributed to sustainable development that took into account the interests of the people

108. The Base Operations Center, built by BP (British Petroleum) in 1974 near Prudhoe Bay, Alaska, served as a facility for workers at the Endicott oil field.

living there. When he moved to Alaska—because he didn't like living in New York and wanted to move away from his famous father—the country wasn't yet a full-scale state of the US. He became an advocate for Alaskan statehood, served as a coauthor of Alaska's constitution, and was elected as a senator in the state government. After eleven years in Alaska and one year at Harvard, he worked for a time for the federal government in Washington, tackling the problem of overpopulation in big cities. But then he moved back to the far reaches of Alaska.

From the pipeline, they drove to a bay surrounded by glaciers and ice-covered peaks. They breathed in the fresh air and spread their arms as if to embrace the whole world from this spot. They were filled with the feeling shared by everyone who experiences untouched nature on this planet that can be so beautiful. At that moment, all their childhood dreams returned: their vision of a just world, and their wishes to discover the world's secrets for themselves and to contribute to a better society. Many years ago in Moscow, they had greatly appreciated the research done on the Arctic Ocean and made their own plans to discover Siberia. On the flight over the mountains to Prudhoe Bay, Koni told them about his journey to Kamchatka. Only the narrow Bering Strait divides eastern Siberia from this part of America, which the Russian czar sold for $7.2 million. Russia's proximity is ever present. Here in Alaska, during conversations with Victor, with pipeline workers, and at the university, the thought occurred that people who live in similar circumstances, who do similar jobs and who share similar environmental conditions, must also have similar thoughts. Koni and Vitya spoke a lot about the similarities between Alaska and Siberia. There was not only a similar landscape, but there were also physical similarities in the features of the people. They were people who live, one might say, at the very limits of civilization, and who live voluntarily in the wilderness in order to discover the land and its riches. To a certain extent, life was easier here. In one way or another, working people were alike all over the world. They were friendly and communicative, and their faces and hands carried the evidence of their labor. Koni listened while, at the pipeline, Victor translated the patient explanations of the workers about the technical processes, which were second nature to them; their jobs; and the rhythms of their life.

It was here that the growing confrontation between the US and the Soviet Union was felt especially painfully. Some of the friends' conversation was preoccupied by this anxiety.

Koni addressed this subject during the screening of his films to his audience of students and staff at the University of Alaska in Fairbanks. His presentation was understated, because it was more important to him that the audience form their own opinions on his films and, therefore, about the country where they were made. He spoke about the purpose of his work: that his films should introduce people to ideas that might help them understand each other better. He placed his emphasis on what unites people rather than on what divides them.

With the vivid impression of their visit to the pipeline still in his mind, Koni told Vitya that art for him was, in many respects, like an unexplored terrain; he needed the undiscovered. Following well-trodden paths would be of interest neither to him nor the viewer. Koni remembered his 1964 film, *Der geteilte Himmel* [*Divided Heaven*], based on the novel—controversial at the time—by Christa Wolf. It was about the problems experienced by a young couple in divided Germany. In a completely different way, the sky above Alaska, which is the same sky as above Siberia, reminded him of the ominous divisions in the world.

Vitya discussed his feelings concerning his trip to the Soviet Union. Making contact with people there was very easy. Because of his command of Russian, there were no language barriers. Everywhere—in Moscow, Leningrad, Murmansk, Novgorod, and Irkutsk—whether on the plane or in a restaurant, he met open-minded people who freely spoke their minds without inhibition. He often felt as if he was back home, but he also had certain reservations. The poignant memories of his youth usually evaporated fairly quickly, and he sensed a political divide separating him from the country where he no longer wished to live. This didn't affect his good relationship with his many Soviet colleagues and the many vodka toasts and relaxed hours spent together. These toasts were not only about peace and friendship; they also expressed the desire for a close, long-lasting cooperation. Victor worked hard to maintain and enhance the teamwork between his organization and the corresponding departments of the USSR's Academy of Sciences in Moscow, Novosibirsk, and Irkutsk. The personal relationships he built through his work were especially important to him. Despite issues that divided him from them, they were still people of the country in which he had spent a significant part of his life.

He recalled that he fell ill in Moscow at exactly the same time as the American President Nixon's visit to the Soviet Union. He felt how much the people hoped for a successful outcome. Nixon, whom Victor personally didn't like, was working toward a detente. By the time of the Troika's current reunion, all those hopes had disappeared. Victor argued that if the high and mighty exchanged insults, then we must maintain even closer contact. They decided that their next reunion must be in Moscow.

Koni and Vitya earnestly considered how links might be forged between the Siberian and Alaskan people. Much later, Victor would introduce a resolution in the Alaskan Senate for a nuclear-free zone in the Arctic.

Throughout these conversations Lothar stayed on the sidelines. He was there, and he agreed to the meeting in Moscow. There was no repeat of the New York outburst, but the politics here were not his. He could, however, attempt to act as peacemaker to help the Fischers with their marital problems. Soon after their arrival the friends had noticed the signs of a relationship in trouble. Things came to a head when, of all things, Victor told his wife that he was going to leave her during their stay. Consequently, the relationship hit the rocks. Vitya apologized to the friends for burdening their visit. The men talked about it until the early morning of their departure. Lothar advised: "Don't rush into things."

Vitya and Koni discussed matters at great depth. Koni told him about Meni and her admirable attitude toward his father's infidelities. Meni had died two years before this journey, and Koni still felt the pain of that loss very sharply. He reflected on how much Meni meant to him and how, when he was sorting out his parents' estate, it became clear to him how irreplaceable Meni had been to his father. She was the center of the ever-growing family, which included his father's illegitimate children. She had been the lifelong soulmate to the writer and his work. Koni also talked about his second marriage, about the important part Christel played in his life.[109] With her personality; her bright, cheerful manner; and her open-minded curiosity about a variety of subjects and her love, she was the first person to make him feel he was walking on solid ground. He didn't mention Margot at all in these talks. Even the passing of a quarter of a century could not heal that wound.

At Lothar's departure the next morning, Gloria burst into tears. She clung to him for a long time. The moment he boarded the Lufthansa flight for Hamburg at Anchorage's airport, Lothar was transformed once again into the self-assured man. Koni was astonished by his cheerfulness. When Lothar saw the German Lufthansa Airlines sign, he said: "At last! One can speak German again!"

They assured each other once more that they shouldn't wait so long for the next reunion. It should be either in Moscow or somewhere in Siberia, or perhaps at Lake Baikal. Koni wanted to reciprocate the hospitality shown by the Americans and Lothar in putting this journey together.

With Lothar gone, Koni and Victor had another casual conversation. Vitya was enormously impressed by their meeting. Like the others, he couldn't forget the time of their youth in Moscow. It was something intangible but also something that obviously had a strong influence on the entire life of each individual member of the former Troika.

There was much in Vic's character that reminded Koni of the young Vitya in Moscow: his composure, his ability to concentrate, his introspection—but, nevertheless, his openness toward other people. Immediately he felt very close to Vitya, more so than to Yura or Lotka. They talked about the others, and about the differences between older and younger brothers. The younger ones took more after the mothers, the older ones after the fathers.

Victor said that he and George had not been very close when they were young, but that this had changed at the end of the war. In 1945, when Vitya was due to embark for the war in the Pacific, Yura came from Marseille to see him off. The brothers spent three or four days together, which they later counted as the best of their lives. This marked a change in their relationship.

109. Christel Bodenstein (1938–2024) was a celebrated German film and television actress, best known for her work in numerous East German productions.

Yura was a good person, but he had become an outsider and a loner. In spite of the radical transformation in his life, from having had a good job as a Sovietologist to becoming a sociologist who was respected and liked by all his students, he wasn't able to change the world. Nowhere could he find a political system that realized his revolutionary ideas. Lothar, on the other hand, tried to suppress the irreconcilable differences between his humanitarian principles and his profession—which was clearly hostile toward people and the environment—by driving himself to the limit. "He should have stayed with you, should have become a politician, or should have come to us in Alaska when we'd suggested it—he would have been a different man. It's too late now—well, it probably is at fifty . . . " said Victor.

Koni flew from Alaska to Los Angeles to see Lion Feuchtwanger's widow, Martha. Through the *Goya* film and her contact with the Academy of Arts of the GDR, a close relationship had formed between Koni and this remarkable old lady. Once, when they went to a restaurant together, the president of the Academy of Arts amazed the staff and guests present by ordering one hundred grams of vodka and downing it in one gulp. It was the thirtieth anniversary of the liberation of Bernau, the day on which he, the former first commanding officer, was awarded honorary citizenship of the city.

On his way back, via New York, Koni stopped in on Markoosha in Greenwich Village. She was also one of the major mother figures in Koni's life. Markoosha had a close relationship with her sons. Unlike Louis Fischer, who disappeared from the family with increasing frequency, she could understand and share her sons' longing for a reunion with the land of their childhood and youth. She could also understand the divide that ran right through the Troika. Markoosha talked to Koni about Lothar and called him "*Nash burzhuichik*" ["Our little bourgeois"]. She felt their rift acutely: "It was much harder for him. He chose a different path and he's much further away from me now."

During the flight, Koni had time to sort out the many thoughts swirling in his mind.

Was Markoosha accurate in her affectionate characterization of Lothar as "the little bourgeois"? He certainly had a lot of the middle manager about him, as well as the trappings of a businessman's lifestyle. He convincingly represented the viewpoint of a liberal citizen; and yet, in his own way, he had tried to remain true to their common childhood dreams. He had had to work hardest of them all to train for a profession in the first place, and to create the means to fulfill his ideas. His staff and his clients loved him. He had no need to feel ashamed when he looked in the mirror.

Even if Vitya was closest in nature to Koni, he shared with Lothar, despite all their differences, similarly strong roots in the society in which they lived. Each maintained a critical outlook, and each, through his achievements, was able to remain independent. At the same time, they had both turned away from socialism. There was never a moment's doubt for Koni about his own socialist standpoint. Everyone has their own opinions, and represents them with varying degrees of temperament and tolerance. And that was also true of George, who brooded constantly and liked to describe his position as fifty-fifty. His ideal was directed toward the convergence of all the great intellectual and social currents of humanity.

With Koni's flight back, the adventure of the reunion of the Troika ended.

"The world of childhood dreams had returned, but it was impossible to bring it into the here and now."

All photographs are from the Markus Wolf papers, Hoover Institution Library & Archives, unless otherwise noted.

Louis Fischer

Bertha Fischer, called Markoosha

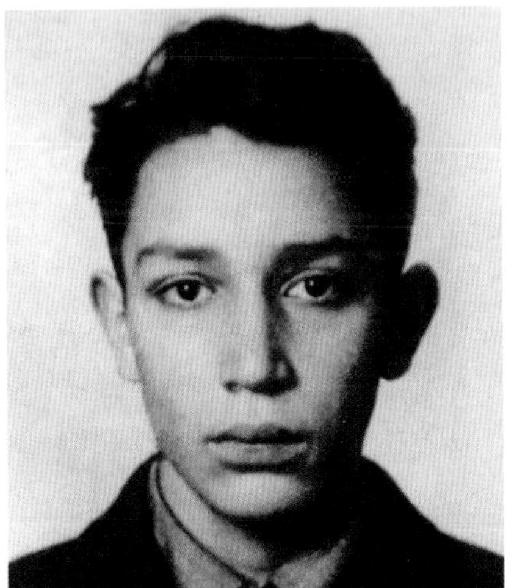

Victor Fischer, called Vitya

George Fischer, called Yura

Friedrich Wolf

Else Wolf, called Meni

Markus Wolf, called Mischa

Konrad Wolf, called Koni

Wilhelm Wloch

Erna Wloch

Lothar Wloch, called Lotka

Margot Wloch, called Mausi

Lenin (circled at left) and delegates, including Louis Fischer (circled at right), at a meeting of the Central Executive Committee of Russia, October 1922

Friedrich Wolf and Kurt Ahrendt during a voluntary work assignment, a so-called Subbotnik, at the construction site of the Karl Liebknecht School in Moscow, 1935. Kurt Ahrendt, who was the Pioneer leader of the Wolf and Fischer boys, was later among those arrested during the Stalinist purges. Despite his innocence, he was sentenced to death in a show trial and executed on February 20, 1938.

Pupils of the Karl Liebknecht School in Moscow (Markus Wolf at the center of the picture)

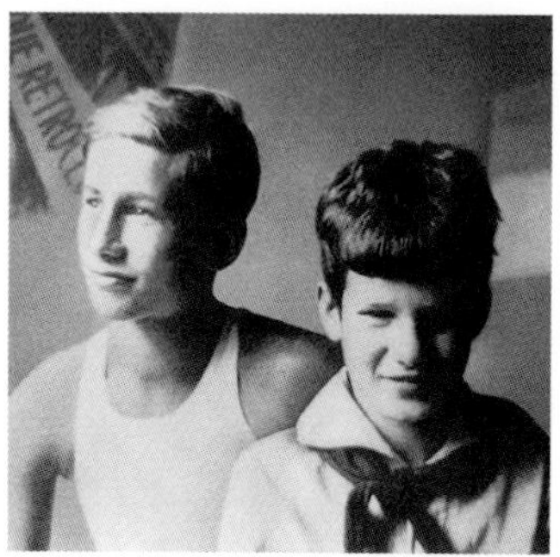

Markus and Konrad Wolf, Moscow, 1936

Victor Fischer and Lothar Wloch in the Fischers' apartment in Moscow

Konrad Wolf, Lothar Wloch, and Markus Wolf with German shepherd, Dosor

Excursion of the Fischer and Wolf families in the Moscow region, 1935

Bertha Fischer and Else Wolf, Moscow, 1939

Erna Wloch in Peredelkino, summer 1939

Friedrich Wolf at the Le Vernet internment camp, 1940

Lothar Wloch, shortly before his departure from Moscow

Lothar Wloch serving as a sergeant in the German Air Force on the Eastern Front

Konrad Wolf as an officer in the Red Army

George (left) and Victor Fischer

George Fischer (left) as an officer in the US Army during the Yalta Conference, Sevastopol, February 1945

The Fischer family in the United States, summer 1943

Reunion in Berlin—Margot Wloch, George Fischer, and Lothar Wloch, ca. 1945

Konrad Wolf (left) with his comrades in arms after the victory of the Red Army

Louis Fischer with Mahatma Gandhi, February 1948

Konrad Wolf, 1951

Lothar Wloch, early 1950s

Markus and Konrad Wolf, 1950s

Friedrich Wolf (left) as the first ambassador of the GDR to Poland, February 1950. *Courtesy of Bundesarchiv*

Konrad Wolf, Lothar Wloch, and Victor Fischer, Alaska, 1975

George Fischer, Lothar Wloch, and Konrad Wolf re-create the iconic Troika photo from 1945, New York, 1975. *Courtesy of Susan Heuman.*

Victor and George Fischer visiting the GDR in October 1985, standing before the former Soviet city command headquarters in Bernau near Berlin

Konrad Wolf, shortly before his death

Markus Wolf during a reading and book discussion of *Die Troika* at the Deutsches Theater, Berlin, November 12, 1989

Markus Wolf during the *Troika* book launch, Friedrichsfelde, March 9, 1989

Markus Wolf, 1998

For years, Markus Wolf was famously known as "the man without a face," his appearance remaining a mystery to the West. That changed in 1979 when a secretly taken photograph of him—captured during a business trip to Scandinavia—surfaced and was published in the German newsmagazine *Der Spiegel.* In March of that year, the image appeared on the magazine's front cover, revealing Wolf's face to the public for the first time. © *DER SPIEGEL* 10/1979.

Epilogue

Story of an Unmade Film

Lothar's death followed the events in New York as if it had been scripted. He died in June 1976 in a hospital in West Berlin. The doctors couldn't establish for certain whether he took an overdose with the intention of killing himself or whether his death was the result of his ignoring his doctors' advice about a long-diagnosed illness: an unfortunate conjunction of excessive drinking, the failure of his weakened heart, and a bout of depression from which he had suffered frequently and with increasing intensity. One has to ask at this point how far his death was attributable to the stress of being a manager; the awareness of his unresolved life; and the conflict between his desire, as a building contractor and Berlin citizen, to contribute to the improvement of people's lives versus the continuous pressure to assert oneself in the economic wonderland. And on top of all that, the trauma of his youth . . . Did the meeting in New York stir up too many things? Did it perhaps even foreshadow the end?

After the death of Lothar, the "Chkalov," the middle horse of the Troika, Koni was constantly on edge. This story, the story of his own life, had to be dealt with and captured; all his previous ideas were now flowing ineluctably together.

Lothar's wish was for his ashes to be laid to rest in an unmarked grave in the city cemetery in Berlin-Wilmersdorf. Koni knew about unmarked graves from the war . . . On January 6, 1977, on six and a half typewritten pages, he created "A short description of the material. First rough ideas for a possible story—*The Troika*."

From this day on *The Troika* became his parallel reality. In his head he had various ideas for the film. Again and again he relived the story: the story of his life. He had tried once before to reflect his own life in a film, when he had made *Ich war neunzehn* ten years earlier. But that film was more about the events of a few days just before the end of the war. Now, taking the story of *The Troika* as his medium, he wanted to present the fate of a whole generation.

Is it any coincidence that, on this 6th of January, in the morning, he visited Fritz Cremer, the sculptor, in his studio on Pariser Platz, and looked at the death masks of murdered communists, and listened to the stories behind them? After that he disappeared from the Academy of Arts, agitated.

The notes for *The Troika* from this day end with thoughts about the middle horse: "He broke off from the carriage, turned away from everybody (except for one person, who seemed, in recent days, to be like a savior—a woman . . .). And then—the death . . . in the hospital, and nothing should remain of all the illusions and dreams of youth: The ashes disappear into the anonymity of a collective grave. The Troika has ceased to exist—without the middle man, the leading horse, there is no point to it! Or is there . . . ?"

The Troika itself no longer existed. But its story remained a challenge for the film director, and also became increasingly challenging for the communist, the man, Konrad Wolf.

At the birthday party of the author and screenwriter Günther Rücker, whose life in 1933 in his German Sudetenland *Heimat* overlapped with the lives of the American Troika heroes, he asked Koni: "Will the adventure called 'Life' begin at fifty, or can it even come about after fifty?"

Koni celebrated his fiftieth birthday in 1975, the year of the get-together in New York. The fabulous party at the Berliner artists' club Die Möwe, attended by many friends and family, was all about the pelmeni. Under Koni's guidance, all the guests had to make these little meat dumplings, and only after meticulous inspection were they allowed to pass into the kitchen to be cooked.

Koni's adventure called Life lasted for another five years, from the first notes for *The Troika* in January 1977 until the hospital in Berlin-Buch in 1982. What years they were! They were filled to the brim with the creative work of a film director and the onerous responsibilities of the president of the Academy of Arts, on whose shoulders rested both trust and expectations. And they were thoughtful years, often filled with distressing introspection about his own life experiences and the difficult issues raised by current events. There were also problems with creativity, not to mention an enormous personal struggle, and both took him almost to the breaking point. Many of his friends had the impression Koni would not be able to cope with the catastrophic separation from his wife. Nobody, including Koni, knew of his illness. He immersed himself in his work and followed his path through to the end.

He had repeated meetings with his friend and screenwriter Angel Wagenstein. From 1977 on, *The Troika* became their shared artistic project and was a subject on which they continuously exchanged ideas. It is impossible to describe his connection with Angel Wagenstein, whom he, like all their friends, called "Jäcki." Their collaboration went back to the time of making *Sterne* and *Goya,* films which Koni felt were among his most important works. The men complemented each other; their arguments were productive. Jäcki wrote the screenplay for the only film in which Koni cast his second wife, the actress Christel Bodenstein—in the role of the Little Prince. But it was not only the work that united Koni and Jäcki; it was the bond of friendship between two communists who were committed, body and soul, to their common cause. They were two restless men, often difficult people who refused anything that resembled complacent narrow-mindedness or uncritical toleration of mistakes, weakness, and distortion. Their personalities were fundamentally different; but both were impatient and wouldn't defer to sacred cows. This solidarity was invaluable for their work on the *Troika* material. Koni and Jäcki fought hard over the design of *The Troika.* They had periods of doubt but then recovered their courage with new ideas. They had a rare affection for each other and related easily and very openly. Jäcki's wife, Zora, played a special role in this. She liked to call herself a "witch," but she was a very kind witch—both to her family and their many good friends all over the world. Zora was a marvelous cook and had a talent for creating a welcoming atmosphere [at their house in Sofia, Bulgaria], for all Jäcki's many guests. Koni was at home at the Wagensteins'. He felt comfortable there and enjoyed the beautiful countryside, the sun, the sea, and the mountains. He especially adored the locals' "Slavonic soul" and the culinary pleasures of their kitchens. He called Bulgaria his third *Heimat.* There, he opened up and was able to relax, which he was rarely able to do in Berlin.

Koni sent the first notes on *The Troika* to Jäcki in Sofia. By March, he had already gotten an initial response that was brimming with ideas and unanswered questions. The material, which covered a period of more than forty years, gave rise to many concepts about the film's potential structure. The consideration of alternative approaches led to the idea that the film should be modern, made by combining a variety of artistic methods, with an emphasis on a maximum self-discipline in film dramaturgy—and on employing the simplest methods of expression. Because it was the characters in the story that had to appeal to the audience the most, Angel Wagenstein saw difficulties in casting actors who might compromise their authenticity. To be successful the film had to be objective, completely truthful, and absolutely sincere. These thoughts seemed to accord with Koni's own. He had just finished work on another film that was also all about authenticity. Almost every day, and well into the summer, there were screenings of *Mama, ich lebe* [*Mama, I'm Alive*], which he made in collaboration with Wolfgang Kohlhaase and Werner Bergmann.[110] The film illustrated the difficult choices facing young Germans in a Soviet POW camp when taking their first steps toward consciously fighting fascism. In its own way, this film was a link between Koni's earlier successes, *Sterne* and *Ich war neunzehn.*

Koni participated in innumerable discussions about this new film. The debates often focused on one scene in particular: the one in which a young Soviet soldier was killed because his new German comrade hesitated to fire on his countrymen in their Hitler uniforms. Among young GDR soldiers the film provoked the burning question of whether Germans should shoot other Germans.

Koni often used those film discussions as the opportunity to talk about his own life experiences, his views on armed conflict, and the defense of power once it has been won. His views were just as unambiguous as those of his father, Friedrich Wolf, who came to his conclusions following his experience of the failure of the November 1918 revolution, which he used as the basis for his writing. Sometimes Koni deferred to his father.

110. Werner Bergmann (1921–1990) was a German cinematographer best known for his collaborations with director Konrad Wolf. Of the twenty-one feature films he worked on, fourteen were made in partnership with Wolf.

In May 1977 in Gommern, near Magdeburg, we were both invited to take part in the swearing-in ceremony for young soldiers of the GDR's Tank Regiment Number One, called "Friedrich Wolf." That evening in Colbitz, in the cellar of a pub called Heidekrug, there was an interesting discussion about young people and whether and to what degree they understood us. In a televised discussion, Koni had reflected on a quotation from Maksim Gorky about "the revolutionary romantic"[111] and had said that young people should be allowed to dream, and that their dreams were not necessarily the same as adult dreams. Young people, he thought, should be permitted to look for adventure, to be curious and questioning. They should be granted more autonomy and be free from continuous constraint or direction. These ideas were not received with universal approval. Koni had come to his conclusions following many discussions with young people after screenings of *Mama, ich lebe*. These conclusions reflected many issues that didn't match the commonly held views about our young people. At that time, when such truths and recommendations were spoken publicly, they were received very warily, with foreboding. The year 1977 was a tumultuous one.

At the beginning of the New Year, on the very Sunday when Koni had written the first *Troika* sketch, he and his wife, Christel, came to my place for lunch. On the menu was wild boar. Culinary get-togethers were very competitive occasions, and when it came to venison dishes, even Koni conceded that I was the authority. The lunch was followed by a long and very harmonious afternoon. But even on a day like this, problems couldn't stay hidden. The following day I wrote some notes on our discussion about what was happening in connection with Charter 77[112] in neighboring Czechoslovakia; about the activities of the Workers'

111. Konrad was probably alluding to Gorky's "revolutionary romanticism," a period in his development in which he used romantic motifs and allegorical narratives to inspire a revolutionary spirit. This phase later transitioned into socialist realism, an art movement defined by the party, which Gorky helped shape as one of its key important figures.

112. Charter 77 was a Czechoslovak civic initiative and human rights movement that emerged in 1977. It consisted of an informal group of individuals who spoke out against the communist regime's human rights abuses and demanded compliance with the rights guaranteed by the Helsinki Accords and the Czechoslovak constitution.

Defense Committee[113] and dissident intellectuals in Poland; and the constant problem of Andrei Sakharov[114] in the USSR: "In our country the situation has calmed down again. There are rumors about Manfred Krug and about the frenzied activities of Western journalists.[115] These are probably going to be the battleground on which the most spectacular skirmishes of 1977 will occur. One can only hope that everyone stays calm and that no one responds to these provocations tit for tat, because certain fundamental questions can only be tackled by long-term political measures." This was Koni's greatest anxiety that day as well, and on days to come.

The normalization of relations with the social-liberal government of the Federal Republic of Germany [FRG, or West Germany] had unsettled some GDR artists and writers. Loud voices of protest were also raised in other socialist countries. These were immediately picked up in the West, widely publicized in all the media, and labeled with the vague term "dissidents." In view of that, our side's response was not always nuanced and sufficiently patient.

The names "Robert Havemann" and "Wolf Biermann" became very emotionally charged words in the GDR.[116] The conflict escalated, providing all concerned with renewed reasons for controversy. Gradually, artists and writers in Koni's immediate circle were also affected by the clashes. Some were acquaintances of Havemann and Biermann's, but most of

113. The Workers' Defense Committee was the strongest and most influential democratic opposition organization in the People's Republic of Poland during the 1970s.

114. Andrei Sakharov (1921–1989) was a Soviet nuclear physicist who played a crucial role in the development of nuclear weapons after World War II. He was instrumental in the creation of the Soviet Union's first hydrogen bomb, tested in August 1953. Over time, Sakharov grew increasingly critical of the arms race and gradually transformed into a prominent dissident. He was awarded the Nobel Peace Prize in 1975.

115. Manfred Krug (1937–2016) was a German actor, singer, and author. In 1976, the East German government banned him from working as an actor and singer after he took part in protests against the expulsion and revocation of citizenship of singer and dissident Wolf Biermann. On April 20, 1977, Krug applied to leave the GDR, and upon receiving approval, he relocated to the Schöneberg neighborhood of West Berlin.

116. Robert Havemann (1910–1982) and Wolf Biermann (born 1936), two of the most prominent dissidents in the GDR, had been close friends since 1963–64. Both were humanist Marxists and outspoken critics of the repressive SED regime. As Wolf describes below, Biermann's citizenship was revoked by the GDR in 1976, barring him from returning. Havemann publicly condemned the decision and was placed under house arrest for more than two years. Shortly before Havemann died, in 1982, the regime allowed Biermann to visit his terminally ill friend.

them had nothing to do with those two opposition spokesmen; they had their own struggles with the reality of our social development.

For many people Koni was the man they could simply call on the phone, or meet up in person, with whom one could talk things over. His diaries of those days recorded these personal conversations and what impressions they left on him: Christa Wolf,[117] Sarah Kirsch,[118] Franz Fühmann,[119] Fritz Cremer,[120] and Frank Beyer[121] . . . Sometimes after these exchanges, he would phone me and tell me about the often valid questions raised in those discussions, and he would report of callous conduct. Koni struggled to get the authorities to understand the anxieties of the people who confided in him.

The situation came to a head when, having given a concert in West Germany in 1976, Wolf Biermann was denied reentry into the GDR.

Sometimes Biermann was compared with the fifteenth-century French poet and rebel François Villon.[122] This was a far-fetched and surely overrated comparison. If you wanted to give him credit, then you might have compared him to his contemporary, Vladimir Vysotskii, the Moscow Taganka Theatre actor.[123] Like Biermann, Vysotskii set his own poems to music. His songs are full of emotion; there are also bitingly critical ones. Many of the songs were officially circulated—Vysotskii gave public

117. Christa Wolf (1929–2011) was a leading East German novelist and essayist, renowned for her critiques of authoritarian regimes. Her best-known work, *Divided Heaven* (1963), grappled with the political and moral questions of the GDR and its eventual collapse. Wolf's work shaped literary and culture debates across East and West Germany.

118. Sarah Kirsch (1935–2013) was a German writer who gained particular recognition for her poetry, alongside her stories and children's books.

119. Franz Fühmann (1922–1984) was a significant German writer of the GDR working across multiple genres, including poetry, prose, essays, and children's literature.

120. Fritz Cremer (1906–1993) was a German sculptor, graphic artist, and illustrator, regarded as a key figure in the art and cultural policy of the GDR.

121. Frank Beyer (1932–2006) was a German film director who worked in the GDR and is regarded as one of its most important and internationally acclaimed filmmakers from East Germany.

122. François Villon (1431–ca. 1463) was the most renowned French poet of the Late Middle Ages. His life was marked by criminal activity and frequent run-ins with the law, experiences that he vividly wove into his poetry.

123. Vladimir Vysotskii (1938–1980) was a Soviet singer-songwriter, poet, and actor whose powerful voice and uncompromising artistry left a profound and lasting impact on Soviet culture.

performances—but some of the more severely disparaging verses criticizing Soviet social conditions of those years had to be copied via the samizdat process and distributed from hand to hand. Vysotskii was enormously popular and after his death in 1980 thousands of people attended his funeral.

Biermann had nothing like that kind of reputation and influence. When the decision to expatriate him led to a major uproar, most of the people in the GDR asked with some surprise: Who is this Biermann? The government had not anticipated that this could create such a persistent controversy. If it had, perhaps it would have made a different decision. Like most of the members of the management of the Writers' Association of the GDR who could not accept the expatriation, Koni also foresaw negative consequences. Together with other leading functionaries, he tried to help this anarchist from a communist/antifascist home who had moved to the GDR from Hamburg, but without success. The problem grew in magnitude when some writers and artists wrote a protest letter and sent it to Western media before informing anyone in the GDR government. When the news came out, most writers condemned this action just as emphatically as they had condemned the expatriation during the Association's previous meetings.

The day after the publication in the West of the artists' protest against the Biermann decision, the newspapers printed statements from many eminent people expressing solidarity with our country and their opposition to Western propaganda. But Koni's statement—although it had already been written—was missing. Some of the old party comrades felt the need to reproach him for his lack of party loyalty. Koni published his statement on the following day, and some of those who were still doubtful took his side. But to other compatriots, some of whom had been comrades in arms with our father, his statement didn't seem forceful enough. Koni's relentless search for reasons why a member of the artistic intelligentsia was driven out of the country, and his efforts on behalf of each individual, even the waverers, were frowned on as liberal conciliation. This accusation hit him hard, but his courage, about which his father had written in his letter to the front in 1944, came from his deep commitment to our cause.

It was only natural that Koni wanted each individual case to end with a positive outcome. Sometimes he was naive in trusting people and was later deceived or disappointed. But what he really wanted to understand time and again was cause and effect, in order [to encourage the government] to build a better, more principled, and in the long run more empathetic relationship with the artists and writers.

These matters were complicated, and in our assessment of individual cases Koni and I had different opinions, because, owing to our separate responsibilities, the basis of our knowledge was not the same. But that didn't mean that we differed in our basic convictions, and there was no contradiction in our attitude, no contradiction in the relationship between artistic intellect and political power.

Much more clearly than his Academy of Arts colleagues, Koni recognized the hopes and expectations revealed by the nerve centers of Western politics when they discussed actions in the socialist countries. We talked about it. After all, we shared common experiences of the past. In times of crisis, writers and artists have often become catalysts of social upheaval without knowing or wanting to.

We were all very troubled by the revelations at the Twentieth Communist Party Congress in the USSR about the atrocious symptoms and consequences of what was simply called "Stalin's cult of personality." Never again should we allow our ideas and aims to become so deeply corrupted.

The intelligentsia's 1956 uprising in Hungary was understandable in the light of Mátyás Rákosi's hard-line imitation of Stalin, the results of which were particularly dire.[124] The reaction to the launch of the correction of mistakes and reparation of crimes committed was horrific. A whole range of forces had begun to move with the calls for unlimited freedom and the abolition of all norms imposed by the socialist state. Protests began at the monuments of the revered idols of the past, Petőfi[125] and Kossuth.[126] Within a few weeks, events had spiraled into catastrophe and the country

124. Mátyás Rákosi (1892–1971) was a Hungarian communist politician who ruled Hungary as a Stalinist leader from 1947 to 1956.

125. Sándor Petőfi (1823–1849) was Hungary's most renowned poet and a prominent freedom fighter. He played a key role in the outbreak of the Hungarian Revolution against the Habsburg dynasty in March 1848.

126. Lajos Kossuth (1802–1894) was a Hungarian freedom fighter who led the country's struggle against the Habsburg monarchy in 1848–49. He has been regarded as a national hero ever since.

was in danger of degenerating into bloody anarchy. Europe stood at the brink of war.

During these tragic weeks, an acquaintance of our family's from our Moscow days, Hungarian playwright Julius Hay, played a prominent role. In 1941, during the first winter of the war, he and our family had been on the same train to the Kazakh capital, Almaty [then known as Alma-Ata], to which we were evacuated. We also lived in the same hotel in front of a picturesque backdrop of the snow-covered Ala Tau mountain range. When, a little later, our father was recalled to Moscow, our parents and Koni went back; I stayed and studied in Alma-Ata. The Hay family took care of me and put me up in their hotel room. We met up again after 1945 in Berlin, I think at the premiere of Hay's play *Haben* [*Have*], one of the first postwar productions of the Deutsches Theater.

In 1956, we came across Julius Hay's name again in the Western media's widely publicized reports on the events in Hungary. He had become one of the most prominent spokespeople for the rebellion, which culminated in the counterrevolution.

It is natural that writers should respond especially sensitively and critically to painful historical processes; that they should feel drawn to demands for greater individual freedom and for more democracy—and, sometimes, that they may become pawns in the games of demagogues. A writer is generally believed to be a sensitive person who seeks out conflicts and represents them realistically without glossing over anything. But this essential work ethic for each writer is always linked to the expectation that the criticism will stop at the level of a mayor or factory manager, and that it won't touch on current taboos. The combination of artistic and political matters in practice will always remain a difficult area. The basic requirement is a steadfast viewpoint, to keep from falling off the wagon during dangerous bends.

Julius Hay wasn't the only acquaintance to have changed sides. At School Number 110 in Moscow, Koni had been in the same class as Andrei Siniavskii.[127] Siniavskii was one of the first dissident writers in the Soviet

127. Andrei Siniavskii (1925–1997) was a Russian writer best known as one of the defendants in the landmark Siniavskii–Daniel trial of 1965. In this show trial, Siniavskii and fellow writer Yuli Daniel were convicted of "anti-Soviet agitation and propaganda" for publishing satirical works critical of Soviet life.

Union. His trial was spectacular; he became a hero in the West. He was forgotten soon after. Much later, Lev Kopelev gained the status of a permanent guest on FRG radio and TV.[128] During the war he had been a political officer and one of Koni's superiors. Koni described this in his war diaries. One of my companions in the Soviet Union, and in the early postwar years in Berlin, was Wolfgang Leonhard.[129] He had changed sides shortly after the war and with his book *Die Revolution entlässt ihre Kinder* [*Child of the Revolution*] made sure that his successful career as a Kremlin expert got off to a flying start.

In contrast to those few acquaintances who chose to go different ways from ours—and about whom much was written, and who also wrote about us—were the great number of friends from those years who continued to stand side by side with us. Among them were quite a few people who had experienced injustice in the Stalin era, who had been arrested or dismissed from the party, but who still stood by their convictions. They held as fast to them as to life. They spoke about their experiences in the gulags and places of banishment and how they kept true to our ideals, how they never missed a revolutionary holiday, and how, in order to preserve their belief in a better society, they sang our songs together with the former commanders of the Red Army and with relatives of murdered revolutionaries. When the time finally came, these people were among the most active comrades in arms and the most faithful friends of the Soviet Union. It is our failure that so little has yet been written about them. Why are those pages of people's biographies being written only now—and why with such timidity? Aren't they witnesses to the power of our ideology too?

Working on *The Troika* was an opportunity to think over all these things. What happened to the heroes who are no longer among us? Are life's circumstances to blame? Would our friends turn into enemies and

128. Lev Kopelev (1912–1997) was a Russian literary scholar and human rights activist. In 1945, he was arrested for criticizing the Red Army and spent ten years in Soviet camps and prisons. In 1980, he was expatriated as a dissident and lived in West Germany thereafter.

129. Wolfgang Leonhard (1921–2014) fled to the Soviet Union with his mother after the Nazis came to power. He returned to Berlin in 1945 and taught at the SED party college from 1947 to 1949. After breaking with Stalinism, he eventually moved to the United States, where he became a leading expert on Soviet politics and history.

traitors only because fate has led them astray? Don't we have to fight for every single one of them, and—in telling their story—do them justice?

And here, Jäcki Wagenstein and Koni's thoughts coincided: "In our film, it wouldn't be possible to portray an accurate political confrontation without allowing our opponent to think his thoughts freely and to speak his mind . . . and not as we would wish, so that the answer would be easier for us. We can't replace the truth with half-truths; we can't pretend, in our film, that we had overlooked the other side's strongest and most convincing arguments—especially those to which the correct answers are the basis of victory in our battle for the hearts and minds of the people. Battles are lost in every war. The most important thing is to win the final battle. Stalingrad wasn't located at the German-Soviet border, but deep in the heart of Russia, and that was the final frontier![130] We must be able to lose battles in our film as well, if we really believe in our strategic advantage in the endgame."

With this in mind, what Louis Fischer wrote in his autobiography about the childhoods of the Troika members should be considered. At the time Fischer's book was called a malicious anti-Soviet fabrication. Is this verdict still valid in the light of what we know today? Louis Fischer, an American liberal, was certainly wrong about many things; but with his immediate sense of disappointment, how could it have been possible for him to be an objective historian? Is objectivity possible at all? You cannot deny him the capacity for critical analysis when you read his account of the trials under Stalin. Who of us had that kind of critical capacity prior to the Twentieth Party Congress of the CPSU? But even so, it wasn't the disappointed critics who won at Stalingrad, but those indomitable people who never gave up their belief in the justice of our cause.

Koni kept returning to the idea of this *Troika* project, which time and again touched on current political difficulties. Whether in meetings or in conversations he had, it was never far from his thoughts. The *Troika*

130. The Battle of Stalingrad, fought between August 1942 and February 1943, was a brutal and decisive World War II conflict in and around the Soviet city of Stalingrad (now Volgograd). Nazi Germany and its allies clashed with Soviet forces in one of history's deadliest battles, with enormous casualties on both sides. The Soviet victory marked a major turning point in the war, shifting the balance in favor of the Allies.

idea was on his mind during his long walks with Franz Fühmann through the woods in Märkisch Buchholz, in Brandenburg.[131] Koni agreed with many of the ideas expressed by Fühmann in his books. But neither man changed his mind. There were disagreements and even angry letters from Fühmann, who wanted the academy to publish an anthology of young, frustrated poets who opposed the direction in which the GDR was heading. Koni was against the one-sidedness of such an anthology. He was interested, however, in why these poets had come to think as they did. Each maintained his own opinion, but their dialogue continued. No matter how bitter his experiences, Koni never deviated from his conviction that the problems and contradictions can only be solved by us, on the basis of socialism.

In countless conversations, Koni time and again tried to communicate his own experiences and beliefs; this was not always helped by his reticent manner. The fact that the president of the academy found the time to visit colleagues at their homes or in their studios and talk for hours on end came as a surprise to many people. Certainly some tasks did not get done, but Koni understood profoundly that it was those artists—especially the ones who worked in isolation—who needed a sounding board for their ideas.

After these talks, he often seemed particularly reflective. Sometimes he deserted his presidential desk at the academy and didn't answer the phone. On these occasions he was assailed by doubt and began to brood. However, these moods did not last long, because he believed that positive results could be achieved only through active participation in life and the courageous defense of one's ideals. Dodging and hiding away was out of the question, as was sidelining yourself or letting others sideline you.

Consequently, he was always trying to discover how an individual can be given the sense that they were needed, that their voice was being heard, and that they had a part to play in shaping the future. Essentially, he was trying to solve the same problem that would be expressed as a demand

131. Franz Fühmann (1922–1984) was a German writer who lived and worked in East Germany. His diverse body of work includes short stories, essays, screenplays, and children's literature. Initially influenced by Nazism in his youth, he later became a committed socialist—only to eventually grow disillusioned and publicly renounce it.

for greater transparency and more public involvement in government in years to come. We had always believed that saying you were listening to the people was not enough. The listening had to be active; politics had to become more public and more legible. From his discussions with individual colleagues, Koni knew that for many intellectuals, the incongruities arising from their not knowing how political, social, and economic decisions were made, both in inner government circles and beyond, was frequently the cause of discontent and uncertainty. There was a direct connection between this knowledge and his demand for people to feel they were needed. Koni's organization of meetings at the academy with leading members of the government was a step in the right direction.

We experienced and recognized, like many who felt responsible, the difficulties and contradictions inherent in the development of democracy in socialist countries. At the same time, we didn't overlook the proximity of our German capitalist neighbor and its media, who used every public utterance and every critical statement to their advantage in their ongoing battle against us. In those days, Lenin's words (popular again today)—that there is a need to openly admit mistakes, even if the enemy can use them to his advantage—were not heeded. But Lenin's warning always corresponded to our way of thinking.

And Koni knew only too well that, without proportion and discipline, socialist democracy could not progress. He had a strong instinct for what was possible, and he always believed in openly confronting one's own weaknesses and mistakes.

On a small scale, he demonstrated his position in his final film, *Solo Sunny*. It kept him busy for the whole of what turned out to be an unhappy year for him, 1978, and gave him strength throughout his great personal crisis—a strength that, in such situations, you can derive only from work.

The material for the film came from his friend Wolfgang Kohlhaase and was originally something of a diversionary project for him. It is the story of a minor pop singer's unfulfilled dream. It was not an epic; in its structure it was perhaps more like one of Maupassant's novellas, and it had none of the scope of the *Troika* story. For this reason Koni asked Wolfgang to codirect, so that when the practical work on the *Troika* project was due to start, he would be able to withdraw from *Solo Sunny*.

But new obstacles got in the way of the work for *The Troika,* and it became increasingly apparent that in the seemingly trivial story of Sunny, the true problems of the individual in our society were reflected. The theme of being needed, of the acceptability and unacceptability of a certain lifestyle in the real world, assumed a philosophical dimension.

These themes were also discussion topics at the plenary session of the Academy of Arts in Dresden in the spring of 1978.

During the opening of this conference—which was also attended by Koni's friend Hans Modrow, the party secretary in Dresden—Koni gave the impression of being tired and distracted. In a low voice he made his welcome address as though he found it a burden. Uncharacteristically, he didn't refer to the conference's purpose, about which he had thought long and hard. During breaks he made long phone calls to Berlin. Then he got in his car and drove to Berlin, returning shortly before midnight to take part in an especially interesting discussion with a small group of people. He was very upset.

I was on vacation at the time. For days Koni had been asking after me and was waiting impatiently for my return. Finally, a day before the Dresden conference, he had found me at my weekend house in the woods. It was a warm spring. Over a bottle of whiskey, my little brother opened up about his grief. His wife, Christel, had told him that she was leaving him. Koni was convinced that this time it was more serious than it had been on previous occasions. Shocked and helpless, he stood before an abyss that seemed to be opening up in front of him. In the previous weeks he had nearly ruined himself with alcohol and pills. He was now merely a shadow of his former self. He needed to talk about it. He clung to every shred of hope and kept expecting help that no one was able to give.

Troubled, he went to Dresden. During the evening session of the conference, the topic was the search for historical truth. It was all about the difficult path to knowledge, the artist's right to speak the truth, and the appropriate time to speak up. With that, Koni was back on the *Troika* project. He participated in the discussion, appearing especially soft, open, and thoughtful.

How could these thoughts be reconciled with the *Troika* project? Jäcki needed not worry that the director of *The Troika* would, as one of the heroes of the story and simply because he was the filmmaker and lived in the GDR, "stroll through his own film with his hands in his pockets, certain in advance that in the end he would be victorious." No, they wouldn't make it that easy for the third horse of the Troika. It would have led them too far from the life of one of the story's heroes and from his truth as well: "As if there were no crossroads in our lives that disrupt people's existence, no disastrous abnormalities or tragic passions . . . as if the model of our lives would be poorer than anyone else's."

When, shortly before the Dresden conference, Koni called Jäcki in Sofia about one particular character in the story, he said: "Maybe his marriage is breaking down . . . " Jäcki told him, almost annoyed, that he shouldn't come up with such banal suggestions. His friend had no idea what Koni was going through.

And, in truth, it was not just because of the breakdown of his marriage. This is how Angel Wagenstein described things: "The authors of the film are communists and naturally they are familiar with the general ideological strategy of our party. To translate this strategy into the language of art, however, cannot mean the burial of uncomfortable facts; the easy victory over lesser opponents that have been nurtured in dubious artistic-ideological incubators; or the timid avoidance of tricky problems. Because avoiding them doesn't mean they don't exist, and it merely invites people to get answers from elsewhere, from other sources. We don't mind admitting that there aren't always simple answers to every question! The shortcomings, errors, and slipups that are blown out of proportion by Western propaganda are not always only the fruits of their imagination. But if *we* aren't the ones providing explanations or analyzing the causes, then someone else is bound to do it, and usually in a way that is to our disadvantage. From a historical perspective, we are right. But that doesn't mean that we are right every minute of the day, that each of our bureaucrats is correct; that we are always moving in the right direction, or that we bond with any musty old comrade simply because he can regurgitate Marxist-Leninist slogans from memory . . . In short: It has to be an honest and courageous film!"

But for the time being the president of the academy and director of the forthcoming film *Solo Sunny* was almost derailed by his personal drama. For days he was in deep despair, unable to function. He couldn't be found.

He was in hiding. He told only me that he was seeking refuge on the outskirts of Berlin with the sculptor Wieland Förster.[132] Once, when that sensitive artist was himself in difficulties, Koni had supported him—and now Koni, in turn, was seeking peace and sanctuary through hard work with stone. Among all the arts, sculpture was the one that Koni found increasingly fascinating. The sheer physical labor on an object that can be touched and can be viewed from all angles was something that impressed him. Presumably, that is why he also had especially close relationships with Fritz Cremer, Ludwig Engelhardt, and Werner Stötzer, the latter of whom contributed material from his experiences to the film *Der nackte Mann auf dem Sportplatz* [*The Naked Man on the Sports Field*].

Koni tried to save his marriage with Christel. He could not and did not want to understand that Christel was not leaving him because she had found love with another man, but because he didn't give her the feeling of being needed, of being as necessary as the air we breathe. He took their living together and their much-loved son for granted; he didn't realize that his social position, his acclaim as a film director with all its attendant responsibilities, had increasingly become a burden for her. She didn't think he took her seriously enough as an artist, and he, the profound, sensitive one, who was there for so many other people, didn't notice the disaster happening on his own doorstep. Only later did they both recognize the depth of his feelings, but by then it was too late.

Koni had always had difficulty opening up to others. Even with his closest colleagues there was a certain distance. He could stimulate and engage them in his work and his way of thinking; his collaborations of this kind were widely acknowledged to be generally creative and productive. But he wasn't often able to convey to those closest to him that he recognized and valued their work. After the separation from his beloved wife, which he never got over, he had other relationships, because he couldn't bear to be alone. But he looked in vain for friends to whom he could reveal his deepest feelings. The Troika no longer existed. Jäcki and Zora, with whom he could talk about anything, were far away in Sofia. Only his brother and Ule Lammert, the old friend from Moscow days, remained.

132. Wieland Förster (born 1930) is a German sculptor, painter, and writer.

When work on *Solo Sunny* progressed and began providing Koni with some strength, he still didn't understand how much the central theme of the film—the desire to feel needed—related to the breakdown of his marriage. It was, however, certain that his emotional turmoil, his own personal drama, helped his work on this film about a young woman.

Sunny's story could have come from an interview conducted by Maxie Wander, a writer with whom Koni felt a strong bond.[133] During one of our talks about his personal distress, he and I also discussed our worries concerning the dangerous stagnation in the progress of our second *Heimat*. We talked about the people in the Soviet Union who had to do without so much of what is needed for a good life and yet who still managed to achieve such great things. We also discussed the lack of openness on the part of the government in the treatment of these wonderful people, and at that point Koni recommended a newly published book by Maxie Wander.

After reading the book, I wrote: "A little bit more courage to be open would certainly be a good thing for our cause. I agree with Maxie Wander, whose letters and diaries have, after her untimely death from cancer, been published only now by Fred Wander, and which have impressed me actually more than her book *Guten Morgen, du Schöne* [*Good Morning, Beautiful*]. She's very much in favor of openness, frankness . . . there is also bitter criticism—but she still roots for "the cause," our cause. There is a kinship between like-minded people that manifests itself in a certain sensitivity, a similar artistic taste, tolerance toward others, readiness to engage in critical self-analysis, rejection of outward display, and other things. It is wonderful that such contemporaries existed and still exist."

I was sure that Koni felt closer to Maxie Wander's attitude to life than I did. I can't remember if we spoke about my impressions of her words, as we always had so little time.

Preparations for filming *Solo Sunny* began, and in addition there were trips to Japan, Cuba, Italy, and France. There were repeated arguments with artists and writers who wanted to leave the GDR for the West;

133. Maxie Wander (1933–1977) was an Austrian writer and journalist in East Germany. Her influential book *Guten Morgen, du Schöne*, which Wolf discusses shortly, features interviews with women from East Germany, and offers a powerful and intimate portrait of their everyday experiences, struggles, and roles within society.

"individual cases" that grew increasingly numerous. Koni and others tried to convince them to stay—even if he thought the person in question was a bastard. If, in the case of an essential decision or the subsequent reversal of it, he thought it was important and justified, he turned to Erich Honecker, in whom he had a deep personal trust. He phoned him or wrote to him in his almost illegible handwriting. Most of the time, he got what he wanted; the trust was mutual.

Finally, he recovered his old energy. He fought for crucial decisions to be made in the field of cultural politics. In an unusually extensive handwritten letter to the general secretary—long letters were not Koni's style—he described his concerns about the growing numbers of people leaving the GDR. He gave examples of some of the problems the artists were facing. Everyone awaited decisions "from above," but there was an absence of any overall policy. As president of the academy, he proposed an idea for such a cultural/political policy, one that should be part of a strategy in the international debate concerning ideology and that should also function as a positive alternative for groups with dissenting ideas. It should also give the federations of artists the opportunity to become more involved. He warned of the danger of treating the intelligentsia with hostility, because one has to be able to work with skeptical intellectuals, and to clarify, openly, what is and is not possible. One should not treat these people as enemies. Following this letter, he had a conversation with Erich Honecker lasting almost two hours.

In the area of his responsibilities, Koni did everything he could to fulfill his principles in work and in life. He got his proposals on the academy's agenda and let the members scrutinize and formulate them with the future in mind. Alongside his work on solutions for the various problems of daily life, he worked intensively with his closest colleagues on the preparation of a plenary session of the academy in Rostock, the theme of which was Art and Society in the Year 2000. Koni gave the keynote speech. He began with an extensive quote about dreaming from Lenin's *What Is to Be Done?,* and explained that Lenin's words about dreaming and imagination were to be understood as the description of the clearest possible view into the future. He concluded with another long quotation from a letter written by the terminally ill Maxie Wander about the people who had given her hope, which contained the sentence: "To live would be a great alternative!"

In these difficult years in particular, which were also years of deep personal crisis, Koni did a great deal to establish the Academy of Arts of the GDR in the position it deserved within socialist society. The academy was not supposed to be an ivory tower; its members were to have close contact with both ordinary people and those leading the country in positions of power. The members of the academy should acknowledge their own responsibilities but should also feel they are needed by a socialist society.

Demanding and often agonizing thoughts about *The Troika* were ever present.

It was certainly no coincidence that Koni used the photograph of the Troika at the introduction of his paper when Erich Honecker met artists and other cultural professionals on June 22, 1979. This meeting was the result of the attempt to establish a closer relationship between the government and the artistic intelligentsia. It took place on the thirty-eighth anniversary of the Nazi invasion of the Soviet Union. And so the wheel turned full circle—from the key event of Koni's youth to the burning questions of the present day. A few weeks prior to this meeting, he had participated in the laying of a foundation stone in the town of Bernau, where he left a little box of homemade pelmeni in the walls. There, in Bernau, he had been the city's commanding officer for two and a half days at the age of nineteen. Now he spoke in his role as the president of the academy.

The mission of the arts in the antifascist battle, and the responsibilities of artists in the process of establishing socialism as well as in the struggle for peace, were Koni's big themes: contemporary themes, and all interrelated. They influenced all his projects and plans, and taxed his energy and stamina. The time that remained permitted no letup.

Past and present were alive in the *Troika* material, and they demanded an ever deeper scrutiny of one's own relationships and secrets, and of the fates of the other protagonists. The research into these circumstances—the search for the keys to the life and death of the Troika's middle horse—developed into an adventure. Together with Angel Wagenstein, a second visit to the US was planned and conducted as a research trip for the *Troika* project. And so it led to another meeting with George and Victor

Fischer. Koni and Angel captured the Fischers' recollections of the events of 1975 on a tape recorder. Everyone was friendly and cooperative. They took pictures of the locations of the events as a photo storyboard for the planned film.

It is exciting to listen to the recordings of ten years ago that Koni left behind and to listen to the Troika members, and Angel Wagenstein, trying to uncover the secret of the life and death of Lothar Wloch. They couldn't find it. But amid the dialogue, each of them reveals his own nature. Angel Wagenstein, the Bulgarian communist and partisan, in whose chest the heart of a Komsomol is still beating, quotes a verse from a civil war song and asks: Was Lothar's Komsomol-heartbroken? On the other hand, George speaks of a broken Moscow-heart. He believes that the ideals formed in Moscow, the pathos of that time, and Lothar's terrible experiences had all determined his future life. The friends try to interpret Lothar's remarks in New York about the dropping of an atom bomb on Vietnam, his clinging to West Berlin, and his petit bourgeois lifestyle. Jäcki finally suggests that Lothar was no longer whole; in the end, he got a new heart, and it broke him.

This discussion about Lothar developed into a serious conversation between Jäcki, George, and Koni about the destiny of the world, where it is going, and which powers will be able to determine its course.

These talks stirred up a lot of things in Koni. Long after his return from the US, they gave him sleepless nights, and he spent many thoughtful hours with screenwriter Angel Wagenstein. What is it that continued to connect the Troika friends—and friends they were—with the ideals of their youth? What is it that separated them from the country that they had all loved, that was so dear to them, and of which they had such fond memories—the country of their common childhood?

The search for an artistic mastery of this material that could also be faithful to the demands of history finally coincided with work on a documentary film cycle, *Busch singt* [Busch sings].[134] This work, too, on the life and songs of the workers' singer and friend, Ernst Busch, became a challenge; it was to provide insights into the history of this century.

134. *Busch singt* was a six-part docuseries that was broadcast on East German television.

The idea for this project was born out of a conversation with Erich Honecker during Ernst Busch's funeral service at the academy. The work on *Busch singt* excited Koni and almost completely preoccupied him during the last year of his life. Recordings of the songs provided the basis for often improvised film montages. In the process of researching parts of the film, Koni played the tapes at top volume to anyone who was interested. At the Tenth Party Congress of the SED in 1981, when Koni was elected to the Central Committee, he even concluded his speech by playing for the delegates an old, scratched vinyl recording of Busch's "Thälmann Lied" ["Thälmann Song"] from the time of the Spanish Civil War.

At the same time he had an idea for a film about Rosa Luxemburg, which would have been another epic project. Koni was fascinated by this revolutionary; perhaps because some of our contemporary political opponents tried to use Luxemburg's disagreements with the Russian Bolsheviks over questions of individual freedom and democracy to attack us. Perhaps it was also because some followers of the alternative political movements of our time took Rosa as their idol. And in this way, the material for his various film projects and his academy duties intertwined with Koni's thoughts about *The Troika*.

The *Troika* project remained the most important one for him. The opinions of the heroes of this unusual story had to inform their audience about their experiences; they were experiences that could prove to be very relevant to life today. Finally, after *Busch singt,* the *Troika* project was set to be tackled with vigor. A journey to Moscow, which was necessary to complete the fifth episode of *Busch singt,* was useful in this respect. Koni was persuaded to narrate this part of the film about the war himself. To do this, he had to stand before the camera in Moscow. Nobody could have known that this journey was a farewell for good.

He visited the places of his childhood and youth with a young photographer who was the spitting image of Christel. She kept a photographic record during his last two years and on this final trip to Moscow. Koni discussed making a photo storyboard for the *Troika* film. The trail wound from our house on Nizhnii Kislovskii Lane to the Arbat with the familiar underground station and the Khudozhestvenny cinema. They walked to the former School Number 110 near Ulitsa Gertsena, and finally to Kropotkin Street, to the building that used to be the Karl Liebknecht School. The Kievskii train station evoked many memories. From there they took a slow train to the much-beloved Peredelkino. What remained of this romantic piece of Russian soil, the writer's idyll from yesteryear? The beautiful landscape of birch and pine trees was now urban sprawl. Most of the houses were hidden behind ugly high fences. The Wolfs' former property had changed, and the dacha had been rebuilt. There was still a hint of nostalgia; Koni looked for some traces in the neighborhood and walked to the bridge by the swimming pond and to the little cemetery. Everywhere they went, Koni was very thoughtful and subdued.

In the evening they walked through Moscow, across Red Square . . . and so the photographer experienced the memories of a big boy pushing sixty.

There was no atmosphere of farewell or sadness. The photographer and the film team saw Koni relaxed and chatty; he acted like this only when he was in the Soviet Union. His fifty-sixth birthday in October 1981 in Moscow was celebrated at Maia Turovskaia's in pure Russian style. She was a former schoolmate from School Number 110 and was now a renowned film scholar.[135] They ate, drank, and sang as only Russians can.

Around this time he and I met up more often, too, and talked about *The Troika*.

And in October there was a very moving reunion with Eva Siao, a friend of our parents' from the Moscow days. Since the triumph of the Chinese Revolution, she and her husband had been living in Beijing with their three sons. With a certain regularity, she visited us in Berlin. She worked as a photographer and had published a few books in the GDR and also worked for the GDR TV station. Then came that cruel episode in the life of the Chinese people, the Cultural Revolution. After that, we did not hear from Eva. She and her husband were kept in solitary confinement for seven years. It had been eighteen years since she had last been in Berlin, and now she was sitting down with us—and she had, in many ways, remained the old Eva. It became a wonderful, very human, poignant reunion, during

135. Maia Turovskaia (1924–2019) was a prominent Russian film and theater critic, historian, and screenwriter, known for her insightful and independent analyses that drew parallels between totalitarian regimes.

which the Troika was very much alive. Eva knew the heroes of the story and had taken photographs of them in Peredelkino. She had learned from Erna Wloch a few details that we did not know about what had happened to Wilhelm Wloch. And now, suddenly the arc of history did not span only across divided Berlin, nor only from New York to Moscow; it included Beijing as well. A few very personal pictures of Koni, taken by Eva, are reminders of this reunion.

The current political situation remained tense and provided the subject for much discussion. The internal state of affairs in Poland became increasingly unsettled and offered fresh ammunition for the rabble-rousers in politics, as did the events in Afghanistan. With the stationing of American medium-range missiles, countermeasures from our side seemed inevitable.[136] During Brezhnev's visit to Bonn, opinions about these fundamental questions led to open hostility. The general secretary of the CPSU set out an unambiguous position. Seeing him on TV, however, many viewers wondered why the most powerful socialist state had to be represented by a man who, physically, was hardly able to meet his obligations. To this often-heard question none of us had a plausible answer.

At the same time, preparations were taking place for a meeting at Werbellinsee near Berlin between the West German chancellor, Helmut Schmidt, and Erich Honecker.[137] Everything was problematic and contradictory.

At first, support for Stephan Hermlin's initiative to hold a peace conference between German-speaking authors was not unanimous.[138] But Koni took up this idea immediately. He recognized that such a conference could mark the start of a new approach to contemporary political problems, a different method of interaction. The phrase "dialogue of reason," while in common usage later, had not yet been coined. Nor had the term "new

136. Wolf here is referring to the NATO Double-Track Decision of December 1979, which offered negotiations but threatened the deployment of medium-range nuclear weapons in Western Europe.

137. Helmut Schmidt (1918–2015) was a German politician and member of the Social Democratic Party (SPD). He served as chancellor of the Federal Republic of Germany from 1974 to 1982.

138. Stephan Hermlin (born Rudolf Leder, 1915–1997) was one of the most famous writers in the GDR.

thinking."[139] But such approaches were, for him, a consequence of *The Troika*, a consequence of the discussions in New York and Alaska, Moscow, Sofia, and Berlin. Koni backed the idea of these peace talks with the full weight of his authority. When he thought the time was right, he and Hermlin requested a meeting with Erich Honecker, who supported the idea wholeheartedly. The academy provided the organizational support for Hermlin's initiative, and so the Berliner Begegnung [Berlin Meeting], unusual and controversial as it was for its time, actually became a reality in December 1981.[140] It was Koni's last major public appearance. I am moved when I watch a video recording of his reply to a contribution from Günter Grass, which he concluded with a quote from a poem by Yevgeny Yevtushenko: "Do you think the Russians want war?"[141]

Watching it back, one can see the signs of Koni's illness.

On my birthday in January 1982, we briefly argued about the benefits of the Berlin Meeting. This was our last conversation outside the hospital.

When I returned from a foreign trip in February, I heard of Koni's terminal illness at the airport. At the hospital we tried not to mention it. We talked about the sixth episode of *Busch singt*, but most of the time about *The Troika*. During those weeks in hospital, Koni always had the black case at his side. He had dropped the idea of making a movie with the material. Instead he thought it should be a documentary film or a book. The uniqueness of the story of three families spanning half a century, between Moscow, Berlin, and New York, had to be treasured.

But then the line between fantasy and reality began to dissolve. Koni was living constantly with the heroes of *The Troika*. He met them and talked to them. He asked me to help him distinguish between the different

139. "Dialogue of reason" was a phrase used by Erich Honecker to support the SED's discussions with the West German SPD to address questions of peace and ideology against the background of worsening East-West relations in the late 1980s.

140. During Konrad Wolf's presidency of the Academy of Arts, the "Berlin Meeting on Peace Promotion" took place in 1981. Initiated by writer Stephan Hermlin, the event brought together one hundred artists and scientists from both East and West to discuss the arms race.

141. Günter Grass (1927–2015) was a German novelist, poet, playwright, illustrator, graphic artist, and sculptor, best known for receiving the Nobel Prize in Literature in 1999.

levels on which he now lived: the past; the present; and in dreams. He still felt the urge to master *The Troika*.

* * *

Koni took many nagging questions and painful thoughts to his grave. What remains is the black case with the idea, the photographs of the heroes, a few recordings of the voices of the witnesses of this story, and his own voice.

Documents to *The Troika*

Werner Eberlein

From: Diary of the First Brigade "Voroshilov" of the German Pioneer camp of the Karl Liebknecht School, Moscow

Summer 1934

A celebration of all Moscow district schools took place on June 10, 1934. Although some schools were already playing volleyball at one-thirty, and some, who were in need of some relaxation, rested in the sun in deck chairs, by ninety minutes after the official opening not all schools had put in an appearance. The opening concert took place at 5 p.m. in the Green Theater (an open-air theater) and afterward comrade Bulganin gave the welcome address. More speeches were given by other comrades from the honorary presidium. The honorary presidium should have consisted of leading political comrades such as Dimitrov, Stalin, Kalinin, Schmidt, and others. Unfortunately, among the well-known comrades, only Bulganin, Bubnov, Schmidt, and Voroshilov were present.

However, when comrade Bubnov came onto the stage, the welcome for him was as rapturous as it would have been for Stalin, Dimitrov, and Schmidt combined. The pioneers and pupils jumped on the benches and screamed and clapped until their hands were sore. The Schutzbund children found it bewildering that pupils would greet their teachers with such euphoric applause, let alone the people's commissar for education. It is common in Austria that pupils detested their teachers, but here, in the Soviet Union, there was a comradely relationship between teachers and pupils. The enormous, enthusiastic noise when comrade Bubnov came on stage dissolved into an iron discipline when he began speaking. The Schutzbund children were even more astonished when everyone participated in "Physiculture," which was directed from the stage. Afterward, the top 180 pupils from each of Moscow's 180 schools received awards for their achievements. And those awards were not inconsiderable. They were presented with cameras and radios. In addition, they received all kinds of books—political, scientific, and entertaining.

The winner for the German School in Moscow was comrade Max Albam. While other prizewinners received great applause from their fellow pupils, only seven people applauded comrade Albam when he was presented with a camera. This was because the rest of the pupils of the German School arrived too late and because they couldn't get into the Green Theater, which was packed to capacity. Those "Seven" had made their own way into the Culture Park and, thanks to their convincing Berliner smooth talk, had wormed their way into the Green Theater. The official ceremony ended with a demonstration by all schools parading across the stage. The Model Aircraft Society carried a homemade airplane engine, a Car Society drove across the stage in little toy cars. And so the Dramatic, Physiculture, and many other societies marched passed the honorary tribune. After singing "The Internationale" at the end, the Schutzbund children chanted to the Moscow pioneers, school directors, and teachers a triple "Red Front."[142]

After that the individual schools, classes, and societies dispersed, and while some visited the attractions of the park, others were interested in the different shows presented at many dramatic and artistic venues in the park. Many also stayed in the Green Theater to watch the cultural program. The Red Army was stationed on the main road with its display of tanks, armored vehicles, machine guns, rifles, and grenades. They answered questions from Moscow pioneers and pupils who were all

142. The greeting "*Rot Front!*" ("Red Front!"), accompanied by a clenched-fist salute, was used by both supporters and opponents to refer to the Roter Frontkämpferbund (Alliance of Red Front Fighters), a far-left paramilitary organization affiliated with the KPD during the Weimar Republic.

thirsty for knowledge. The Seven from the German School went to one of the theaters where there were performances by singers, entertainers, violinists, and other artists. The whole theater became tumultuous when a fife band marched through the park. The Seven jumped from their seats and hurried through the rows of seats, trampling over and pushing aside everything in their way. This was the German School who, eventually, at 8 p.m., had fought their way through to the Green Theater. Their disappointment was clearly written all over their faces. Things only began to improve when an entertainer presented a comic show. Shivering with cold, they listened to some singers. The celebrations were concluded with a fireworks display, which was enormous but without any artistic concept. It exploded, there was smoke, stink, and then it was over. On the way back they saw a similar fireworks display on the banks of the Moskva. A special tram was ordered to take them all back. As could be seen by the singing of humorous songs, the pioneers had finally raised their spirits. They sang until hoarse; songs such as the one from the Crumpled Chapeau, or the song from the Singing Family, the Bavarian March, the song from the Louse on the Wall, or the song of the Baked Pancake. With a triple "Be ready!" the pupils went their separate ways.

Elisabeth Gebauer
Oral report on the Wloch family

Berlin, February 1984

The Wloch couple were the center of political life in Bohnsdorf. All the young comrades and members of KJV [the KJVD, or the Young Communist League] were drawn to them. Among them were Rudi Greulich, Herbert Bachmann, Alfred Bohlke, Erich and Lotte Gensch, Walter Hoffmann and his wife, Alfred Jagielski, and the Gebauer family. After each rally, the comrades went to the Wlochs' house and debated. It was largely due to them that the young comrades became members of the party.

All we knew about Wilhelm Wloch was that he was a trade representative working for Soviet friends. Nothing else was said. Erna Wloch didn't work, but she was politically active and responsible for the work at Rote Hilfe.[143]

There was certainly discussion among the comrades in Bohnsdorf as to why the Wlochs had returned to Germany. Comrade Erich Gensch once said: "He [Wloch] must have done something fishy, otherwise they wouldn't have treated him the way they did." Herbert Bachmann replied: "I don't believe that for a minute. The Wlochs were the people who brought us to the party. You can ask Lis Gebauer as well, she's also on their side."

We always felt that Erna was one of us, and vice versa.

Rudolf Greulich
Memories of the Wloch family

Berlin, January 10, 1985

To my recollection, the Wlochs came to Bohnsdorf in the mid-1920s. I can't pinpoint the precise month or year. It was at a time when we, the politically conscientious youths in Bohnsdorf, were planning to join the party. Our group, which varied in number, had grown out of the petit bourgeois hiking club Die Heimatwanderer e.V. into the Jungproletarischer Bund [Alliance of Young Proletarians].

At this time of growing political awareness, the Wlochs suddenly appeared. There was Willi Wloch, his wife Erna, and they had a boy. That was Lothar. Soon after they settled in Bohnsdorf they adopted a little girl. This was Mausi; her real name was Margot. She was the Wlochs' darling and ours too. When we visited the Wlochs we also had to play with Mausi.

We discovered very quickly that when you had any problems, you could always go to the Wlochs, because there was always a frank discussion taking place. There was no need to be afraid of repercussions from saying something that might have sounded stupid or reactionary to the adults—namely Willi and Erna—such as, What kind of reactionaries are you? That

143. The Rote Hilfe, or Red Aid, was affiliated with the Communist Party of Germany and operated between 1924 and 1936. It was established to support communists who had been arrested or imprisoned.

never happened. We could speak about anything and had no fear of being misunderstood. And that put us at ease and made us very fond of them.

Well, obviously we pestered Erna more often than Willi, because he was often away on business trips. And so Erna was the only one available and had to talk things through with us. She liked doing this. There were constant comings and goings at the Wloch household. When Erna had put one visitor straight, the next one was already on the doorstep. It really was a wonderful and warm relationship. Of course with the really serious questions, Willi had the last word.

Willi was the rather quiet type, not the noisy agitator and propagandist. I think this was his great strength. Erna was similar, but much more impulsive than Willi. They were like two poles. Erna was quick to act and was easily excited. Willi was always quieter, more balanced. Maybe she also craved a little recognition while they worked here in Germany.

But she was reliable. She was perhaps a little less fussy in such things as propriety and order . . . In that respect she was more casual. She didn't care much whether a coat was hung up properly or just casually cast aside. That was Erna, too, somehow.

We were told that Willi was working at the Soviet trade representation. That was enough for us. It was normal that many Germans worked for businesses there. There was hardly anything questionable or dubious about it.

I can't quite recall whether it was shortly before January 1932 or shortly afterward that the Wlochs moved to the Pankow district of Berlin. We went to meet the Wlochs possibly at the Gebauer household, because they were in close contact. They told me: "You know, Rudi, we're almost certainly going to leave the country soon, but we've paid six months' rent in advance on our Pankow flat." That must have been a prerequisite for getting the flat there. So I moved into the Wlochs' flat with a friend and that was the right decision, because five years later everything became much more complicated.

In the meantime, it became 1936.

At that time I was together for some time with my bride or girlfriend Friedel, who still had work. Soon after we got married, we got a letter from the Wlochs from Copenhagen—probably via the Gebauers. I believe they initiated it. And that's how Friedel and I came to have our official honeymoon in Copenhagen. It was a good enough reason, anyway. And in those days it was still possible to travel. So, we went to Copenhagen and had a delightful reunion with Willi and Erna. Erna introduced us to all their new friends as old friends from Berlin. They asked me to report because they were eager to hear what Germany under Hitler was like. I can't quite remember how long we stayed—a week or longer. We had a marvelous time.

Then we packed a box of chocolates with a *Braunbuch*; that means we hid the book under the chocolates.[144] In case we were discovered, we agreed to say that lots of people accompanied us to the station. One gave us a bunch of flowers, someone else a box of chocolates. Who—we don't know. However, in this way we were able to smuggle a *Braunbuch* into Germany.

The Berlin Secret State Police's Request to the Foreign Ministry for Information on the Whereabouts of the Wloch Family

Berlin, December 17, 1936

Re: International communist functionary Wilhelm Wloch, born February 13, 1897, in Berlin. According to credible and confidential information, the aforementioned is working as a courier for the Comintern on an international scale. He carries a German passport number 47, issued on May 12, 1932, in Berlin. His spouse Erna, née Falkenberg, born in Berlin, December 18, 1896, who is also living abroad, carries the passport number 179/29, issued on August 8, 1929, in Berlin. It is possible that the spouses are currently in England or Denmark.

144. *Braunbuch* (*Brown Book*) refers to *The Brown Book of the Reichstag Fire and Hitler Terror*, published in 1933 by the World Committee for the Victims of German Fascism. It purported to show that the Nazis, not communists, were to blame for the Reichstag fire of February 27, 1933. A second Brown Book with the title *Dimitroff contra Göring* was published in 1934, detailing the confrontation between Bulgarian communist Georgi Dimitrov and Nazi leader Hermann Göring during the 1933 Reichstag Fire Trial.

Wloch is supposed to have traveled to Shanghai in 1934 on the steamboat *Porthos* and to have lived there with a nonpracticing dentist called Dubowski. Dubowski is also supposed to be working for the Comintern.

I request that inquiries be made via the German consulate in Shanghai and the consulates in the other European countries as to if and when the expired passport of W.'s wife has been renewed. I also ask that the abovementioned offices do not reissue W.'s passport, which will expire in May 1937, without my permission. The reason for this is to gain knowledge of their whereabouts.

On behalf: signed Müller

Reply from the German General Consulate Shanghai to the Foreign Ministry about the Whereabouts of Wilhelm Wloch

Shanghai, June 26, 1937

The communist functionary Wilhelm Wloch has lived in Shanghai from October 12, 1934, until the end of 1935. In December 1934, he opened a dental clinic at the French Concession, 542 Avenue Joffre, and appointed as director an otherwise unknown Dr. W. Dubowsky. To this end he spent more than $8,000—origin of which is unknown. At the end of 1935 Wloch retired from the business and traveled, presumably to Hangzhou (Zhejiang Province), and has since vanished. The local police have not yet been able to establish his whereabouts. Since it is questionable whether Wloch is still in China, I have, for the time being, refrained from the disclosure of the Secret State Service's letter to other police stations in China. It might be advisable to inform the German consulates in all European countries of the non-reissuing of the abovementioned passport.

Wilhelm Wloch
Questionnaire

Moscow, February 19, 1937

1. Wloch, Wilhelm (Wilhelm Paul)
2. February 13, 1897, in Berlin
3. Working-class background

4. Parents:

Father:	Mother:
Wloch, Wilhelm	Wloch, Martha
Engraver, metalworker	Housewife
No assets	No assets
Factory worker	Cleaning lady, Berlin
Died 1929	Fritz-Schulze-Str. 4

5. Construction worker
6. German
7. German Citizenship
8. Married, 2 children:
   Lothar, 13 years
   Margot, 9 years
   Wloch, Erna, nee Falkenberg
   EKKI[145]
9. Spouse's parents

Father:	Mother:
Falkenberg, August	Falkenberg, Anna
Construction worker	Seamstress
Died 1930	Died 1916

10. (...)
11. 8 years Elementary School, 3 years Vocational School
12. English not very well, Danish well
13. Business trips to different countries and within Germany
14. Stays in foreign countries for illegal work
15. Mother and sister are living in Germany, but no contact
16. Drafted into the German Imperial Army during the Great War in the years 1916, 1917, 1918
17. Have not served in the army or in any offices of the Whites
18. No relatives or acquaintances in foreign missions
19. No service in the Red Army

145. Abbreviation for the Exekutivkomitee der Kommunistischen Internationale (Executive Committee of the Communist International, 1919–1943), the leading governing body of the Comintern between its world congresses.

20. Not registered for military service
21. Member of the Communist Party Germany since 1920
22. From 1911 to 1915, Member of the Social Democratic Workers Youth; from 1915, SPD; 1916–1920 USPD
23. Was arrested a few times after the revolution for different reasons. Have not been in prison; prosecuted for buying a weapon
24. Was not in any inner political faction or grouping
25. Party penalizations: reprimand in the KPD in 1930 or 1931 in connection with a strike of construction workers
26. Active participation in the revolution in February and October of 1917 and in the civil war. In Germany in January 1919, 1920, 1921, 1923 on the order of the KPD
27. Union member from 1912–1933 in Germany; currently not a union member for work reasons
28. Moscow, Hotel Lux, 36 Gorky Street, room 210

29.–31. Occupation:

Franz Federmann Company—engraver workshop, apprentice from 1911–1914

S. Bergmann Co. from 1914 until beginning of 1916 until conscription into the Wehrmacht

Betonbau AG in Berlin 1925, dismissed because of participation in the strike committee

32. I'm known by comrade Abramov, comrade Stassova
33. Occupation after the October revolution:
    1. Schwarzkopf Company Berlin, Metalworker, 1917, three weeks
    2. Military service, soldier, 1917–1918, released
    3. Haberland AG, concrete works, construction worker, 1918–1925, dismissed because of participation on a strike, at my own request, staff reductions etc.
    4. From 1925 until 1937 work at OMS; Collaboration with EKKI—always illegal work[146]

146. OMS is the Russian abbreviation for the Department for the Otdel Mezhdunarodnoy Svyazi (International Relations of the Comintern).

Wilhelm Wloch
CV for the application of citizenship in the USSR

Moscow, May 15, 1937

As the son of the metalworker Wilhelm Wloch and his wife Martha, née Peste, I was born on February 13, 1897, in Berlin. Father and mother are working-class. Father and mother participated from about 1900 until the war, in the working-class movement: Free Union and Social Democracy. During the war they joined the left wing (USPD) and in 1920 the KPD.

I went to elementary school from 1903 to 1911 in Berlin, and from 1911 until the beginning of the war in 1914 I served an apprenticeship as an engraver. After that, worked as a metalworker. Drafted into the army in 1916 and, after training, sent to the French front. At the end of 1916 ordered to retract from the front and start work at Rumpler Company. After the strikes in February 1917 I was dismissed and shortly afterward started work at the Spandauer Werke and was drafted again. After garrison time sent to the Landwehr-Inf-Reg. 48 at the Russian front. On the transport back, member of the Soldiers' Council. Participation in the demonstrations in January 1919 in Berlin. Work as construction worker since February 1919.

Union member from 1912 until 1933. In 1911, after leaving school, I joined the Socialist Workers Youth, from 1915 member of the SPD, from autumn 1916 member of the USPD, and from 1920 on, member of the KPD.

My father died in 1929. My mother has worked since 1929 as a cleaner; since 1930, as a cleaner for the DEROP AG or similar institutes. I can't make any statement about what she's doing at present as I have no contact. Address in Berlin is: 4 Fritz-Schulze-Strasse.

Furthermore, I also have a sister who is married to a postman. The last address known to me was: 114 Grosse Frankfurter Strasse, Marta and Otto Herbst. I have no contact with them.

Erna Wloch
Application for citizenship in the USSR

Moscow, May 15, 1937

To the Headquarters of the Central Executive Committee

(Via the section for Workers and Peasants Police)

I would like to apply for citizenship of the Soviet Union and make the following statements:

1. Wloch, née Falkenberg
2. Erna Augustovna
3. Berlin, December 18, 1896
4. Married
5. German citizenship
6. Moscow, 36 Gorky Street, 50th police district
7. Work situation: office worker
8. Member of the KPD since 1922
9. Elementary school
10. Shop assistant
11. Member of the Comintern, Mochovaja 16
12. Member of the Comintern
13. No previous convictions
14. Never have been a citizen of the USSR
15. Entry into the USSR on December 23, 1936; entry visa was obtained at the Consulate of the USSR in Copenhagen on December 19, 1936.
16. Visited the Soviet Union before from September 1934 to March 1936—business trip.
17. Reason for application for citizenship in the USSR: Since I was actively working in the Communist Party I was forced to leave Germany. I would like to stay in the Soviet Union and want to work as a citizen with equal rights.

18. Relatives in the USSR and abroad:
    1. Wloch, Lothar, son, German citizenship, 1923, pupil, Moscow, 36 Gorky Street
    2. Wloch, Margot, daughter, German, 1928, pupil, Moscow, 36 Gorky Street
    3. Lehmann, Wally, sister, German, 1889, housewife, Berlin-Heiligensee
    4. Falkenberg, Walter, brother, German, 1891, construction worker, Berlin
    5. Wloch, Martha, mother-in-law, German, 1873, works at DEPRO AG, Berlin, Fritz-Schulze-Strasse
19. Citizens of the Soviet Union who know me:
    Müller, Boris Nikolaevich, Comintern
    Stasova, Elena Dmitrievna, ZK MOPR[147]
    Schawer, Maria Abramovna, Moscow, Bolshoi Gnesdnikovskii 10
20. I hold a residence permit from OVIR GURKM of NKVD[148] of the USSR in Moscow on 29th December 1936—Number A 090164
21. Address: Moscow, 36 Gorky Street, 4

Erna Wloch
CV for the application for citizenship of the USSR

Moscow, May 15, 1937

I was born on December 18, 1896, in Berlin as the daughter of August Falkenberg, molder, and his wife Anna, née Priess. Father and mother are working-class.

147. The International Organization for Aid to the Fighters of the Revolution (Mezhdunarodnaia Organizatsiia Pomoshchi Revoliutsioneram, MOPR), commonly known as International Red Aid, was founded by the Communist International (Comintern) in 1922. Its mission was to support political prisoners and revolutionaries worldwide.

148. OVIR (Otdel Viz I Registratsii, or Office of Visas and Registration). It was the subdivision of the NKVD responsible for passports and visas, exercising extensive control over the movement of Soviet citizens and imposing strict restrictions on travel abroad. GURKM (Glavnoe Upravlenie Raboche-Krestianskoi Militsii, or Directorate of the Workers' and Peasants' Militia) was the NKVD division that functioned as the Soviet Union's regular public police force. Its responsibilities included maintaining social order, combating crime, and overseeing the internal passport system.

Both were members of the SPD, but I don't know when they had joined. I only know that my father, born in Pomerania, was expelled from Prussia because of the anti-Socialist law and emigrated with his family to Ückermünde in Pomerania and returned in about 1901 to Berlin. Then he worked on building sites, because he couldn't find work as a molder. At the same time he joined the German Construction Workers' Union where he was, without any interruptions, very active. He did not actively serve in the war but worked during this time as molder at the *Heereswerkstätten* [army workshops] in Berlin-Spandau. After the war he became an employee at the *Baugewerkbund* [building trade association] and later worked as a recruiting officer at the *Städtische Arbeitsnachweis* [municipal employment office] in Gormann Street. From 1917 until 1921 he was a member of the USP [USPD]. He rejoined the SPD from 1921 until he died in January 1930. My mother worked first as a domestic servant and later, without interruptions, from 1894 until her death in May 1915, as a homeworker (seamstress). She was a member of the SPD and the Union. The name of this union is not known to me (something similar like "Federation of Tailors and Neckwear Producers"). At that time there was no union for homeworkers. My mother died in 1915.

We were four children. My oldest brother was a ladies' hairdresser and died in 1930 in Switzerland. He had moved there in 1917 because of lung tuberculosis. Until 1917 he was a member of the "Hairdressers and Wigs Guild."

My sister worked for fifteen years as a shop assistant for the Konsum Cooperative Berlin and District. She no longer works, is married to the chauffeur Paul Lehmann, and lives in Berlin-Heiligensee, Street 165, plot 216.

My younger brother is a stonemason and used to be a member of the KPD—he lives in Berlin, his address is not known to me.

I have no contact with either of my siblings.

From 1903 to 1911 I went to elementary school no. 56 in Berlin. Because I had excellent grades in German and math, my headmaster arranged a job in an office for me. I began working there the day after I finished school. Since this kind of work did not suit me, I soon looked for an apprenticeship in the food industry and started work as a shop assistant on October 1, 1912, at Konsum Cooperative Berlin and District.

I was employed there until April 1, 1918, until I resigned of my own accord. After that I worked as a clerk at the raw material stockroom for Bergmann-Electricity-AG Seestrasse. From 1921 until 1928 I worked at short intervals as a temporary worker back at the Konsum Cooperative.

I was a union member of the Association for Trade Workers from 1912 until 1918, and a member of the KPD from 1923 on.

Günther Rücker
Yura and Vic

May 30, 1988

On a summer's day in 1933 my parents told me that two boys from Berlin had come over the border, and I would get to meet them at a hut in the Jizera Mountains. They were called Yura and Vic, and I wasn't supposed to ask much about where they were from and where they were going to. We met them and from the first moment I was enchanted by the two boys. Everything I admired in a human being was gathered in them. They had black hair, spoke the Berlin dialect, had no respect for anybody, and everything associated with them was surrounded with secrecy. Even their family name was never called out. The rumor went round that it was Fischer. Some questions they never answered. They had this kind of wit that I admired and did not myself possess; their approval was like praise and their silence, the hardest criticism. They were like the yardstick of my life. I felt more than I knew that with those two the dangerous world came closer, and so did the images of nearby Germany or the images of the faraway world of the Soviet Five-Year Plans. I knew these images from John Heartfield's photomontages. Yura and Vic didn't attend a public school. They were home-educated by a governess in their villa on the edge of a forest that went steeply uphill and led into the Jizera Mountains. Once, my father took me to this villa, and I saw the two bent over their books and exercise books that I wasn't able to read. Then we left. I took away a feeling with me that I had experienced something that I would never understand

and that would stay with me for the rest of my life. I couldn't suppress a feeling of inferiority and envy.

One day they were gone. I was told not to ask for them and not to tell anyone what I knew of them. Some said they were in Moscow, others in America. The loss hurt me. The only thing I could do for them was not to speak of them. I imagined them on the streets in Moscow as I knew it from Panteleev's books. And in New York I imagined them in the area of Madison Square Garden, where the big boxing matches took place. And I imagined that I would see them again one day—the day I had always fantasized as the day of victory, a good and happy, holy and righteous day on which humanity's pain had ceased. And we would be sitting next to each other and Yura and Vic would tell all of their secrets because it would be a time in which man wouldn't have the need for secrets any longer.

Then came Spain, Austria, and then the German Wehrmacht, first to Reichenberg, then to Prague, and then came the invasions of other European countries. Then the guilty people crawled out of their ratholes and capitulated, and then the emigrants returned to their homelands and the day of victory proceeded to be different from the one of my childhood dreams. I asked everyone who I thought could have met Yura and Vic during the emigration, asked everyone I knew from the Jizera Mountains—but no one was able to tell me anything about Yura and Vic's fate.

In 1979, I flew with Koni to Belgrade in order to sign a contract for our academy. Koni was in a cheerful mood and on the return flight he talked a lot, and when the subject came to films, he spoke about his life project, *The Troika*. He told me about the years in Moscow, the school the children of the emigrants attended, photographs, memories. And I thought I should ask Koni about Yura and Vic. But he was talking so excitedly about the past, got so carried away that I forgot my question. Two years later Koni died. Kohlhaase told me that on the occasion of Koni's sixtieth birthday two friends from the United States would be visiting: Yura and Vic. I felt as if all the days that made up my memory would knock against my heart. The long-awaited day was finally there, victory's distant cheers. It was like the passage in a fairy tale where it says: . . . and when half a century had passed, they were reunited and embraced each other. In front of the cemetery gate I met them. I told them everything and they listened and looked at me thoughtfully for a long time. Yes, they said, everything happened as I described it, but the fact that they should have met this boy, who now stood in front of them as an old man, Yura and Vic didn't remember.

Friedrich Wolf
Letter to Else Wolf

Stuttgart, April 13, 1930

Meni Dearest!

Quick, a little kiss, very quickly! It is wonderful how you manage everything! If I could only see it so clearly too when I'm home . . . all those times when you annoy me! Why do you have to do this? Or better: Why do I feel annoyed??? Meni Dearest, we really should not make this short life, three-quarters of which I'm devoting to books, unnecessarily difficult!

So that your eardrum can properly turn inside out again, your ear must be blown from the mouth through the Eustachian tube. Do you want me to do it? What a nuisance! I still don't understand it.

And Bäutzlein is a good boy and goes swimming? The way you put it in writing: Marvelous!—Here, since last night, it's raining cats and dogs. I'm slowly getting back into work; my brain cells apparently have to readjust, and that's not easy. But the exposition is finished and later I'll start the first scene . . . it has to be done with great care, because the blow at the end has to hit the bull's-eye . . . The first word, the first page—that is tremendously important; can you actually know what I mean?—But now to the more important things: I need urgently Fischer's *Oil Imperialism* (it must be at the bottom of my bookshelf, next to the red Lenin edition; I also need Alfons Goldschmidt's *Mexiko*); and lastly, please look up "Huerta" and "Mexico" in the encyclopedia and copy down for me what you find!!

The letter is posted to Meersburg despite the rain.

100,000 kisses for the dear Meni and the boys

Pitz

Please send me also a copy of *Matrosen*,[149] which I forgot. It's on the top shelf.

Louis Fischer
From: Men and Politics *(autobiography, 1940)*

I was born in the Philadelphia slums to poor parents. My father worked as a laborer in a factory and then graduated to selling fish and fruit from a pushcart. I can still hear his cry, "Peaches, fresh peaches." Sometimes I hauled the empty pushcart to the stable. My mother took in washing. The family moved whenever it could not pay rent—which was often. Until I reached the age of sixteen, I never lived in a house with electricity, running water, or an inside lavatory, or any heat except from a coal stove in the kitchen-living room. We frequently starved, and for many years the only good meal my sister and I ate each week was the one given us by a rich aunt on Friday evenings. A long, intimate acquaintance with poverty killed my dread of it. In later years, I could always reduce my needs to my means, and I never craved security. But life as I had seen it could certainly stand improvement. Especially did I feel that society has an obligation to help us overcome the accident of birth. It does so often, but not often enough.

[. . .]

With the exception of teaching school in Philadelphia for half a year in 1917 and work in a New York news agency in 1920, I have never held a job and I have always tried hard not to get one. Once when I weakened for a brief moment and thought of applying to the *New York World*, Markoosha warned me off. She always supported herself and the children while I free-lanced, and it was not till 1929 when by doing just what I wanted I earned more than I needed for myself that I accepted partial financial responsibility for the family. Markoosha made some money by translations. I never

149. Friedrich Wolf is referring to his play *Die Matrosen von Cattaro* [*The Sailors of Cattaro*].

owned any property—beyond a typewriter and now a steel filing cabinet—or any stocks or bonds. I have never held any insurance of any kind. I have never been a member of any political party or of a trade union or, after my youth, of any club. I am essentially a libertarian and resent shackles, even personal ones. I can impose discipline upon myself, but I would fight its imposition on me by others. This applies especially to intellectual discipline. For me the question of joining the Communist party never arose because I would not allow another person to tell me what to write or what to think.

I nevertheless sympathized strongly with the Soviet regime out of a conviction that, despite all the repression, it had brought a new freedom to workingmen, peasants, women, youth, and national minorities, and that, in time, the dictatorship would yield to a democracy that would be real and better. That was my big mistake. [. . .]

Markoosha Fischer
From: My Lives in Russia *(Autobiography)*

I went to Berlin to work for my old boss of the Railroad Mission in New York, Professor George Lomonossov, one of Russia's great railroad experts. He was supervising the building of German and Swedish locomotives for the Soviet government. [. . .]

In April 1922, one of the most exciting events of my life took place. Professor Lomonossov, upon Maxim Litvinov's request, lent me to the Soviet delegation going to the Genoa conference . . . Being the only one on the staff who knew several foreign languages, I was present at most sessions and secret conversations, and saw highly confidential documents. But I never really understood the meaning of the talks. [. . .]

I knew that Soviet Russia was fighting in Genoa for her very existence. She had against her extremely polite, well-mannered enemies, who, having failed to cut her throat with a knife, now tried to choke her to death in an iron economic grip.

To me the Soviet delegates stood on a high pedestal. I saw in them the embodiment of all the hopes of an unhappy post-war world. When the Soviet delegates walked in the streets of Genoa, the eyes of the Italian workers reflected these hopes. So did the modest gifts which Italians and others in Italy sent to the delegation: field flowers, baskets of fruit, homemade cake, etc.

In the beginning the presence of men like Chicherin, Litvinov, Krassin, Rakovsky filled me with breathless awe, and every member of the Soviet delegation, including the youngest messenger boy, seemed to be slightly more than mortal. I was relieved to discover that they possessed the qualities and weaknesses of all normal people. Dreaded conspirators loved to show family snapshots. They flirted and they fussed over a boiled egg. They sang sentimental songs and competed in buying presents for their wives. We had parties where Foreign Commissar Chicherin composed on the piano, where Litvinov entertained us with clever jokes or a fist fight with a fellow delegate, and where Krassin directed a chorus. All displayed great skill in folk dancing. [. . .]

I caught my first glimpse of Soviet Russia late one night in September 1922. I entered Russia in a splendor too rich for my taste. [. . .]

Some stories told by Soviet Russia's enemies were correct. They saw destruction. I saw it too. They saw dirt, ugliness, and brutality. I saw it too. But I also saw a magnificent edifice emerging from the battle. The most exquisite cathedral is born in ugliness: Human sweat, piles of rubbish and junk cover the site of future beauty. Man, the king of creation, comes into the world in all the ugliness and pain of birth. I did not expect the birth of new society emerging against the resistance of all the powerful of this world to be something like Venus coming out of the foamy waves, all pink, lovely, and peaceful.

[. . .] I wanted to be part of it.

Else Wolf
Letter to Friedrich Wolf

Moscow, March 9, 1935

My Darling Man,

Right now your ship is leaving. I felt tremendously relieved when the telegram arrived with the confirmation of your visa. [. . .]

In the evening I went to the get-together (*vetcher*), of which you know.[150] It was a very small circle of people who were treated to magnificent hospitality. Budzislawski was mainly interested in communicating to everyone the material he needed for his journal. He was quite clear and unambiguous. Then followed an interminable discussion that continued long after I and Reich left the party at half past two in the morning. By then the discussion had turned into boundless chatter that was not exactly productive. Budzislawski said aloud what so many here think, especially those who have just arrived; that there is an atmosphere of security here and that many consequently lose the feeling for the state of things in the West. They lose the ability to fully understand the difficult situation and when they write about life here so indiscriminately, it all too easily turns into a boast; a boast that would have no influence at all for this journal and its target readership, because nobody believes these hymns of praise. As examples of articles that have been hugely influential, Budzislawski cited those written by Louis Fischer. He found these articles indispensable, because every now and then they also include a question mark. It's not just about results but also about the way of achieving those results, and that wouldn't always be an easy task. (Maybe it wasn't entirely clever to mention LF of all people, because now the mob descended on this bourgeois journalist.) He further said that with such fragmented developments there are bound to be a few sprained ankles and that one would have to mention them as well because without pointing this out the reports become implausible. And people in the West are by nature skeptical. He especially emphasized the needs of his journal and that reports about life in Russia—if they are just boasts—are better left for a different kind of press. More than anything he demanded up-to-date coverage; as an example he mentioned how he had a real problem getting a report when the new election law was published, and that he even sent a telegram but received no answer, and how this was commented on with glee over there and brought out the usual malice. He was simply lacking relevant articles that illustrated the nature of such elections for instance, using as a concrete example: the preparations for an

150. *Vetcher* is a transliteration of the Russian word for "evening."

election in a factory—that is what he needed. Someone said that in this case the best thing would be to provide a passage from Molotov's speech. But he warded off that kind of contribution because no one would be convinced by speeches. [. . .]

Budzislawski's simple request was obviously difficult to understand. He didn't ask for concessions in the way that you try to turn an already convinced communist into a sympathizer, as the United Front Movement[151] is often wrongly understood to do. He demands the truth in its natural development, which could sometimes be contradictory and certainly not without difficulties (think "dialectical"). In the end, he's aiming for more committed and suitable collaborators and aiming not to have to put aside all the many manuscripts he receives because they're useless to him. His journal, *Die Weltbühne,* has changed. No longer is it just a forum where all sorts of people can express thoughts they couldn't publish anywhere else. Today the journal has a political face. The tiniest thing he demands from the communists when writing their articles is that they think about the form, the tactic, in which they write. Well, there is not much point in describing the rest of the evening and what everyone said in any more detail. I just wanted to let you know what contributions Budzislawski asks for because you are planning over there to work for him as well. [. . .]

I wonder how you feel when you get this letter. Don't forget about us while you are in the big new world. I'm thinking of you often. I'll always love you, but I don't have to tell you that, as my always standing by you and often in difficult times must have shown you. And I hope I will continue to remain this sort of comrade to you. [. . .]

For today many good kisses

Meni

151. The United Front Movement, introduced by the Communist International (Comintern) in 1921, was a strategy aimed at fostering cooperation between communist parties and other working-class groups—primarily socialists and social democrats—to advance workers' interests and counter the influence of big business and fascism.

Hermann Budzislawski
Letter to Louis Fischer

May 2, 1935

Dear Mr. Fischer, Thank you very much for the three articles, of which one has already been published. Many thanks also for the letter that your wife wrote at my request. I have forwarded the information accordingly.

You wish to receive an extended report about the banquet that the German writers organized for me in Moscow. The evening took place about two months ago and it's not so easy for me now to summarize. But I'll do my best.

The evening took place in the rooms of the International Union of Revolutionary Writers.[152] The following were present, among others: Ottwalt,[153] Lukács,[154] Gábor,[155] Béla Balázs,[156] Hans Günther,[157] Leschnitzer,[158] Frau Friedrich Wolf, and Reichenbach.[159] As far as I remember,

152. The International Union of Revolutionary Writers was an umbrella organization founded in 1927 and dissolved in 1935. The Union of Soviet Writers, established in 1934, was one of its branches.

153. Ernst Ottwalt (1901–1943) was a German writer and playwright. A committed communist, he fled Nazi Germany in 1934 and sought refuge in the Soviet Union, where he later became a victim of the Great Purge and died in a gulag.

154. György Lukács (1885–1971) was a Hungarian Marxist philosopher, literary critic, and key figure in Western Marxism. He introduced the concept of reification and expanded on Marx's theory of class consciousness. A proponent of Leninism, he helped shape its revolutionary philosophy and vanguard-party theory.

155. Andor Gábor (Greiner) (1884–1953) was a Hungarian novelist, poet, humorist, publicist, and lyricist.

156. Béla Balázs (1884–1949) was a Hungarian writer, Symbolist poet, and a pioneering figure in film theory.

157. Hans Günther (1899–1938) was a German writer in exile, a Marxist economist, and literary critic. During Stalin's purges, he was arrested and sentenced to five years in the Gulag, where he died in 1938.

158. Franz Leschnitzer (1905–1967) was a German journalist, author, and peace activist. Due to his Jewish background and communist beliefs, he fled Germany in 1933. While in Moscow, he was stripped of his German citizenship in 1939. From 1933 to 1959, he lived in the Soviet Union, working as a political journalist and educator in Moscow and Tashkent.

159. Bernhard Reichenbach (1888–1975) was a prominent member of EKKI. As a representative of the Communist Workers' Party of Germany, he served as the party's delegate to the Third Congress of the Third International.

at the beginning, Ottwalt, Gábor, and Leschnitzer made speeches in which they pointed out the importance of *Die Weltbühne*, and expressed the hope that there should develop a better collaboration between the journal and writers living in the Soviet Union. I was invited several times to say something about how I imagined this collaboration might take place.

I think I might have taken this request, which was made at a well-laden table with quite a bit of alcohol, too seriously. I explained to them why most of the submissions coming from the Soviet Union are unsuitable for *Die Weltbühne*. I told them that composing hymns about the Soviet Union finds little favor in Western Europe and that they had to realize that life in the Soviet Union can't be described so indiscriminatingly, because it is viewed in Western Europe in much more contested terms. When I said that, I referred to your articles for the first time, which, in spite of your certainly Soviet-friendly attitude, nevertheless contain some criticism and have therefore come across as more honest, much more convincing, than the enthusiastic outbursts of staunch communists. Unfortunately I had chosen a comparison that was taken as far too absolute, and which then set the tone for the subsequent discussion. This is roughly what I said. There are many ethnic groups in the Soviet Union who are now breaking out of Asian feudalism and are taking a tremendous historical leap into new and modern times. This is without doubt something that will enthuse any observer. But the observer's report is probably more valuable and will sound more genuine when he also truthfully reports how the Muslim people might sprain their ankle when taking such a giant leap. It is most certainly curable but will remain an acute problem, and we want to learn about those problems too in order to experience the full development of the Soviet Union. Though the entire Soviet development is commendable even and especially in this leaping, each individual stage needs to be correctly presented.

Well, the phrase about the sprained ankle was immediately worked up into a theory by some of the authors. They said a lot of intelligent things, which I have forgotten now, but above all they defended their right to sing hymns. Ottwalt explained: "When I, Ottwalt, am really enthusiastic about something, I can expect my Western European readers to believe my genuine enthusiasm and not demand that I will discover sprained feet just to please him." And then Ottwalt launched into a polemic against Louis Fischer's articles, which were written from a bourgeois perspective, especially the article about Trotsky, published last year. In the article Trotsky is criticized, but it also criticizes the current policy of the Comintern. (Apologies, I have to add that Ottwalt was enjoying a bit too much vodka.)

Béla Balázs, by contrast, defended my point of view and Fischer's articles. He said that the writer has no right whatsoever to demand anything from the reader, but that his duty is to write so that the reader can understand him. Lukács added that it is the mistake of many communist writers who had only been living in the Soviet Union for a short time to take every stage that is accomplished in the process of development as being already the zenith and heaping praises upon it. One had to recognize that "sprained feet," which obviously do exist, are not meant as a reproach to the Soviet Union, but just as phases in the overall process of development.

After that the conversation got quite confusing. Animosities between Ottwalt and Béla Balázs became obvious, with Ottwalt darkly predicting that all those colleagues who agreed with my point of view could not understand the United Front politics of the Comintern; and, in turn, writers who took Fischer as a model and followed my demands would be following a misguided united front politics and would betray their own communist convictions.

I cannot deny that I got somewhat rough at this point and replied that Ottwalt's view completely contradicted what the leading men in the Soviet Union had recently told me.

It would seem, according to my report above, that we mostly discussed your articles, but that wasn't the case. They served as an illustration, from my point of view, as a model for what I expect as objective reporting and, from Ottwalt's intransigent side as an example, that a communist author writing for *Die Weltbühne* could easily be in danger of becoming a bourgeois. I also have to add that after the banquet, which lasted half the night, some individual writers came up to me and agreed with almost everything I said. Among them, it occurs to me now, was Willi Bredel, whom I forgot to mention in my previous list of the writers there.

All in all, my impression is that German writers who haven't been long in the Soviet Union feel the need to deliver excessive evidence of their

Soviet loyalty. Lukács and Gábor, whose ties to the Soviet Union go back further, were completely at one with me, as were the Russian writers with whom I spoke before and after—Koltsov, for example—who stressed the indispensable need for friendly criticism.[160] Additionally, I want to mention that, in a private conversation, Béla Kun for instance praised *Die Weltbühne*'s reportage on the Soviet Union and only took much offense at some of my personal remarks regarding Litvinov's speech about the Saar plebiscite.

I don't want my account to give you the impression that I left the Soviet Union upset. Almost everything I saw was enjoyable, and when I was asked in Moscow about my impressions (and that naturally happened a lot) I gave more or less the same answer: It's impossible to get an overall picture of the Soviet Union in only a few days. With what I was able to gauge I can say Louis Fischer's balanced articles in *Die Weltbühne* present an accurate picture.

I hope you don't mind that I often spoke about you in Moscow. Also, I always share your position.

I remain, with best wishes,

Yours

Budzislawski

Louis Fischer

"Soviet Journey," in Die Neue Weltbühne, *38/1936*

Louis Fischer left Moscow in mid-July to undertake a research trip through the vast Russian Empire. The outcome of this journey, which lasted until the end of August, is now ready to be published. Immediately after Kiev [Kyiv], the author continued his journey via Prague and Paris to Spain and will here report his experiences in due course.

160. Mikhail Koltsov (1898–1940) was a Soviet writer, journalist, and prominent public figure. He served as head of the Foreign Department of the Union of Soviet Writers.

Kiev, end of August 1936

In the Soviet Union the signs of the past are disappearing, and her future face is beginning to emerge. The many ugly traces of the czarist days, the scars of revolution that claimed many victims, are vanishing and now the outlines of the new era become visible.

Tiflis [Tbilisi] has been given a new sea promenade; new straight arterial roads cut through the hills of the inner city; new student accommodations grew out of the ground in blocks and the workers' houses stretch in long lines. The hundreds of new and beautiful school buildings, which started to be built months ago in all of the Soviet cities, are coming to completion; in Leningrad alone, 116 were erected during this summer. In the last year many splendid apartment blocks have been built in Kiev; beautiful buildings, and not the kind of cold cubes that characterized the uncomfortable architectural atrocities of a past formalistic period. Everywhere, innumerable newly created parks delight the tourist's eye and sometimes, as in Baku, the park is a large garden dedicated to sport and recreation; and elsewhere, there are a few flower beds and benches to rest on: An empty plot of land turns into a place of relaxation. In double and quadruple rows, millions of freshly planted trees line the avenues and alleys—those shadeless, excessively broad thoroughfares of the czarist times—who gave a thought for the individual and his aesthetic needs in those days! On sun-drenched country roads, benches and wooden sun shelters anticipate the traveler; in the overcrowded ships on the Black Sea there are playrooms for children, and in cities you'll find generously equipped club rooms for the girls' and boys' Pioneer groups. As part of this initiative, Kharkov [Kharkiv] donated one of its most beautiful palaces—the former seat of the Ukrainian government. Rostove [Rostov-on-Don] has just finished building the most marvelous theater that has ever been constructed under the Soviet regime and is rightly proud of the trolleybus route through its new main street. In Novorossiysk ever more factories are being built, more houses, and it is currently devouring a neighboring village. Nal'chik, the pearl of the North Caucasian republic of the Kabardins, is becoming ambitious and is spreading outward. Since the last time I traveled through the Soviet Union (the previous year), its forty thousand inhabitants have added twenty two- and three-story new buildings to their ubiquitous single-story houses. Even the permanent Moscow resident is surprised at the growth of his native city when he's on the lookout for a new apartment. Leningrad, too, albeit somewhat belatedly, is striving to create new housing for its growing population. The building of the new Moscow–Minsk highway is well under construction, and the modern road from Moscow to Kiev will be finished next year. In the countryside, you see new brick kilns everywhere, village communities' new pigpens or cowsheds, and, every now and then, a new farmhouse. These are just a few spontaneous examples of the outwardly visible changes in the country which is now developing at an even faster rate.

Every collective farm that I visited owns a "laboratory hut," a little building equipped with diagrams, display boards, models, agricultural tools, and a microscope. Here, the peasants receive instruction in the preparation of seeds, the correct use of machinery, the treatment of diseased animals or plants, fertilizers, and the efficient cultivation of the land. And so the results of scientific research are communicated right down to the very last link in the production chain, to the muzhik [peasant], who, of course, doesn't like hearing this word any more. It reminds him too much of serfdom and backwardness. Today he is a kolkhoznik. During the past years many kolkhozy have equipped themselves with light-duty trucks. The harvest is brought in more quickly and with less waste; man and animal are treated more gently; as well as being the tractor driver, the driver now becomes a new link between farm and city, and the peasant suddenly develops a previously undiscovered concern for well-maintained roads.

The two-wheeler has moved into the villages; tractors and trucks can be seen everywhere—and in greater numbers than ever before. There is the manufacture of electric threshing machines. On the huge state farm Zernograd near Rostov-on-Don, even now, specialists are experimenting with an electric tractor, an electric truck, and a tractor with pneumatic tires. A tractor equipped in this way needs less horsepower and uses less fuel than the standard kind with heavy, ridged iron wheels or caterpillar tracks.

The value of mechanization and improved technology is proved this summer; only because of this a potential crop failure was avoided in the

USSR. The largest part of Ukraine, which produces a quarter of the state's wheat, had only one proper rainfall between sowing and harvest. However, Ukraine is proud to have achieved a greater harvest than last year. It was the same in the Northern Caucasus, the second largest of the Soviet granaries. In the collectives everywhere, I asked them to explain this phenomenon and everywhere I got the same answer: Observing the fallow period, which improves the soil and brings greater results, has become common practice. The tractors can plow the fields when the ground still retains winter moisture, much earlier than a horse would ever have been able to work the heavy soil. They used high-quality seeds and planted deeper than before and so safeguarded them from drought. And when in July and August a smoldering heat covered the fields, the wheat and rye would have burned had it not been for the trucks that quickly gathered in the grains at a faster pace. On August 15th of the previous year about 57 million hectares were harvested; at the same point this year it was more than 62 million. A few days earlier, on August 10th the difference was even greater: almost 8 million hectares.

The USSR is now reaping the benefits of the costly collectivization process. It is quite possible that there will still be poor harvests in the future, but the wayward tyranny of nature is being countered by the will of a collective group with mechanical wonders springing from their richly inventive brains—not to mention the better living conditions in the countryside. In one of the Kabardin peasant huts I asked what they had recently bought. Among the treasures the occupants listed each two pairs of shoes that they had bought for their wives—a pair for Sunday and one for working days. There was also a new colorful sun umbrella. You rarely find a household without a cow; the herds are doing nicely. In recent years the number of cattle in Ukraine has grown by almost 27 percent, pigs by more than 60, and sheep by more than 42.5 percent. On the roads and in the fields, one comes across mares and their foals. A kolkhoz near Kharkiv proudly showed me a stable full of young horses that had never been worked. The animals are carefully tended by specialists. More is expected of peasants than before; I met special workforce brigades and Stakhanovite people in the collectives. They're better off now; never before had a peasant so much to eat. In a village in Crimea where tobacco is grown, I spoke to a peasant, who, together with his wife, earned eight thousand rubles last year and in addition had fruit, nuts, vegetables, and cheese. At first I didn't want to believe him, but the accountant showed me his books in black and white. And this couple is not exceptional; many of their neighbors have had similar earnings in this year. An annual salary of eight thousand rubles is what two competent city workers would earn. In rye-growing areas the income is lower—but still enough to embarrass the earner wondering what to spend his money on. A shortage of consumer goods remains, because the main emphasis is still on heavy industry and weapon production.

The peasant has not enjoyed the collectivization process; but he understands, and he has learned to think collectively. The kolkhoz has destroyed the fence that separated his fields from his neighbor's and with it the fence around his thinking also came down. Once, his world consisted only of his little piece of land, his basic housing, his family, his primitive agriculture, and the church. Today he's a member of a collective and the task of the collective is his task—and it is a complicated one. And to the same extent to which he applies himself to this task, by seeing and hearing what others will contribute to getting the job done, he has to think ahead. The existence of the collective depends on industry, on the provision of machines and fuel, and on domestic politics. The politics of the Bolsheviks, which also necessarily includes international relations, are intertwined with his day-to-day work. His horizon is widening. He wants to read a newspaper and listen to the radio. Talented boys and girls are sent to the cities to be educated at the best institutions. A new generation of capable, intelligent organizers and leaders is growing up. You can meet them everywhere—strong individuals even in the smallest village and the most forlorn factory. And this year there are also more noncommunists among them. Bolshevik party members no longer monopolize jobs in the higher levels of administration. It is almost impossible to overestimate the importance and constructive consequences of the intellectual revolution that was triggered by agricultural collectivization. One hundred million individuals who, before 1917, were in hibernation for half a year and during the other half hardly produced anything, have now metamorphosed into fully fledged, mature people.

The way they think and feel has been revolutionized. A young engineer showed me the Dnieper dam. I asked him to tell me about his life: Once upon a time he herded cattle in a village in Azerbaijan. The director of the tea plantation in Chakva, near Batumi, also used to look after animals. In Rostov-on-Don I passed a Hall of Residence, went in, and unceremoniously knocked on one door after another. Three women were just preparing for a history exam. They gave correct and intelligent answers to my questions about the American Civil War and the French Revolution. Two of them came from villages. They used to work as maids in the city and, on top of their jobs, attended an evening school. Now they were village teachers and went on a special course for six months. The third woman was an Armenian Greek, thirty years old. Five years ago she could neither read nor write and worked in a coal mine in the Donets Basin. Now, since last year, she teaches at a school. This woman asked me the most astute questions about the capitalist world. She was typical of thousands of others. The Bolshevik Revolution did away with the thin sheet of royalty, aristocrats, and plutocrats who once kept the Russian masses from the light and the sun. The new harvest is burgeoning. Their time is now. You have to take note of these people now. They can withstand any scrutiny. They are the new Russia, the future. They possess a remarkable dignity and self-respect. They want more out of life. They will take the new constitution very seriously.

And in those areas inhabited by minorities, dignity is the overriding impression. The Soviet victory was a milestone in the history of the old Russia with its repressed ethnic minorities. It made possible their first emergence as communities, each with its own individuality, culture, and government. There is no limit to their gratitude for the gift of a fledgling national existence. The government will find many loyal supporters among their ranks; but, for their part, the Bolsheviks also did a lot to meet the requirements of those minorities. In this way, they created a strong bastion against each form of nationalism. Everywhere in the Soviet Union the observer encounters enormous pride in the country's achievements. But there is not pride simply in "Russian" achievement, because half the USSR isn't Russian. It is made up of dozens of national minorities. The Georgian

Stalin, the Jew Kaganovich,[161] the Georgian Ordzhonikidze,[162] the Armenian Mikoian—all of them members of the Supreme Politburo—they can't feel a "Russian" pride. At the same time they will not think that Georgia or Armenia are alone the creators of the Soviet successes. Each of the country's national groups has played its part. And thus the free development of innumerable nationalities warded off nationalism. The USSR is a true Internationale. The American may boast about special "American" predispositions, the German about the superiority of his race. The citizen of the multicolored patchwork that is the Soviet Union can see their recent triumphs entirely due to a social and economic system. He admits gladly that socialism would function better in the US or Germany. Therefore, when he glorifies the Soviet Union, he glorifies an idea that knows no national boundaries.

The general enthusiasm is now stronger and more widespread than I have ever experienced it during my fourteen years of living in the Soviet Union. This is as much an unassailable fact as it is easy to explain. Here, enthusiasm isn't a hollow sentimentality that has to be generated by noisy spectacle, as it is in certain other states—here it grows naturally out of the solid foundation of material advancement. In the past five weeks I traveled thousands of miles throughout the country, visited many villages and twelve cities. I asked everyone I met what they earned. I must have asked a thousand people, men and women. In all cases I was told that the respondents earned more than the previous year, and usually a lot more. At the Kirov (formerly Putilov) plant near Leningrad, a worker's average salary in 1935 was between 250 and 311 rubles in the first half of the year. An engineer's and technician's salary rose in the same period from 475 to 599 rubles and the salary of an office clerk from 223 to 269 rubles. My estimate is that in the past twelve months average income rose by 20 percent throughout the Soviet Union. At the same time, prices fell—although not as much as the people expected or hoped for. Prices for bread, shoes, and

161. Lazar Kaganovich (1893–1991) was a Soviet Communist Party leader and a close ally of Joseph Stalin.

162. Sergo Ordzhonikidze (1886–1937) was a communist leader who played a key role in bringing Georgia under Soviet control and in the industrialization of the Soviet Union.

various items of clothing are still too high. Since the Stakhanovite movement began (in the final days of August last year) production has risen by 30 percent. The importance of this movement is easy to explain: better utilization of the individual's capacity to work; more efficient use of technical equipment leading to improved wages for the individual worker; better employment opportunities; and further cost-cutting measures in the factories. According to a recent decree, half the savings must go back into housing. There is, however, greater investment in heavy machinery than into the production of consumer goods. But the quantity of available consumer goods determines the general price level. Toward the end of the year, a further reduction in prices is expected. Each price reduction means an improvement in living costs, which is on a much higher level than at the time of the Czar, but for a socialist state is still too low.

The greatest need now is housing. Considerable progress has been made, but there is still a sad disparity in the rate of building with regard to the potential in this area. Seven years ago the Soviets laid down the foundations of a new state industrial policy. The industrialization process provided the prerequisites for construction: iron, steel, brick, glass, and so on. Since 1929 all this material went into the new factories and the housing associated with them. The diversion of this building material from the needs of the person to the needs of the industry causes a disruption in house construction. And this diversion is still noticeable today: factories, schools, military facilities, offices are built; school building must be a priority, and next year, maybe it's time for hospitals. And there is also an ongoing lack of skilled workers. In Moscow I know whole blocks of buildings that haven't been completed because of a shortage of tradesmen. Their productivity is quite low because their work is hardly automated at all. Even fewer homes were built in 1935 than in 1934. The quality of plumbing and other installation work is deplorable; the design of features and fittings is poor; and modern comforts such as cooling systems or air filters are nonexistent. The Soviets must now concentrate their attention on the quality of living. A gifted and energetic Commissar for Home Décor, backed by the authority of men like Kaganovich or Ordzhonikidze, could achieve a great deal, because the overcrowding of living areas causes serious personal and economic problems, as well as severe deprivations.

Certainly, the Russians are used to living four or five to a room and simply accept it as just the norm; outside observers think they should actually do something about it. The problem is that this lethargic point of view can be applied to other circumstances as well, and, if that's the case, there seems to be no urgent need for action. But new housing is immediately needed. There is no reason why concentrating on this problem should not produce positive outcomes, just as the Bolsheviks battled on difficult economic "fronts." Nothing will eradicate the memory of the time of the Czar as thoroughly as a new line of beautiful houses at the place where once stood a cluster of miserable barracks. Only when prices come down and better housing goes up will the USSR stop reminding everyone of prewar times, and will it begin to stand comparison: that is, comparison with the progressive states of the Western world.

E. Dotschkal

Article from the Pionerskaya Pravda*, Moscow 1938*

This is our international obligation!

(Report from the young members of the Workers International Relief)

On the wall—a red flag. On it, photographs of victims of the fascist terror. A pencil drawing shows a disheveled boy who stands on a woodpile, holding a flagpole firmly in his hands.

This is Gavroche, the French boy who fought with the revolutionary workers of Paris on the barricades and met a hero's death.

The children have read about him in Victor Hugo and saw a film about him in the cinema.

The cause, for which Gavroche gave his life and for which thousands of Communards fought and died, has triumphed for sixty-seven years in our country.

The flag, which is held high by the Paris Communards, flies high above the liberated Soviet soil.

It won't take long for this flag to fly over the whole world. The fight for peace and against fascism is going on everywhere.

Children are following the war in Spain with particular excitement. Every time the newspapers report the situation on the battlefronts, the children move the flag pins on the map of Spain. They register every victory of the Republicans. Often arguments take place in front of the map about how the insurrectionists could be better attacked.

Here at the WIR[163] news corner, in front of the map, the children tell each other what they have read about the battle in Spain. Maya Uralova tells us about a little female machine gunner. The fascists had conquered the city. Catalonia is overrun by enemy troops. Two Republicans are manning a machine gun. It is an unequal battle. The Republicans, who have fought against the fascists, are killed. Then, a fourteen-year-old girl leaps behind the machine gun—and the rows of the insurrectionists begin to thin out. In their minds the image of the little Parisian revolutionary appears. "Like Gavroche!"—shout the children.

They know a lot about Spain: from books, newspapers, and radio broadcasts. They have written a letter to Spanish Pioneers. The letter was sent some time ago, but no reply has yet reached them. The children are not worried, because there is the possibility the letter couldn't have been delivered because of the war in Spain, and the fascists might have intercepted the letter. The Pioneers wrote again.

Then they decided to collect money—international five kopeck pieces—to send to the Spanish children. But each of them brought more than five kopeks; one brought fifty, another seventy, and a third, one ruble.

In order unceasingly to help the resistance fighters, all Pioneers and pupils became members of the International Organization for Aid to Revolutionaries. The children created news bulletins about this organization and the first was published on March 18, the sixty-seventh anniversary of the Paris Commune. They wrote about the life and battles of comrade Thälmann. Each new bulletin reported on proletarian fighters. In the summer the children often listened to songs sung by the German, Ernst Busch. Thereupon they learned German revolutionary songs themselves: "Komintern," "Einheitsfrontlied," "Die Moorsoldaten." The children sing

163. WIR, or Workers International Relief (also known as International Workers' Aid), was created in 1921 as a response to a call by Lenin in order to channel relief from international working-class organizations and communist parties to famine-stricken Soviet Russia.

the songs in German. In each geography lesson the children, one by one, talk about recent world affairs. And the military side is not forgotten either. The children have already completed the requirements for the medals PWCHO [Air and Chemical Disarmament] and BGSO [Ready as Paramedic for the Defense of the Homeland]. To mark the anniversary of the Paris Commune, the class organized a shooting club.

The Pioneers and pupils of this class do important work. This should be organized in every Pioneer group or class because it is the international obligation of each Pioneer to help their foreign comrades.

E. Dotschkal

Moscow

32 School 'Lepeshinski'

7b

Friedrich Wolf
Letter to Louis Fischer in New York

Paris, January 18, 1939

Dear Louis Fischer,

By way of Else, I've just learned your address. She also wrote that you saw *Mamlock* and that "there's great hope of getting you [F.W.] over there." That's also my hope. But what I need is the following: Although I tried everything, I can't get a "*Titre de voyage aller–retour*" and consequently no visitor's visa for the USA; further, the situation here is becoming ever more difficult for us—untenable, actually—and as a result, the only option for me (since the quota of German emigrants is overflowing) is a Preference Visa. A few prominent writers have already received such a visa. In order to get it, one needs an official invitation from an American institution to give lectures etc. As you know, I already gave several lectures in 1935 at the

Theater Institute of Columbia University in New York and at Brooklyn College on "Theater and Film in the West and the Soviet Union." I believe that, after the success of my *Mamlock* film, my name is as well known today as it was at the time of the *Matrosen von Cattaro* [*Sailors of Cattaro*]. Someone would have to try to send or cable me an invitation as quickly as possible. My friends here are 100 percent behind my attendance at the World's Fair as representative of the writers and film and theater people. Everything is held up only because I can't get this damn "*Titre de voyage aller–retour*" and therefore only a Preference Visa will get me entry into the USA. Dear Louis Fischer, help me from your side and, if possible, help me quickly.

A while ago, my acquaintance, Sydney Ross, asked his lawyer, the counsellor Leo Taub, 521 Fifth Avenue, Murray Hill 2-0514, to take care of this matter. Taub did write to me once, but nothing further happened. Please give Taub a call in any case. You probably have even better connections and more influence. I'm stuck here, like a mouse in a trap. No work—only harassments!

The most important thing is this:

The renowned director Leo Mittler, who's coming to New York in February, and I have just finished a play about refugees and people exiled from Germany in *Niemandsland* [*No Man's Land/Hell on Earth*]. I think it is one of the most important and best plays, not just on this subject.

The play is called *The Forgotten Ship* and is about a poignant episode where about two hundred Catholics, scholars, and Jews, all exiled by Hitler from Austria, live and starve for weeks on end between the borders on an old Danube ship, until—through their own discipline and through great solidarity of action—they make contact with the outside world and are rescued. I can't tell you the whole thing, but I've rarely been as excited about a play as I am about this one. Today, when ten thousand Hitler refugees shuttle back and forth in a no-man's-land between different borders, it would be a magnificent, vivid, and inspiring play particularly if produced for this summer's World's Fair! For Americans especially it would also be just the right melodrama, due to its currency and its suspenseful action-based plot. It could be staged on a moored ship, or on a real ship in the open air, or at Madison Square. You know that I know a thing or two about theater, and you can trust me on this. What could you or a committee do in this matter? Might Moritz Wertheim be interested?

Mr. Mittler will be in New York by the end of February. From a director's point of view, we keep imagining an open-air show production. Mr. Mittler, whose work as a director in Germany, France, and England I have known for years, already has some valuable ideas for the staging that seem to me very convincing.

So, dear Louis Fischer, please don't put this letter in the wrong pocket of your jacket, and answer me as quickly as possible, maybe by the next mail ship! I very keenly await your reply.

Cordially,

Yours, Friedrich Wolf

I had a phone call from Else in M. three days ago. Your Markoosha and our boys are well.

Friedrich Wolf
Letter to Markus Wolf

Paris, January 21, 1939

Mischa, what a bad papa you have, who has even forgotten your sixteenth birthday! The fact alone, that you are already sixteen, is beyond my imagination—I can still see you then as if it were yesterday. You were a rosy, lovely little bundle in my arms with silky blond hair and a smart little parting; but exactly for this reason I, the thoughtless papa, should have remembered this day! Please, don't take it the wrong way, pal; here is a big birthday kiss! I hear that now you'll get your own Soviet passport and will become a true citizen of the great Soviet people. My congratulations on that as well. And so you can understand the importance of this a little better, I will tell you about the situation here in the West and about those strange creatures, who—although they do exist—don't exist. There are, for example, a hundred thousand—soon to be a million—emigrants without papers. I really don't want to cry about it on your birthday, but you'll see how much more meaningful your life is compared to that of a hundred thousand boys your age, who now shuttle between borders for years, can't receive an education, and are regarded everywhere as irritating nobodies. Tomorrow for instance I will meet a number of Jewish refugees who have been living for the past six weeks in the open air without shelter, in the winter, like wild animals prowling around on the German Western border in Hitler country and surviving only on farmers' charity. A little child who died had to be buried somewhere in a field at night. Now they are here but have permission to stay for only four weeks and then they will be forced out. Will they be allowed to leave for England? No. Honduras? Madagascar? Some pestilential area or desert? If some are lucky enough to have money, then it's taken off them by one of the little rogue states or agents; and once they set foot in Uruguay or Chile, they're told that it's all a pack of lies, they have been swindled by some fraudulent consul, and they are sent back! But Europe is denying them reentry! And so they're hanging around in quarantine centers all over the entire world.

You could say this toughens people up. Well, if he could fight and work, even under the hardest conditions . . . that would indeed toughen him up! But this passive waiting and hanging around: that only creates dropouts and the worst kind of lumpen proletarians, scroungers, and disreputable people. You need to know this too, since that's the reason why emigration is so hard these days, because you're not allowed to work! It's the first thing you notice printed on your visa everywhere here in the West. Heinrich Heine in Paris . . . he got—and was unfairly criticized for this—a monthly annuity from the French state! Fabulous! Or the émigré Russians between 1905 and 1914, they travelled to London, Zurich, Kraków, went to conferences, to Capri, etc. Today you can't get across a border if you don't have a lot of money as well as endless papers. Often, however, difficult situations create solidarity. The same people who invited me for "potato dumplings" tomorrow have created out of their own hardship a little working group led by a true "Yiddish Mamme," a wonderful woman. They have hardly enough to survive, but then six to ten German Jews in utter rags appear and without batting an eyelid, Mamme takes them in, feeds them, and gives them new clothes! And, of course, what's the first thing they have to do? Tomorrow morning they have to go to the Boulevard Montmartre to see the *Professor Mamlock* film! That's first on the list of Mamme's priorities; she, who comes from Łódź and knows each and every twist and turn of life from the age of twelve. And she speaks with such pride about the Soviet Union even though she has never been there, and even though the Poles have beaten up her son so badly that he's paralyzed; she is unrelenting and stands by her convictions. A woman like that can restore courage, time and time again, to people like us as well. You are so lucky. You boys live in a world of transformation. Luckily you haven't encountered economic crises, unemployment, or exclusion. And that's why you need to know how boys in the West live. Certainly, there are lots of nice things in the shops and they are not even particularly expensive. But the workers have no voice here. The decisions are made by the big companies, which, for example, had so arranged things that, via the Creusot cannon factory, the shares of the allied Škoda factories in Plzeň/Czechoslovakia were sold to Krupp/Germany. And that happened in July—long before the supposed Hitler crisis. Then, in September, mobilization follows and there's a huge row that today, although it is far too late, is denounced even by honest lawyers and patriots like de Kérillis, who, while antisocialist, are passionately defending the alliance with the Soviet Union.[164] In the country itself, however, they are all for repressing the workers who are on strike against rising prices. It's all completely mad and hypocritical. What's urgently needed is the unity of the people. But when it comes to taxes and wallets then a wild brawl begins, like dogs fighting over a bone. And Mussolini and Hitler use these for ever-new extortions. And that's why, I'm afraid, neither England nor France will be able to withstand the dictatorships, because the battle around the money is still stronger here than all "national pride." For a third of the Western democrats, Mussolini and Hitler are still the "lesser evil."

How is it going with *school, Misch*? *Please write a bit to your dad again!* How did you like *Der Kampf geht weiter!* [The struggle continues]? *Write about it!!!* You have all the rights and obligations of a bigger brother toward

164. Henri de Kérillis (1889–1958) was a French writer, journalist, and politician known for his right-wing nationalist views.

Lenochka, the little toad; if she doesn't listen, you are allowed to give her a little slap on the bottom.—

At the moment I'm preparing a huge scenario that is called *Das vergessene Schiff* and is about the fate of a ship that drifted for months on the Danube, in this no-man's-land between the German and Hungarian borders, with two hundred refugees from Vienna on board.

I don't know whether I'll be able to travel to America. It's out of my hands. I wrote to Mins but he no longer replies, and I wrote to Hede four months ago, also no reply. I wrote to two lawyers in New York and have been waiting for a month for a reply. Now I have written to Louis. However, I will only get a visitor's visa and only if the authorities here give me a "*Titre de voyage aller–retour*." The fact that you still need US$500 for a visitor's visa and US$3,000 for an emigration visa is a different story. But if the political situation carries on at this rate, perhaps there will no longer be any need to go overseas. Although I'm sitting here in a real mousetrap, maybe one day I will be of use somehow.

If a fascist government in the style of Adolf comes to power, though, then we should all look for a family burial ground. But since that concerns a whole lot of people, it's only half as tragic.

Have you read your father's novel, Misch? What's your opinion? You don't get away by just saying "Shoemaker (playwright), stick to your last." That would be too easy. You are now a high-cultured *chelovek*, so write a detailed analysis about it, what you like and don't like.

But for now, Mischa, good night, it's late. I still remember that winter's day in Hechingen, when you, a tiny tot, came into this world . . . Meni bit my hand, because you hurt her so much. Today I remember this fondly and I wouldn't mind experiencing it all over again. Give Meni a big kiss as well and be my brave, big boy.

Warmly

Yours Papa

Kisses for Meni, Koni, and Lena!

Eleanor Roosevelt
From: This I Remember, *1949*

My friend, Mayris Chaney, was with us this Christmas for dinner and the night. The day Mr. Churchill arrived, young George Fischer, a son of Louis Fischer, the writer, had come down to spend the night, not expecting anything like the galaxy of important people whom he met in the house. When he was told that he had to wear a dinner coat he had a very difficult time trying to borrow from his friends and his final ensemble was not quite all that it should have been.

Several years earlier I had learned from Louis Fischer something about conditions in the USSR when he told me that his wife and his two sons were not being permitted to leave the country and join him in the United States. He asked me if there was anything I could do about it. I talked it over with Franklin, who suggested that since it might be unwise to do anything officially, I might ask Ambassador Oumansky to tea in my sitting room in the White House, tell him the whole story and get his reaction. I followed that suggestion and Mr. Oumansky said he would find out about the situation. However, I heard nothing from him until one day we happened to meet on the plane from New York to Washington. It was a rough flight and neither of us had any desire to talk, but just before I left the airport the ambassador came up to me and said: "The people you are interested in will soon arrive in this country."

Letter from NSDAP[165] Headquarters, Berlin, to the Secret State Police Office, Berlin

March 4, 1938

Re: German Returnees from the Soviet Union

165. The acronym stands for the Nationalsozialistische Deutsche Arbeiterpartei (the National Socialist German Workers' Party, or the Nazi Party).

With reference to the conversation between Superintendent Schroeder and our party comrade Bürksen, we ask the Secret State Police office to send us a copy of the questionnaire used for interrogation of German Returnees from the Soviet Union for the purpose of evaluation through Reichsleiter Rosenberg.[166]

We would be grateful to receive previous and also all forthcoming materials.

Heil Hitler!

Dr. Leibbrandt

Letter of the Chief of Secret Police and the SD[167]*, Berlin, to NSDAP Foreign Affairs Office, Berlin*

July 29, 1941

Re: Returnees from Russia

Enclosed for your perusal is one copy each of the interrogation protocols of below listed returnees from Russia.

You are requested to forward the documents after use to the Reich Ministry for People's Enlightenment and Propaganda.

1.)

2.)

[. . .]

166. Alfred Rosenberg (1893–1946) was a German Nazi ideologue and one of the party's key theorists. He held several influential positions within the Nazi regime. From 1933 to 1945, he led the NSDAP Office of Foreign Affairs and, from 1934, oversaw Amt Rosenberg, the official Nazi bureau responsible for cultural policy and ideological oversight.

167. The SD (Sicherheitsdienst) was the intelligence agency of the Nazi Party. It operated as a branch of the SS (Schutzstaffel), the elite paramilitary organization led by Heinrich Himmler.

100.) Wloch, Erna, DoB: December 18th '96 in Berlin-Weissensee

[. . .]

Eva Siao
Memories, 1983

I can only talk about Koni in relation to his parents, because I was friends with them, especially with his mother, Else Wolf, for many years. My husband, the Chinese author Emi Siao (Siao San), and I lived in Moscow in a home for political émigrés. One day in the autumn of 1935 or 1936—we hadn't been married long—the phone rang. It was Friedrich Wolf. He was writing a piece about China and wanted to get some advice from Emi. We then visited the Wolfs one evening. They lived in a small apartment near the Arbat.

The Wolfs also had a small dacha near Moscow, in Peredelkino. I was often there, and it was there that I also met their child, Koni. When our son Lion was born on July 7, 1938, I came from the maternity hospital and went directly to Peredelkino and spent the whole summer with Else. She was very hospitable. Her friends, the doctor Hette Lammert, and her husband, sculptor Will Lammert, and their two sons Till and Ule, were also permanent guests in the house in Peredelkino.

In the summer of 1938, another friend of Else's, Markoosha Fischer, the Russian wife of the American journalist Louis Fischer, together with their sons Yura and Vitya, lived there too. Vitya and Koni were inseparable friends. And there was a third boy, Lothar Wloch. I got to know his mother, Erna Wloch, after her husband Wilhelm Wloch was arrested. That was after 1937. I remember a conversation with her. Wilhelm Wloch was held at Lubyanka Prison. The wives of the prisoners were allowed to do their laundry; one time she got blood-soaked clothes back. We often talked to Erna Wloch, and Else Wolf especially took care of her.

In 1939, I went to Stockholm while my husband went ahead to China. In 1940, I came back to Moscow in order to travel on from there to China. I lived once more at Else Wolf's in Peredelkino, and it was there that I met

Erna Wloch for the last time. She was already in possession of a visa for Germany. She went back to Germany because her husband was no longer alive. It was depressing for us too. That summer wasn't as happy as 1938. Friedrich Wolf was at that time on his way to Spain and we were all a bit anxious, but on the other hand, the children demanded all our attention. We had called our son "Lion" because it has a Chinese sound to it and at the same time Lion Feuchtwanger was my favorite author. I took a lot of photographs in Peredelkino.

In 1951, Emi and I attended the "Festival of Youth" in Berlin. Our friend Joris Ivens made a documentary film about the festival and Koni, a student at the film institute in Moscow at the time, was his assistant. It was a wonderful reunion. Our thirteen-year-old Lion was there with us as well, and he spent some lovely hours at the Wolfs' in Lehnitz. In the following years, whenever I had to come to Berlin for my film or photography work, I always stayed in Lehnitz, mostly over Christmas and New Year's. On such days the whole family came together, just like in Peredelkino. Mischa and Koni made pelmeni, competing with each other. We saw them for the last time in 1963. After that my husband and I experienced the painful situation in our country, but we survived.[168] I saw Koni again in 1981 in Berlin. That was the last time.

Ule Lammert
Memories of Peredelkino, 1987

Eighteen kilometers from Moscow—the Wolfs' dacha was an island at this time, which shaped us in many ways. It was a tragic, rough, yet at the same time inspiring time, about which nobody spoke for twenty years, and subsequently avoided bringing it up. At least that was how it seemed to me. After the dissolution of the Schutzbund's children's home and the loss of a tight community of rowdies (as Koni called us later), I came to join my parents in Peredelkino. After a fruitless search for a room in Moscow, my parents had found permanent accommodations, thanks to Else Wolf, in their dacha. Peredelkino was an idyllic place, especially during

168. Siao here is referring to the widespread repression during the Cultural Revolution in the People's Republic of China.

the summer holidays and on beautiful winter Sundays. The house back then was full of people; guests came and went all the time. Above all, there was the suggestion of a matriarchy. The men were far away, and the mothers ruled the house, garden, and conversation. They smoked and looked benevolently over the boys playing outside. Lammert, the only resident man, frequently retreated from this atmosphere. His target was usually Adam Scharrer, who lived twenty minutes away and who had a radio receiving news from all over the world.

We boys went swimming in the lake. The one bicycle, perpetually broken, was constantly under repair. Enthusiasm for sports was part of it, too. It was difficult to find an excuse not to join in. When Spartak Moscow played, that was a great event. Erna taught us mah-jongg and Hette, skat. Wickedly, we shot crows with air rifles in Peredelkino's cemetery; Pasternak wasn't yet buried there. We played soccer and later volleyball and with it came the friendship with Zilya, who emanated warmth and togetherness. It was a selfless and brave friendship to which we all owed much. Once, half-asleep, she took us foraging for mushrooms very early in the morning and tried to teach us how to dance: without much success for Koni and me.

Later she helped wherever she could. When we were scattered throughout the enormous country during the war, she was the one who got us together again.

And then were the long walks, often deliberately lengthened, to the shop to buy bread. Most of the time Koni and I had to go because we were the youngest. Grumpily, we enjoyed these walks. You could make up wonderful stories, dream and talk, all the while nibbling on the fresh bread. Koni already then spoke cautiously, slowly; I, mostly hurriedly, with my words falling over each other . . . He loved animal stories and cats. Thompson Seton's *The Pacing Mustang* and *The Biography of a Grizzly* and the films *Chapaev* and *The Thirteen* inspired him. After we read Ethel Voynich's *The Gadfly*, he and Lothar especially raved about Garibaldi. I stayed true to my love for Saint-Just, Robespierre, and Danton to Napoleon coming from my time at the children's home. Charles de Coster's *Ulenspiegel* [*The Glorious Adventures of Tyl Eulenspiegel*] and Heinrich Mann's *Henri Quatre* were dear to me. Especially we younger ones, Lothar, Koni, Vitya, and I, argued about our heroes passionately and unconditionally. Groups were formed. As can be expected for our age, we debated very personally and insultingly. The older ones, like Till who was nearly twenty, Mischa (who spent some of the summertime at the writers' Pioneer camp in Koktebel and almost certainly had a circle of friends there too), but Yura as well, probably had other problems and kept their distance most of the time. The year after the Fischers left stayed more vividly in my memory, but maybe that's due to the fact that I was then more involved.

On my walks with Koni, we also inevitably talked about the things we didn't understand when we had overheard our parents' discussions. The questions usually revolved around themes such as the arrests, the Hitler–Stalin pact, but also the suspension of the *Mamlock* film from all theater repertoires, and the delayed duplication of Lammert's Thälmann bust. Often we glossed over things and never questioned the larger cause itself when we were seeking answers in a childish naive way. We would have loved to find the answers. When abortions were banned in the Soviet Union too, Koni felt especially close to his *Zyankali* father.[169] And so the innocent thirteen-year-olds argued and looked for socially equitable solutions.

We read a lot—German and Russian. I had my difficulties with the language. When later, at the beginning of the war, I started to be fascinated by Tolstoy and, with him, Russian literature in general, I read *War and Peace* in German. The assimilation process was more slow and painful for me, because of the Schutzbund children's home and because my father couldn't gain a foothold; but certainly because of other social preconditions as well. But we didn't just read "good" books; we also devoured crime, especially Edgar Wallace. And Felix Dahn's *Ein Kampf um Rom* [*A Struggle for Rome*] excited us probably no less than it did our peers in Hitler's Germany.

Besides the short holidays, which were like celebration days for me, there was also the long, gray, everyday life in Peredelkino. Then, we Lammert boys were alone with our parents' unrest and worries about work and survival. Now the dacha became a sad place, a home without water and sanitation and with long, laborious public-transport connections into the city. For months everything was covered under a thick blanket

169. Friedrich Wolf's 1929 drama *Zyankali* (*Cyankali*) powerfully highlights the potential devastating consequences when abortion is made an illegal act.

of snow. Very early in the morning, still in the dark, you had to get up and trudge through the deep snow for half an hour until you reached the railway. Then the journey continued in overcrowded and smoky carriages to Moscow's Kievskii Station. Then on the underground and tram to Nikitskii Vorota to the School 125. It was an especially hard journey with temperatures around minus forty degrees. Opportunities and conditions to make new friends didn't really arise. After school I dawdled aimlessly through Moscow, went to the reading hall for foreign literature, waiting for my mother so that I didn't have to go back home by myself. I tried to make myself useful with grocery shopping, which, after the start of the Finnish war, usually meant queueing for a long time.[170] Hette, the doctor, also went to work in the city every day. Too often she was the only breadwinner for the family. Till was home most of the time, because he couldn't get into architectural school immediately after finishing his studies, though he had recommendations and good grades.

Lammert, however, was hit the hardest. On his arrival in Moscow he was greeted by artistic, like-minded, modern sculptors and architects, but his arrival coincided exactly with a wave of dogmatic, realism-oriented changes in arts policy. And so he remained for years without work. It has to be said, though, that his situation and isolation kept him out of trouble, because he was then still a man prone to flare up. Only in 1939 did he get a sculpturing job, but he didn't have even the most primitive studio. He created the larger-than-life Thälmann bust in one of the two little rooms that we inhabited in Peredelkino. One day Walter Ulbricht and Kurt Funk (Herbert Wehner) visited him, as the cultural association had asked for a consultation.[171] Somehow they were not in agreement with Lammert, who refused to crown the beautiful round form of the bald head with a Red Front fighter's cap. The already existing tension between Lammert and Walter Ulbricht was certainly not diminished because of that. Later, Ulbricht is supposed to have said at Lammert's return: "The formalist

170. Lammert here is referring to the 1939–41 Russo-Finnish War.

171. Richard Herbert Wehner (1906–1990) was a German politician who belonged to the KPD from 1927 to 1942 and joined the SPD after 1946. He served as a member of the Bundestag from 1949 to 1983 and held the position of Federal Minister for All-German Affairs from 1966 to 1969. During his exile in Moscow between 1937 and 1941, he used the alias Kurt Funk.

is back again." But with his work, no matter how hard it was, Lammert's natural optimism returned. The year before the war, especially after we moved to Moscow, was certainly the most hopeful one for him. At that point he was also less hesitant toward integration.

Even if Peredelkino comprised more than a summer resort, my time there, especially measured against what was to follow, belonged to the happiest of my youth. There were friends, and relationships were built that last a lifetime. The last time I was there was for a few days in September 1941. Despite the war, the air raids, and an uncertain future it was like the "old days." Zilya came around for a few hours. The next day she and Koni and other children of writers were evacuated from Moscow. We took the often-walked path once more to the station. In my memory, this was the farewell.

Zilya Voskresenskaya

From: Ein ganzes Leben lang. Erinnerungen *[An entire life long. Memoirs], 1984*

Lothar . . . this male name is probably the dearest to me. He's standing in front of me laughing, blond hair hanging over his forehead, the eyes almost closed, the left eyebrow slightly raised, and the foot poised to jump. He's wearing green shorts. He always wears green shorts. (What did Jerome K. Jerome say? "Red drawers rather suit him.") The boys have come to pick me up to play volleyball. It's seven in the evening. We always play around that time of day. We are five—four boys and me. Ule, being eleven, is the youngest of them. His brother Till is the oldest—sixteen, Koni—twelve, and Lothar, the same age as me, is fourteen. Sometimes we're joined by Lothar's friend Anarch Eisenberger from Moscow. (His father was an anarchist, that's why the son got this name. We call him Anarik. And Lothar's name is derived from an area called Lotharingia.) My boys are German. Their parents are political emigrants who had to flee fascism in Germany when Hitler came to power. They all speak terrible Russian. Till is the one with the best command of Russian and the worst, in my opinion, is Lothar. I like how they mistreat the Russian language. It makes me laugh. Lothar speaks very slowly, chooses his words carefully, and tries to speak correctly. But he uses the cases and gender as it comes into his head. In his note from the station Lothar wrote: "I wanted to call you from the station. You were not home. Yours, Lothar." Or Ule's text on the back of a photograph from 1950: "The best hours of my life were those when I was beside you." Koni always said "*okadelonchik*" and that's what my family later always called eau de cologne. And all of them said "*karasho*" instead of "*khorosho*." None of the boys suspected that I was in love with Lothar. How surprised they were when it came out after Lothar's departure. Till, in particular, couldn't understand it—he, the adult, didn't see it. "You behaved the same toward all of us." Much later a teacher at the circus school where I worked remarked, aptly: "When Cecilia Alexandrovna likes somebody, she flirts with everyone."

While writing these memoirs, I always have the images of those years in front of me. I sit by the sea and write. I imagine Lothar is walking there. Yes, that boy looks like him, I think, when I see some slender blond guy walking along the beach. I rejoice as if this guy would actually be Lothar and as if we weren't separated by an entire lifetime . . .

Happy days. This was the last summer before the war. Lothar and I were already seventeen. For some time Lothar had been coming to see me on his own. It was the first time that it was just the two of us. At some point I said that I would be worried about an inferiority complex; that I would be worth less than other people. That was what I felt. Lothar looked at me seriously and said slowly: "Once you step into life, you meet many more people, and then you get to know your own value." I've kept a postcard depicting two children: one laughing, the other crying. The text beneath one says "optimist," and the other, "pessimist." When Lothar saw the postcard, he pointed to the laughing child saying, "This is your face." And then he pointed to the crying child and said, "And those are your thoughts." Lothar was very bright and caring. He was convinced that he, as a man, was responsible for everything. The whole "burden" of the person next to him would be his to carry.

In my room up in the loft he once said, "If someone calls my father a spy in my presence, I'll beat him . . ." And looking at his gritted teeth, the clenched fists, and the look in his eyes, I could imagine how he would have. That remained a trauma for him throughout his life. Not long ago I learned from common acquaintances that shortly before his own death, Lothar spoke about his father's arrest as a German spy in the USSR. "Father worked in the underground," he told me during one of his visits. "We seldom saw him. He was forced to hide. When we met it was at night on a small path over some canyon. And when the fascists came to power, we emigrated to the USSR, a country where we thought we could live freely and undisturbed. And then he was accused of being a spy . . ."

That was in 1937.

They have no civil rights—the mother, the sister, and him. A friend of the mother, Else Wolf, the wife of the antifascist writer Friedrich Wolf, takes the whole family in. Wolf himself is at that time in an internment camp in France. Solely through the efforts of Vsevolod Vishnevskii, he gets a Russian passport and comes to Moscow. Else is an amazing woman. I can only bow before her, or now, the memory of her. It was a terrible time. Endless arrests. Endless betrayals. Friends, children, parents spied on each other. One was afraid to meet and talk to one another. But Else isn't afraid of anything. She takes in the family of someone arrested and is herself without a husband but with three children. The Wloch family lived in the Wolfs' apartment at Nishnii Kislovskii Lane, fourth floor, until December 16, 1940. That day the Wlochs left for Germany. Lothar had applied for an exit visa on September 13 because he thought that would be a lucky number. He received the visa on December 13. "I want to tell you something," said Lothar, while we were passing the gate of the office of the writers' town. (There is an office there now; in our time there was a forest.) In a voice wooden with tension I asked: "What is it?" We were on our way to the railroad station. End of August. Sun. Earlier, I had picked raspberries for a long time—the season's last fruit, the sweetest. With effort, I filled a glass, because I so wanted to give him a feast.

"No, I probably should not tell you, when I'm going away . . ." "Why?" My God, how much I wished he would say it, though I well knew what words Lothar would say. "So, say it?" I asked him gently. We walked on silently for a while.

"I love you."

Silence around us. A locomotive whistles. I tried to be calm. "It would have been better for you not to have known . . ." He didn't ask whether

I loved him too—he was probably convinced I did. It caused him grief that there would be no prospects for me . . . he was worried for me. But that was Lothar: He will manage somehow, but he feels responsible for helping the other person. When his mother died, Else Wolf wrote to me: "Lothar refuses any help. He wants to do everything for her by himself . . . he's always helping everyone else, takes care of them. After Erna's death he remains restless. The whole load is on his shoulders." [. . .]

"I want to build up socialism. No question about it, but not that kind that you have here," Lothar says to me, walking up and down in the room.

And then he became very rich. He was a manager. He was an architect and built all over the world, but not in our country, of course. But he didn't believe in a happy future for the people. The contradictions with which he was confronted from his earliest youth and which he was never able to resolve, tormented him. He committed suicide. He requested that his ashes be blown away in the wind, which was what happened. He was fifty-two years old. [. . .]

A whistle. The boys have come to pick me up to go swimming at the pond. They are always whistling from the gate because we have a big German shepherd dog, Jef. He doesn't let anyone in. Merely the sight of him instills fear. He loves me very much, more than anyone else in the family . . .

Lothar also had a big dog, a Saint Bernard. His name was Troll. A magnificent dog. Lothar loved it very much. I remember that this dog once got ill with distemper, which developed into pneumonia. How Lothar nursed this dog! He made it compresses at night and didn't leave it, which, of course, made me sad. I prayed to God that the dog would soon recover and that Lothar would join us once again in our walks and games. [. . .]

We didn't meet during winter. It was only a "summer friendship," for when we came to Peredelkino during the holidays. All the boys lived at the Wolfs' dacha. Only in the last winter before the war did the boys come to visit me at the Moscow apartment to celebrate the 7th of November. All of them were wearing dark suits with a red carnation in the buttonhole. Lothar wore a dark suit too and he was of course the most handsome one of all. [. . .]

And then Anarik came after Lothar's departure. He brought me a note from Lothar and told me how sad Lothar was when he wanted to hear my voice one last time and say goodbye, but I wasn't home. Like a madwoman I dashed out of the apartment when the door closed behind Lothar forever. Forever! No! It couldn't be! Why? I went down on the street in tears and ran to my friends Soya and Vera. We walked through the city for a long time, and my poor friends calmed me down as best as they could. But could they?

When I heard that Lothar had received the exit visa, I asked my friend Prolet to talk to him (his father was also assassinated in 1937) and convince him to stay. "I don't see any prospect here for me and us and that's why we have to leave." And as much as Prolet tried to convince him that it would be even worse for Lothar in Germany, Lothar was convinced that he was doing the right thing. From today's point of view one can say he was right. But back then . . . ? The Germans knew very well that his father wasn't their spy. What kind of trap were the Wlochs putting their heads in? For the life of me, I couldn't understand it. It only became clear to me after the war, when I read [US Ambassador W. Averell] Harriman's daughter's book: Hitler, who was busy preparing for war, sought to return to the Reich as many expatriate Germans as possible. That's why the Wlochs were allowed to enter.

Lothar gave me his passport photograph that was made for the passport for stateless people. I have enlarged the photograph and framed it. The passport photograph itself got lost. I also can't remember what was written on the back of it . . .

In the beginning the picture hung above my daybed. Then I took it with me when we were evacuated. En route, I gave the picture to Koni, who took it safely and in one piece to Bersut. Now it hangs once more in my old room at the head of the bed. The picture has returned to its "original" place from where I removed it when I got married. It made me somehow calmer: I had my old order back . . .

Once, during the day, the rain surprised the boys at my house. All of them were wearing shorts and it got very cold. I gave Ule, the youngest of them, my fur coat. My god, how beautiful he looked. We couldn't take our eyes off him. He is a handsome boy, and in this jacket he looked like a prince, a Little Lord Fauntleroy. My cousin Raja's eyes and mine followed him lovingly for a long time. This picture is fixed in my memory.

Early morning at 3 a.m. I jump out of bed, prepare sandwiches. A whistle. I walk with baskets to the garden gate. We are going to pick mushrooms. We also have to pick up Sofia Bespalova. We arrive at her dacha but in her garden two dark cars are parked. All the windows are open, and it is silent. We looked at each other and walked slowly into the forest. For a long time nobody said a word. Then, gradually, our youth, the sun, the birds, and the aromas of the forest prevailed. We picked mushrooms, called out to each other and laughed. Ule didn't leave my side the whole time; he clung to my skirt, so to speak. He constantly asked for one of the sandwiches and claimed that he should get more than the others because he was carrying the basket with the provisions. I made it a condition, however, that he earned a right to eat only when he found ten porcini mushrooms.

Lothar found a lot of oak boletes, which I envied. Finally he felt sorry for me and gave me a mushroom. Ule immediately demanded that I should kiss the mushroom (which I did, of course, with joy) and then grumbled: "I can't pick mushrooms, I carry the sandwiches. Ziloosh, give me something to eat."

We took the train back and Lothar never took his eyes off me for the entire journey.

Later, during the war, in their letters all the boys referred to this mushroom-picking expedition with great joy.

But the 16th of December drew ever closer. The train departed at 8:45 p.m. At 7:30 p.m. Lothar called me from the station, but I wasn't home. He had come to my house at 4 p.m. It was already dark outside and the meeting was short. I only remember that he told me he'd changed the tram several times (at that time trams were still going over the Maly Kamenny Bridge) in order to get rid of any pursuers. A man and a woman in civilian clothes had followed him. That's why he came so late to me. But he'd managed to shake them off. He couldn't stay long as he had to go to the station soon. He implored me to take care of myself. "What will become of you when I go?" In the hall he shook my hand and said twice: "Goodbye."

That was all. I kept the cigarette butt even to this day. The entire life consisted only of thoughts, ideas, and dreams. [. . .]

The Fedins visited the Ivanovs. Nina allowed us to read Zweig, whom her father didn't yet permit her to read.[172] With a key she opened the little bookcase and got the book out. One after the other we read it, listening to the novella while alternately standing guard by the window to see the return of the Fedins in time to put the book back. But Nina's parents didn't come back that soon. "And he thought of the invisible woman, incorporeal and passionate, as one might think of distant music," is the last sentence in *Brief einer Unbekannten* [*Letter from an Unknown Woman*]. We were silent for a long time. Then Nina put the book back in its place and closed the case. That was all. We had actually only read a novella. But the way it penetrated me, my heart and my thoughts, it left such a deep channel that never went away for the rest of my life. The scar never healed. This day was the start of my inner woman's world. I started to dream and to wait. *Brief einer Unbekannten* shaped me as a woman. I, too, wanted only one man throughout my entire life. [. . .]

When I worked during the evacuation at a theater, I assumed his name as my stage name—Z. A. Wloch. I didn't care for anyone else; I didn't need anyone, although I was only eighteen years old. Everything passed me by. When I left Chistopol, the girl in the box office found the courage to tell me at last: "Many pilots asked me to introduce them to you. But I only said that I wouldn't even dare to put this idea forward to you." [. . .]

And then I had to say goodbye to Else Wolf, who left for Berlin in 1945. I knew that Lothar was still alive. I gave her my first letter to take with her to Lothar. It was just a miracle, that after such a horrific war we were both still alive, just living at different "poles." In the beginning, even with his first letter in my hands, I still couldn't believe that this was reality and not a dream with which I had lived for five years . . .

But enough of that. I had waited five years. Now I had to act. We had to see each other, but how? I rack my brain. I ask Else Wolf to help me, but she is not yet able to. I talk about it with Koni. He is our main postman. He is in love with Lothar's sister Margot. I think that he loved her most of

172. Stefan Zweig (1881–1942) was an Austrian writer distinguished in poetry, essays, short stories, and drama. He was especially renowned for his vivid portrayals of both fictional and historical figures. At the height of his literary career in the 1920s and 1930s, Zweig was among the most widely translated and celebrated authors in the world.

all, but he was confronted by a dilemma: either do the work that he wants to do or marry Margot. Once, when he flew in from Berlin, he drove directly to me from the airport and, as soon as he came into the room, started to cry inconsolably. I was so shocked. He couldn't say a word. I didn't know what to do and was in complete despair. The most horrific scenarios went through my head—even that his father was arrested. I went to my parents to ask what I should do. I gave him some water to calm him down and finally he did and talked of his great love for Margot who, in the meantime, had gotten married. Only now did Koni realize that he couldn't live without her. Up until that point he had only tried to decide whether or not to live with her. I didn't donate one of Koni's letters, in which he reveals his innermost thoughts in great detail, to his father's museum along with all the others. I think the key to his problems was that he could never do what he wanted, but always did what he had to. That was his tragedy. [. . .]

Eight years ago Emmi Wolf, Mischa's former wife, came to visit me to record my memories of Friedrich Wolf on tape. In passing, she mentioned that Lothar had died the year before. The name "Lothar" upset me all over again. I never thought that his death would "bring me back to him." There wasn't a single day in this year in which my thoughts didn't revolve around him. Lothar is, once again, inseparable from me. As a dead man. I look at his photograph with Koni, which was given to me by a DEFA film crew and see . . . two dead men. But they are always with me, in my thoughts, before my eyes . . .

I have never again asked anyone about Lothar. When the subject came up, I listened. Just once (a long time ago) when Else came to the Soviet Union and we invited her for lunch. The lunch was a failure. Maybe Il'ia Lvovich was annoyed about something or deep in his thoughts, but he didn't take part in our conversation. Impatiently I waited for lunch to be over. Finally! I went with Else on a walk. I was dying to get some information out of her, but she kept her lips closed tight. Suddenly, when we had almost reached the pond, Else told me that Lothar was planning to come to Moscow in the autumn. "Please ask him to call me. Give him my telephone number." "But of course, without a question. He has your telephone number."

Why did I never ask after Lothar? I think this was mostly a matter of self-preservation. Why upset everything again, reenter his life, disturb his peace? He had a wife and two sons. And as far as I know, at the outset he was happy. And now this . . . Now that he's gone, I'm full of questions and want to know everything. How much I longed to meet him and how much I was afraid of it. "No, no, we mustn't meet"—this was my firm resolve. "I was seventeen then and now . . ." But I so wanted to see him, to talk to him. "What does it matter that so many years have passed? It doesn't mean anything." And my firm resolve was that we had to meet up. Somebody told me that he was very much afraid of traveling to Russia and now suddenly . . .

But, as always, life has made decisions for us. In the autumn of 1961, the wall was built between East and West Berlin. He lived in West Berlin, and he wasn't able to surmount this wall.

Konrad Wolf
From: War Diary

August 16, 1943

2:15 p.m., a sovkhoz[173] southeast of Boromlya (Svyoklovychny)

Another redeployment and I couldn't finish writing my notes. So, we were driving on August 10 for about two hours and then—a breakdown. Something wrong with the engine. We prepared to sleep in the car. I slept badly, it was very cold, it rained, and things pressed onto me everywhere. Early in the morning of August the 11th we continued and arrived at 8 a.m. at the village Raznoe, about 20 kilometers south east of Krasnopol, where three days before the Germans had been driven out. We are nicely accommodated: Tsygankov and I are in one house, the rest next door. There is more work today. There are prisoners of war. They hid in the forest, but hunger had driven them out. I interrogated two of them: a lieutenant who was terribly stupid and only knew one thing: "The Führer is thinking for us," "The

173. A sovkhoz was a state-owned farm in the Soviet Union, organized on a large, industrial scale. Unlike kolkhozy (collective farms), where members shared in the profits, workers on sovkhozy were employed by the state and received fixed wages.

Führer will know," and so on. The next day I interrogated the young gunner from the 7th tank division. He was more interesting, because he only arrived here on July 30 from Mainz, where he was on leave. He described interesting things about Germany. Then I had a look at the looted literature that had piled up. Then I translated a flyer and slogans for loudspeaker use. [. . .]

February 10, 1944

Today there were a few incidents, if you can call them that. But with the little material we have, every little thing, every bit is an "incident." Today we had a meeting of all members of staff. And something happened there that hurt my self-esteem a bit. Because it was a meeting for all members of staff it was only natural that I went there too. Everyone was gathered, and after Kalashnik entered and looked at everyone in the room, he said casually that Wolf doesn't need to be here. Well, I left the room of course immediately and, admittedly, everything inside me was boiling with rage. In my view I'm a member of this department and I'm entitled to take part in general meetings. But now, suddenly, when secret things are talked about, my presence is not needed. What have I done to deserve this distrust? Well, in this case I felt mortally offended. I would understand if it had happened in the first months of my stay in this department. But I've been here for more than a year now. I can see clearly that many look at me as if I were a young braggart whose only value is in knowing the language that didn't cost him any effort to master. Oh well, in a way I can understand that. But I will prove that youth doesn't always mean inexperience and immaturity. This year of service in the army has taught me a lot—most of all, that you can't take insults too much to heart, as it only makes people unhappy. In the work of everyday life one can protest, fight back, or discuss things. You can't do that in the army, and that is why you have to get used to it. You have to bury these feelings deep inside you, for when this period is over you can let them out again. [. . .]

September 10, 1944

I made a decision to write more often in my diary, but turns out it can't be a daily book but a weekly book. It seems as if great things are going to happen soon. We've been able to feel it for the last few days. An incredible amount of technical gear of all sorts was moved on the Warschauer Chaussee. Then we had a visit from Rokossovskii,[174] Bulganin,[175] and Telegin.[176] Today the air was full of the thunder of planes flying over us. In short, it will get tough for the Germans, even the SS. So far, we don't know any details about the results and dimensions of this operation, because we're isolated from the intelligence unit, which is our only source of information. I have to break off my notes as I have to be on duty [. . .]

Friedrich Wolf
Letter to Else Wolf

October 2, 1943

Meni dearest,

Sixteen days of being on the move before I get the chance to write to you for the first time. But we have hardly any time to breathe. Always either marching or on the truck. Until we found our formation in the terrain before the march, far away from any train tracks; the best connection would have been a speedboat, but we are landlubbers.

The heat here in October is the same as in Moscow in July. The corn harvest has just finished; wonderful *arbuzy* [watermelons] and sweet *dyni* [honeydew melons], the sea, the silver-gray landscape, similar to Provence, and, up until now, a cloudless sky.

If it weren't for the war! Darkness is rising up from the ground. As recently as last winter I had little idea what those Hitler bastards could do! The city of Mariupol is completely burned and smashed. We arrived there ten hours after the Germans had left. In every house they set mines

174. Konstantin Rokossovskii (1896–1968) was a Soviet Polish military leader who held senior command positions in the Red Army during World War II.

175. Nikolai Bulganin (1895–1975) held a number of important political posts in the Red Army during World War II and served on Stalin's State Defense Committee.

176. Konstantin Telegin (1899–1981) was a Soviet general and political officer who played an active role in the World War II campaigns in Belarus, Poland, Pomerania, and Berlin.

and bombed everything systematically, regardless of whether there were still old women and children inside. The big hospital was also devastated. In Rostov-on-Don the wonderful great theater was destroyed, the Institute of Pediatrics, and all the villages on the way, even the smallest hut! They drove the people into the fields, and their cows and sheep, which they couldn't take with them, were machine-gunned. In the little village of Novopokrovskaya [Novopokrovka] near Melitopol they bashed little children's heads in with rifle butts, murdered and burned down everything like in the Thirty Years' War. Einsiedel is completely shocked.[177] And shocked too about the "*Übermensch*-material" that we capture . . . Eighteen-year-olds from the Bavarian Palatinate who can't subtract or divide; seventy-seven minus twenty-nine they couldn't solve for the life of them. "Who was Goethe?"—"Schiller?"—"Bismarck?"—"He was a strong man."—"When did he live?" (Einsiedel could not believe his ears.) When asked, "Who was Goethe?" the third one replied: "He built Goethe Street."—Those are the eighteen-, nineteen-year-olds! The older ones do know more. I spoke to many Alsatians who had deserted. Up to 30 percent of the Hitler army companies consist of foreigners—Alsatians, Poles . . . Sometimes when you see these boys from the Palatinate and the crimes that they performed without thinking and in such a brutish way, one loses every desire for the old *Heimat*.—

Meni Dearest, excuse my outbursts! But I'm often in despair when I see these "Germans"!—How are you? Are you still working away in your museum? And Mischa, the eloquent speaker and diplomat? Ludwig is heavily involved in action, but more as an economic director and lion tamer, but he is doing fine. We—that is, the boss, Einsiedel, and I—are mostly out among our "*Willi*'s" [*Freiwillige*, or volunteers] where the troops are and where we work. The roads are well maintained, magnificent colorful deciduous trees, but then again flat land like a plate and no trees at all and lots of air strikes with constant explosions and bombs. The main thing is that things are moving forward, *na zapad* [in the background],

177. Heinrich Graf von Einsiedel (1921–2007) was a German World War II officer, politician, and author. In August 1942, he was shot down near Stalingrad and captured by Soviet forces. During his captivity, he voluntarily attended an antifascist school, where Friedrich Wolf was among the instructors.

and probably we will be soon as well! It just has to finish soon with Hitler and all this filth, if possible, this winter!

Is Lena there? How did it work out with the metrics? The school? The maps? What does she look like? And what about literature? Theater? Oh well, it really doesn't matter! It will happen when the right time comes.—Still, if I could only write again! My heart is heavy with things I want to say! If I'm still even able to write? Let's hope for the best! It would be such a shame if I couldn't!

Please give my regards also to Elisabetha and Boris and Hänschen! Are they all well? It's been so long that I've been away from you all! Oh and I nearly forgot my little Koni! How is he doing? Please send him a big kiss from his papa! He must be outside Kiev! When I see the young lieutenants here, I often think of him!

We've got lots of work to do! Let's hope we'll be back at the beginning of November!

Many kisses, Meni Dearest

Manle

Greetings from Einsiedel. Please write Koni my P.P. 19 640

Konrad Wolf
Letter to parents

April 15, 1944

My dears!

The past few days have brought me two letters from you. First, I want to say thanks for the communication of Papa's personal greeting for me. You'll be surprised who brought me his message. It happened exactly as Papa wrote it himself. One of his pupils visited us—Sinzinger, a great guy. He has just gone to the front and is working very hard there. And what do you think of our recent successes? It really is a catastrophe for the German army, simply for the fact that in only forty days, thirty-seven thousand prisoners were captured in the Crimea region. Comrade Kobus is going to Odessa, his home city, in the next few days. Naturally he is very much looking forward to it. I can understand him: Returning home after two and a half years is a great joy. Sasha is now working right at the front line as well. To be honest, I envy him, because I can't stand just sitting here anymore. I have been promised, however, that I will soon be transferred to the front as well. And so, I'm doing my work as usual, and nothing has changed much in my life. Gregor is now working hard too, as they have made good progress in their advance. I can't understand what makes him so unhappy, because I think the work gets more interesting the nearer you get to the front. But it'll get busy for us too. That's what we're hoping for, anyway, because we don't want to remain behind the Ukrainian front divisions.

Spring has come, finally, but it's certainly taken its time. The temperatures are already so high that you can go without a military coat. The blossoms on the trees are now near bursting; it will probably soon turn green everywhere. The roads also dry out, which is particularly important for us.

Except for your letters, I hardly get any letters these days. Sometimes Ule writes, Anarik or other friends, but those are rare events. Zilya hasn't written in ages. But maybe that is because I haven't written to her for a long time. All the same, could I ask you please to ask her why she's not writing? Maybe she is sending the letters to the wrong address. Nina has not written to me since my departure from Moscow and I haven't written to her since then either. We had a few arguments, but I don't want to write about it in detail, it is quite complicated and confusing. I just wanted to let you know so that you don't wonder why she isn't writing. If you do want to know the details, you have to ask Zilya. I tried to explain the problems to her and asked her advice in some matters. All in all, I have to admit, that nothing goes right with me in terms of women. Either I'm too naive, an idiot, or I was born a true woman hater and an eternal bachelor. Which of and whether any of those is true, the future will show. Oh well, it isn't all that important, although it is quite nice to receive a letter from a girl every now and then. In this war situation all these questions, which would take first place in normal life, are pushed into the background. Not everyone feels like that though. Even at the front, some manage to prioritize this topic.

I'm probably boring you with my reflections and that's why I send my regards now. Greetings to the Rappoports, Elisaveta Mich., Nyura (I also include the Fischers, and others).

Many heartfelt kisses to you all,

Yours, Koni

Friedrich Wolf
Letter to Koni

Moscow, October 1944

Koni dearest,

Once again, a firm birthday kiss for you! I trust you have received my long letter (written in German) that I sent you two or three weeks ago? Today the other novella, *Heimkehr der Söhne* [*The Return of the Sons*], has arrived still warm from the printer—it's the first copy! The October issue of *IL* [*Internatsional'naya Literatura*] with my new play *Dr. Wanner* has unfortunately not been published yet.

Today was an important day: our Red Army's invasion of East Prussia. I believe nothing can stop the advance now. It might be of importance to Meni and to me as well, although I've taken on different work for the committee.

Sasha tells us that your health has improved recently and that you aren't thin as a beanstalk anymore; it's about time your body filled out a bit more and your hero's chest expanded! It's a shame that you can't do any sports there! And how is your heart? Do you still have discomfort?

Koni dearest, my last letter contains all my best wishes for you. Take a look at what the mother in my novella (pages 114–15) says to her youngest!

When there are difficult situations in life, where no one can give advice or help, then everyone, according to his own conscience, has to make bold decisions and follow this path firmly to the end. The greatest courage—and that applies also in the war—is *Zivilcourage,* which means sticking steadfastly to your convictions in all important matters and speaking up for them! It might make you unpopular with lesser lights sometimes; but in the end it's the right thing to do and the upright person will never regret it. On the Place Danton in Paris you can read on the plinth of Danton's monument: *Pour vaincre les ennemis il faut de l'audace, encore de l'audace, toujours de l'audace*! To defeat enemies you must have audacity, more audacity, always audacity!

You know that Lenin often quoted this phrase in particular. I chose it in 1933 as the motto for my *Professor Mamlock.*

I would be very interested to hear what you think about *Heimkehr der Söhne*? What touched you and what remains unclear or unresolved for you? I wrote this novella in particular with the German youth of today in mind, who are still feeling their way in the fog . . . And will probably have to deal with the Nazi legacy for a long time after the war is over. But the older ones, too—the mother and the old Professor Schittenhelm—will need to struggle hard, very hard, through the self-created jumble of inertia and lies. If you see Sinzinger, you can give him the novella to read as well. The piece is partly a fruit of the work I did with the group that he was a part of.

It is commendable that you are taking account of your life and your experiences. Meni and I were very interested; later it will be an important reminder for you of these tumultuous times.

For now, my Koni, once again all the best for your future! Stay healthy and keep your spirits up! We really want to celebrate your next birthday together, in peace and in a world without Hitler or similar figures who belong in a zoo.

Once again, a big birthday kiss,

From your Papa

Erna Wloch
Letter to Margot Wloch

December 30, 1944

My dear grown-up daughter!

It's great that the book arrived in time for Christmas and that you enjoy it. It is lovely, isn't it, and breathes so much purity.

And this brings me right away to the most important part of your letter. What I was most afraid of has happened, and I'm surprised that you didn't say anything during the holidays. I wasn't going to mention it because I wanted to hear what you thought first. You're almost grown up, fully developed, but still we all enjoyed your childlike goodness. I'm very proud of it, and it is the very thing that brought us together again in all things. I'm a part of you and you stand absolutely on a par with our son, my dear, grown-up daughter. That must give you resoluteness in all the dirt around you, and that must nourish in you the commitment never to let it go.—You want to be a doctor. Try to see it this way and make it clear for yourself. When a young person matures, the sex drive comes into existence naturally, and most people are, unfortunately, sexual animals. They are subject to this drive more than any others that they may have inside them. Most of the time, however, they brag about it more than they actually know, and a really clever person doesn't talk smut but knows that the pairing of two people (man and woman) can be something significant, and must be, if you want to keep your self-respect later in life. When you arrived at the train station, I could already see what was going on inside those other girls. If you can't defend yourself in any other way, then keep your innermost thoughts to yourself and pretend to the outside world that those things are old hat and nothing new to you. Everything usually settles after a while like a worn-out record.—With regard to the bullies, I feel quite uncomfortable. But once you have toughened up against what you hear the girls talking about, then the other pigs will not be able to embarrass you and you'll be able to give them the cold shoulder. Under all circumstances, hit; beat them up if anyone dares to lay a finger on you.

And forget the consequences. This was always my best strategy.—Should anyone talk to you suggestively, you can safely tell them that your parents didn't bring you up to be a sex animal, but that you go to school in order, first and foremost, to get what you need for your mind.—Lothar has probably put up with worse, and I know how often he suffered. But he came through on his own account, and nothing, absolutely nothing, of this nonsense stayed within him. Imagine: Coming from your pure, happy home, right into barracks where, on top of everything, married couples were staying as well. It was really horrendous. But take our son as your model and, in all situations, remind yourself of me and my trust in you both, and nothing can hurt you. And don't think for a moment that you'll miss out on something. Oh no—we are really normally inclined people, and you shouldn't give anything away too soon, because if you do, something might break inside you that you'll never get back. Please continue to let me know how things are going, without exaggeration or untruths, and I will intervene at the right time and in the right place.

You should put all your strength into studying. Study, study, study and if at all possible, go outside. Do some sport. Are you able to do some skiing up there? Or ice-skating? I can send you some skates right away.

Lothar had already seen what was going on in Zakopane and was very worried for you. You know that he feels like a true brother to you and he was glad that you were finally able to come home, and he's now reassured. And wouldn't you agree with me that he should stay like this? It's not easy for you. I know that only too well. But it's the first opportunity to prove yourself. Now you have to show what you got from us; strong characters are always formed in difficult situations. Of course it would have been wonderful if you could have slipped through the next few years sheltered by me. This ordeal, however, serves you better for life. Lothar has passed it, and so will you, so that we can continue to look into each other's eyes fair and square.

You will remember that there were always many people coming and going in our house. And, by God, not everyone was inclined in the same way as Father and I. But when I said to Father: "This guy is not coming into this house again," Father knew exactly that the guy was looking at me in a way that I would not have expected from a comrade.

Unfortunately, only the fewest marriages come into being via comradeship, most come via the bedroom, which is then called love, but it is a far cry from actual love. First of all, you should build your own life and then sidle up with any human being who you would also accept as a comrade; then, one day, at your side will be a comrade who you will need for the rest of your life.

So, my child—I think this letter will help you going forward a lot. Please don't be astonished that I'll be sending this letter to Lothar first. The three of us are as one, and Lothar must also know what's on your mind. And in this way you will always treat each other freely and openly. This is important and concerns all three of us.

I'm pleased that Christmas went well where you are. For me, it was the saddest Christmas of my life. But thank God it is over now. Oh, there is one piece of news that you'll enjoy. I'm parting my hair again. But it has turned completely white. Nice, isn't it?

My dear, that's all for today; the rest of the page is for comments from Lothar.

Many kisses and warmest wishes,

Your mother

Postscript from Lothar Wloch

Magdeburg, January 2, 1945

My dear Margochka!

I have your letter to Ma here and read her reply and, to be honest, I'm not at all surprised. After I visited you in Zakopane I had expected it, and I'm glad you commented on it. Most of all I'm happy that you wrote to Ma first of all, because you know, she is more than a mother to both of us.—She is our best comrade.

I don't want to add anything to what Ma has already written. Just remember one principle, and always act in this way: We both want to live our lives in a way that we can be held accountable before our Ma and our father.

So, and now belatedly, I want to wish you a Happy New Year, a year in which we'll see each other again at home. Warmest wishes, kisses, and embraces from your

Lotka

Konrad Wolf
Letter to parents

May 29, 1945

My dears!

I don't know if my letter will reach you at the address I'm sending it to, but I wouldn't know where else to send it. Jan Vogeler went to Moscow yesterday and he will tell you more about my life and goings-on here. In brief: I'm in Berlin, working as a journalist for the local newspaper *Berliner Zeitung*. Everything happened so fast and so unexpectedly for me. Suddenly, I was called to see Mel'nikov, and from there I was transferred here, where I'm now working. Actually, my service contract formally ends on May 30 but, in fact, I think I will stay here whether I want to or not. My colleagues are the—to you not unfamiliar—[Fritz] Erpenbeck (my immediate line manager), Major Feldmann (Papa knows him very well and he sends his regards), [Alexander] Kirsanov, and others. Through my work I have dealings with [Hans] Mahle, [Otto] Winzer, Pieck and others. In a word, everyone is here. It's obvious that there is lots to do because the work is becoming increasingly demanding. That's how it is; even at the end of the war you can't get a little rest. [Marshall Boris] Shaposhnikov was here as well by the way. I wanted to talk to him—before I get roped in here for good—and get permission to go back to Moscow, at least for a month, but he left earlier than I thought. Of course, somehow I'll try to manage it anyway, but it will be difficult because there is such a shortage of people. But I will insist on it as soon as everything is running smoothly here.

There are all sorts of rumors about where Papa is supposed to go. All sorts of areas were mentioned, except for, of course, Berlin. But you know where to find me and I hope that one day a very familiar face will be in my waiting room . . .

You see, my dears, how abruptly fate can toss people hither and thither. Up until now (and actually even still) I had no idea about the work of a journalist, but now I whiz through the streets of the city on my motorbike collecting material. In any case I will try not to make a mess of it, although it is not easy.

My dears please excuse the obscure, illegible, and short letter, but duty calls.

Best wishes to all acquaintances. Please tell Hilde Plievier[178] that I met her brother near Berlin and he sends his regards. He works in the local administration and is doing well.

Heartfelt kisses,

Yours, Koni

Markus Wolf
Letter to parents

Berlin, June 4, 1945

(Berliner Rundfunk, Charlottenburg–Masurenallee)

My dears!

Well, today I reached the Radio Palace on time. This is going to be my "workplace" for the foreseeable future. I don't really know where to start. There were no problems with the flight. Stopover in Minsk. After the River Oder there was a little strip of devastated ground, excavated fortifications. And then, until Berlin, it was pleasant, clean, and above all undamaged

178. Hildegard Piscator (born Plievier, 1900–1970) was a German actress and writer.

villages and towns surrounded by forests and lakes, magnificent highways and so on. The outlying districts, from the air, look totally unscathed. But then we circled over Berlin! You wouldn't believe your eyes. It looks totally unnatural from the air. Street after street, district after district utterly devastated, nothing but hollow shells, and it is only the traffic on the roads that have been cleared that lets you recognize that below, this really is Berlin and not some scale model from the hand of an overexcited stage designer. Touchdown at Tempelhof airport.

The once magnificent buildings around the airport are all completely burned out. We go into the "waiting room"—which is just in a deserted Nazi apartment. The houses here, which once probably belonged to small-fry civil servants, are undamaged. They are all quite simple but nicely built. The cherries are ripening in the gardens. I was astonished by the amount of green in Berlin. The inner city with its narrow streets no longer exists, but in the outer districts everything is beautiful and green. Since you can only partially rebuild the inner city (if you could see it, you wouldn't believe it), Berlin is going to be a downright "green city." I couldn't imagine it any other way and Herr Stadtrat Schwenk (City Council, Planning Department) entirely agrees with me.

Moving on. I felt very strange at first. The people on the street all speak German. At the same time there are many Red Army soldiers and officers. The first impression: many bicycles, baby carriages, and a lot of young men conscripted for military service. In Tempelhof the people seemed downbeat, and they worked reluctantly. Unfortunately I don't have time to describe everything in detail. When evening came, we were picked up by a bus. We began our journey through dead Berlin and drove along almost all the main roads. The roads are mostly cleared of rubble. We looked for buildings and hoped for at least some that weren't destroyed, but all in vain. Everything, and I mean literally everything, is ruined beyond hope. It would certainly be more viable to build a new city than to clear away the rubble and ruins. Then we drove along Frankfurter Strasse. On Frankfurter Allee every now and then you can see a partially intact house. In Friedrichsfelde almost everything is working again. We are moving into a house there that has been prepared as a hotel for officers. We sat there until the next morning, waiting to be picked up, went for walks, and spoke to people.

These days you could almost forget what we saw in the city center. Relatively little damage, nice streets, beautiful buildings, the shops full, with bread and other staples, well-dressed leisurely people.

The first buses and trams are working, and they aren't overcrowded either. Extensive sections of the U- and S-Bahn are intact as well. As of today, you can get beer in the innumerable pubs, even 9 percent—priced at 50 Pfennigs. Yesterday, a Sunday, you could almost believe that there never was a war. Sport festivals everywhere, restaurants, cabarets, variety shows with colorful programs and dancing.

We went to Schöneweide and Karlshorst. The football stadium was overcrowded. Mainly young men dressed in their Sunday best. In the evening we went to the Capitol variety show; the emcee was Genschow. His wife, Renée Stobrawa, performed as well. What do you say to that? Unfortunately, I wasn't able to speak to her. It would have been pointless anyway. People are not saying nice things about her.

Well, now I'm at the broadcasting station, which miraculously is completely undamaged. Comrade Grünberg, to whom I have entrusted this letter, can tell you a few things about this enterprise. We are six men, Germans, and one major with six hundred of the "old" staff (this has to stay between ourselves). Unfortunately, the clearing out is only partially possible, since many, or in fact most, of them are needed. I think it will work with time. Our human resources boss, Mathias Klein (your acquaintance) told me today that someone you know from Düsseldorf (Krumm or something like that) has asked after you. Maybe I'll meet him.

I want to keep it brief, since there is still a battle to be fought according to the laws of courtesy. (The old men in the administration still exercise their power.)

I want to summarize my impressions:

The people of Berlin, that is from the neighborhood around the broadcasting studio, whom I have met so far, are—and this might sound strange—in complete denial that Germany is a defeated country, and that they all share responsibility for this war and its crimes. After the initial shock and fear, which were overcome in a few days, the Red Army's generosity has been taken for granted, and the complaining has begun. The people don't comprehend the catastrophe into which Hitler has plunged Germany; that they would now all starve to death without the help of the Red Army. They don't understand the significance of what the German people have been given here, and only here: the opportunity for a new beginning. We are the only German broadcasting station (very much to the dislike of Reuters, etc.) that is also listened to west of the River Elbe. People complain that the coffee is often green and not roasted; and they bemoan even more (see the SPD) that people are being sent elsewhere. And, by contrast, how humane and close to us are the Red Army soldiers, and the Russian and Ukrainian girls who are working here now. I could write many pages about that.

And the German arrogance! At a soccer match, you have nicely dressed young men standing there making dirty comments. Or take, for example, the "innocent" Germans from our courtyard: a worker's family. Already there is a lot of talk about which Nazi apartment in the front block they can move into. In discussions with neighbors, it turns out that her father (now a prisoner of war) has handed five communists over to the Gestapo, and so on.

Joy is seldom to be found. On the street I spoke to a seventy-six-year-old working woman. The knowledge and understanding that this old woman had of all the issues are rarely to be found among comrades. She remembers all phases of the workers' movement, remembers Bebel's, Liebknecht's (whom she knew), Zetkin's, Arendsee's, and others' speeches. She said: "If Bebel were still alive, he would have knocked the heads of the Social Democrats and the Communists together until they united. And then Hitler would never have risen to power. Bebel was a true leader of the working-class movement, not like Ebert and the other *Stehkragenproletarier* ["stiff-collar proletarians"].[179] Or: "We heard Trotsky speaking. He wasn't good. The right ones were Lenin and Stalin." Unfortunately such women are seventy-six years old. Still, many old comrades have come back. In order to see the picture clearly you still have to observe and weigh everything. You are going to see it soon with your own eyes.

179. A worker who, no longer identifying with the working class, uses his advancement to set himself above his peers.

Oh, I forgot the most important thing! I met Koni right away. On the first evening I heard that he works at the *Berliner Zeitung* with Kirsanov and Erpenbeck. On the third day he came to see me on his motorbike, "Pony," as a roving reporter. Our meeting was short and a bit "formal." I think as soon as our situation is stabilized, I will see him more often. He'll tell you about his days of battle in Berlin himself. Marianne Weinert wanted to visit us yesterday, as well, but we were out.

Lothar Wloch
Letter to Zilya Voskresenskaya

Berlin, January 24, 1946

My dear Zilya!

I'm sure you have received my first letter and were annoyed with me because it wasn't the expected answer. But you will understand that I was, after reading your letter, completely confused and I couldn't collect my thoughts. Now, after I've read your letter more than twenty times and know it almost by heart, I am somewhat calmer inside and am able to answer you in more detail.

I will certainly make innumerable grammatical mistakes, but this is hardly surprising after so many years and, at the moment, of no importance—the main thing is that you'll understand me.

In this letter I will, just as you have done, write about me and be completely open. It won't be easy for me because I don't like talking about myself. But to you I will reveal everything. Not because I think it's my duty, but because I want you to understand everything.

According to other people, I haven't changed at all. Of course I've grown a bit and I'm older now. But what about my heart?

You write that my life has been a completely closed book to you all. I understand that, but did you feel like that too? After all, I was much more frank and open with you and we always did understand each other. And because of that we are much more and better connected than is usually the case between people. You know that I went away then with a heavy heart and with my arrival here, a new life began. At that point in time I thought this would be a better life but now I know I was wrong. Life is always good, only the circumstances under which each of us has to live are different. It is called destiny, I believe. And my destiny seems to me like a tragicomedy. Tragic because I never find any rest, and comic because I started seeing it from that perspective. The exact dates of the last years are not important even if they played a great role in the inner life. We will talk about it when we meet up again. In those years I have often thought about you. Our time together always seemed like a long-lost dream. More than once I longed for a person like you by my side. When I heard that you are alive, I instantly thought that I had to come and see you and speak to you.

Anyhow, love! If I had to explain what it is, I couldn't find an answer. In my entire life I was forced to put my feelings second and give my mind all my strength. You know very well what I mean. I have gotten so used to this that I currently doubt whether I'm able to love at all. Remember, we once talked about which is stronger: heart or mind. You said it's the heart and, even then, I doubted it. And now it has become reality for me. In all matters it is the mind that is working foremost in me, and personal feelings are secondary. They are somewhere inside me, but I suppress them.

Currently, I'm at a low point of my life—my head has grown tired. The result is that I sometimes don't care, literally about anything at all. The only thing that gets me out of this situation is work and that's why I'm working so much. The more physically demanding the work, the better.

This is how I feel. I'm only too well aware of this. My mind is just able to conceive this, but I can't defend myself. You know that I have willpower, but only for other people; for myself I just can't find it within me.

After I have revealed my innermost feelings so openly, for the first and the last time, you will probably not want to have anything to do with me. I understand only too well, and I would therefore not be angry with, you also because I'm so unhappy with myself. Nevertheless, if you ever have the opportunity to come and visit me, please do. I so long to speak with you. I understand that this is not going to happen soon. I know for sure, however, that we will meet again. Until then, write to me, write a lot and often. I will always answer. I find it difficult to write in a letter what I want to tell and explain to you. But you will understand me, I know that.

That's it for today. I could continue writing a few more pages but Else wants to take the letter with her and for me the nights end at 5 a.m.

I kiss you wholeheartedly and wait for your reply.

Yours, Lothar

Erna Wloch
Letter to Markoosha Fischer

Berlin, February 20, 1946

[. . .] For a week now I've been completely confined to bed. That's not the usual me. But what can I do? Once I've been up for as little as a quarter of an hour, I don't feel myself again until I'm back in bed. A ridiculous state of affairs! It's mainly trouble with my circulation (which runs in our family) and then the heart's weak too. No wonder when you look at the many years one's overtaxed one's body! I was already a living corpse when I arrived here. And all that new energy (from taking on a new job, from regular and mainly nocturnal visits to the Gestapo, from air raids day and night, and from the victorious invasion of the friends from the east) was just a bluff. It's no surprise that typhus got the better of me in the end, is it? . . . Has Fate really preserved me only to get me ready for such a miserable end?

I'm anxious when I think of Lothar who still has three hard years ahead of him; he will certainly not give up halfway. It will take a heavy toll on his health in spite of all the theories about calories . . . We all have to find our way and it's not in our blood to rely on others. There is a good side too: to have gotten to know the absolute highs and deepest lows of life. Our children will benefit from that in their future. Although it has been, and still is, far too hard for the boy. The daughter has been lucky not to have experienced many bad things because the two of us have looked after her and kept her safe. She will have to fight hard for her future; she has a good character and she works extremely hard, and so it's even more difficult for her now that she carries the burden of the entire household on her shoulders, as well as all the errands on top of her school stuff. But she has no choice, because that is how our life is.

Lothar is very much liked by his older colleagues (there aren't any younger ones yet) and everyone wants to help him, with both practical and theoretical things. Everyone likes working with him. And he enjoys it too; every morning he gets up with a smile and goes to the building site in a good mood. Not every worker can say that about his workplace. With his pronounced sense of comradeship and his willingness to pitch in where help is needed, he won everyone's heart. He certainly offers his opinion openly and honestly. But where are the boys his age? You can find only the odd individual in the construction industry, although it promises a better future compared to the opportunities in the other industries here, which are still bleak.

How well I understand Thomas Mann. I can well imagine that it's possible to find a second *Heimat*. He will be able to work much better there for the time being. Fallada,[180] who disappears into rehab for his alcohol and morphine addiction every few weeks, is celebrated here in a big way. [...]

Wolf can achieve something, and is still popular, but he's very abstract and doesn't want to learn to see. Unquestionably, his *Mamlock* struck a big chord we didn't expect. We thought it would still be too early. But its pronounced humanity, in particular, is greeted with great enthusiasm. Well, the Berliners are not quite as squalid as everyone always made them out to be.

Young people in general are regarded as depraved because of twelve years of the Hitler Youth. As of yet, no one has pointed them in a new direction. The political parties have started competing for them, but who will give them something in return for what has been taken from them? And that's not considering that the fascist campaigns have had their greatest harvest among the young people, and that most of them returning home are all left alone amid the rubble, their starving parents and siblings, no opportunities for work, and are plunged into that seething cauldron of the parties who want to play politics and take the country's fate into their hands. They don't have a KARL [Liebknecht] and no ROSA [Luxemburg] as we had. [...]

180. Hans Fallada (born Rudolf Wilhelm Ditzen, 1893–1947) was a German author best known for his socially critical novels.

You can't make young people responsible for what our generation caused and what they now inherit. And I think we are far too burdened [by our mistakes] for us to be able to demand that they trust us. We should provide them with advice and assistance and in other ways give them the responsibility for what lies ahead, because they are serious and keen enough. [. . .]

Now I have reached the topic of the unification campaign. Every thinking worker longs for unification, even a unification of the whole working class. The reaction is already more than impertinent. But what are these workers affronted by? The fact that everyone's in such a rush! They know that what's served up comes from the Russian kitchen and doesn't reflect their own free will. Many still remember the repercussions of this food from earlier times. Everyone knows that the KPD perform poorly in the election before unification, and they want to go ahead with it anyway.

The SPD knows very well the mistakes it has made. Whether it reflects on them in the right way is hard to say. If it did, I think, then it would have from the start removed from party offices any people with all too much dirt under their carpets. Traditional supporters make up the bulk of the large party rank-and-file, and on top of that is the fear of a new dictatorship.

What we really need now is to establish a new socialist workers' party from all branches of society, including even those workers who used to be members of the NSDAP—but only on the condition that they can bring a spotless character reference showing that they always behaved decently. So that the mutual mudslinging finally stops, and the economy can be built up for us all, and everyone gets a political education and so we can work, and I mean really work, toward the welfare of the entire nation. What else can I say about the situation here? Because of the occupying forces everything is more difficult, since they haven't yet decided among themselves on a final treaty about the German problem. Once we have proper guidelines, which every opponent will have to follow without fail, then they can do away with a police force against the Germans and can let them freely develop—and provide only advisory support. I'm always shocked by the attitude of the international workers toward us.

I assert that the problem can be solved with some discernment. One only has to read Stalin's speech. For the past two years I've been saying that the course of history can't be stopped. Fate has taken its toll. No one is trying to find excuses for the crimes that have been committed—not even in the slightest. Every decent person is deeply ashamed. Germany has lost face. A lost war—and a war of aggression at that. One could cope with that, but having said that, it is crazy that it could even come to this: the second one of the twentieth century. Do we Germans really have to bear the blame alone? I often ask myself this question. Are you going to tell me that when you came from the West to Munich, you really couldn't see it? And when you came from the East, as a guest, to the [Palais] Bellevue, you didn't see it either? I'm convinced they would have sacrificed every German emigrant abroad, if it had come to an alliance. Not everyone who praised Hitler and was enthralled by him was a fascist. You only have to read older newspapers. Even in the years 1939 and 1940 when we were already in the middle of a war, there was the war criminal Ribbentrop pictured in Moscow, where once before they shared the plundering of the apparently dead Poland. [. . .]

There are still many glaring problems that need a solution, and until then, in my opinion, there won't be peace in the world. It would be a rewarding task for the Second International. We know very well that it looks bad in all our neighboring countries. And for that reason we have to try and bind together again.

Why are our people, our good people out there, so discouraged? Are they weaker than I am? It especially comes down to them. We can't do much here. Psychologically depressed? Oh yes, I know how it felt when I was already learning over there and was feeling absolutely responsible for it—for something that you had helped build up (What would have happened to the Soviet Union without the Third International?). I was so depressed and in despair because ultimately our soul is made from the same timber. To experience both dictatorships firsthand—I can only warn nosy people: Either you hang yourself or you fight your way through to the better part. I promised myself never ever to lie again, even if it affected the existence of the entire KPD. We can't yet say everything, but our people out there, they can. Are they afraid of the truth? You don't break so easily, if you have the necessary political support. Our life is but a battle. [. . .]

That subset of the emigrants who spit on us as well will find that it only blows back in their own faces. For us there was never a "Jewish problem." But I'm convinced that many a Jewish banker would have sacrificed the entire wealth of his people if he had been gifted his life and that of his family by Hitler. We have to get out of this lethargic mood under all circumstances. A soul alone is not enough. Head and heart have to be in there too, and then, if there is any energy left, knuckle down with both hands. My son shows them how it's done. The food situation, however, is difficult, very difficult. And in the end, everything depends on that. Let's wish that we don't have to sacrifice too many postwar victims now. The worst of the winter is nearly over. When it gets a bit lighter outside, things will look different. May spring give once again courage and strength, love and warmth to all people. [...]

George Fischer[181]
Letter to parents and brother

Berlin, March 9, 1946

Dear M & P!

Dear Vit (extra letter to farm)!

It is the "morning after" after a gentlemen's evening with Lothar, Kon, and me, which we had planned for such a long time but could never make it happen because Kon was only now able to join us from Halle.

We celebrated at my place. At 5 p.m. I picked up Kon from the Wolfs' apartment with a jeep. Then we drove to Lothar, who had just come home. He quickly changed and then shaved at my place and took a hot bath, something he doesn't often have an opportunity to do—as often as he and Margot can go and bathe at the Wolfs' apartment.

181. Although this letter and the following letter from March 11 were written in English, the originals could not be located, and they have been translated here from the German edition of this volume.

Then we talked about Kon's future. His greatest wish is to go back to school again. He wants to have a proper education, something he has always wished for and completely missed out on during the war years. He is skeptical about whether he will be released in the coming years since his German-language skill is needed. On the other hand, there are things that would support his dismissal. He wants to live here in the future, but he is afraid of coming here and then having to live like Mischa—that means having to work for the apparatus, and he wants to avoid this under all circumstances. He wants to study cinematography and believes that the best place is the school in the old part of the city where our old friend Sergei is the principal. (I asked Kon to give him regards from the whole family if he ever gets to meet him. Kon plans to see him during his annual leave in October.)

After many hours of idle and pleasant talk and steady drinking we came onto politics. Actually it was a solid lecture for Kon from Lothar, which I often had to agree with. Kon sat there, head bowed, and I had the impression that he kind of knew that the truth was being spoken. But he asked, what can and should he do? Lothar then spoke about dictatorships. He told Kon that he had to admit that he had wished the whole time for Germany's victory over Stalin, because he was deeply convinced that it would be easier to get rid of Hitler than Stalin. Then he spoke about what had happened to the communist ideals and Leninism under Stalin. He said that the communist world movement had developed solely into a spy network for Russia.

Then we spoke about personal freedom. And Lothar said that he is, in the face of the complete collapse of communism, convinced that the only way forward would be a democracy with personal freedom. We told Kon what is happening to the Germans in Berlin if they actively oppose the party line. Lothar reported on the widely discussed elections of the union congress in Berlin, how predictable they had been. Wedding was the only district where everyone voted for the SPD. Kon simply couldn't understand this. Lothar explained that Wedding is, first of all, the district where the Russians, after the invasion into the city, had been fighting in and living in the longest—with everything that comes with that; and second, that the current politics of the Russians might appeal from time to time to intellectuals, but they will not be able to withstand the careful considerations of a worker.

We continued our one-sided attack, and when I was alone for a moment with Lothar, he assured me that Kon could cope with such a lesson and that he was also due to receive one. [...]

Wolf's historic play *Beaumarchais,* which he wrote in a French internment camp, has its premiere this afternoon. We are all going. I'll take Erna to the theater and Kon will take her home. Tomorrow we—Lothar, Kon, and I—are going to see *Professor Mamlock.* I have already told you that this play has been running for the last few weeks with great success. Tonight we're having a party here in our house to which Lothar and Kon want to come, if Kon can square it with his family that he spends the first two evenings of his three-day leave away from home. He has grown into a very mature young man and has a hearty laugh and the serious forehead of a thinker. We measured our height again and he is now really taller than me, which—I told him—will one day lead to a serious breakdown of our friendship. Before we left the house in the morning (they stayed overnight and slept in the maid's bed; Kon had pushed Lothar out of the bed during the night, which Lothar interprets as typical Russian expansionism), one of our roommates took three photographs of us. I hope they turn out well. [...]

George Fischer
Letter to parents and brother

Berlin, March 11, 1946

Dear M & P!

Dear Vit (extra letter to farm)!

Saturday morning I wrote you a four-page-long letter about the previous night's gentlemen's evening with Kon, Lothar, and I. Today is Monday and I will try and report on the weekend events, which were more exhausting, after the two hard weeks, than anything has been in months or years. On Saturday afternoon I picked up Erna and Margot at 3 p.m. and took them to Max Reinhardt's Deutsches Theater, which is situated in the Russian sector of Berlin and is now managed by Wangenheim. The big event was the premiere of Wolf's *Beaumarchais,* which he wrote while in a French internment camp. Inside, the theater is completely lined with red plush; it was well heated for this occasion and appeared to me to be the most festive and aristocratic of any theater that I had ever visited in Berlin. The play is about the inner conflicts of Beaumarchais, an eighteenth-century French writer who had written *The Marriage of Figaro* (which was a revolutionary play in its time). However, even after many years in opposition to the monarchy, he hadn't bonded with the ordinary French people when they rebelled and stormed the Bastille. The play lasted four (!) hours and wasn't a success. You can imagine that afterward we discussed it a lot—for a variety of reasons . . .

As if we wanted to diminish the play's impression, Lothar, Kon, and I went to see *Professor Mamlock* on Sunday morning. The play, which was magnificently acted, was moving and was enthusiastically received by an intelligent, although not intellectual-looking, audience. It is the kind of play that gives one lots of stimulation and provokes thought. And what else would you expect of a play like that? The great praise for *Mamlock* in most of the newspapers is certainly deserved and I was glad that my fear about the play's topicality was not justified. Lothar and Kon enjoyed it too; and Wolf, who was there as well, had tears in his eyes, as did many of the other people in the audience. I'll send you the poster of *Mamlock* as soon as Wolf gives me some. During the party at our house afterward Lothar, Kon and I spoke mostly about the *Beaumarchais* and *Mamlock* productions.

At the party there were about twenty young Americans, mainly union members and some Germans with SPD and union backgrounds. The party had quite a slow start, but it warmed up later. Kon was very relaxed and delighted us with some solo presentations of songs from the Odessa underground. He quite deliberately sang those songs in a bass voice with a lack of melody and supported the whole thing with concentrated gestures and signs. Both he and Lothar were a good match and each of them had lots of fun. Kon and Lothar left at about three in the morning to go to Lothar's, who only lives ten to fifteen blocks away. It took them three (!) hours to get there. If you were to believe later reports, they staggered along the street and happily sang the "oh-so-meaningful" song, "Immer an der Wand lang" ["Always Along the Wall"]. They must have been walking around the house a few times before they "found" it. [. . .]

After *Mamlock* I had a nap for an hour, which I desperately needed, and then went to Wolf's. All the Wolf family were there, and Lotka and I got ready for another party. Mischa and I found a quiet corner where we could talk, and his lovely wife Emmi listened. We had a long but not at all bitter talk about the domestic political situation in Germany and the confrontation between the Soviet Union and the West with regard to their different views of aspects of the new developments. Mischa thought that Germany needed a limited democracy and that the greatest danger currently would be the return of the reactionaries. You could only prevent this if the SPD and the KPD could unite in a determined opposition toward all right-wing movements that expressed their views. He also said that the SPD leadership's old Weimarian approach would not be able to solve the country's problems. Only a resolute Marxist socialism could do it. He said that the British Labour government has nothing whatsoever in common with this militant socialism. His arguments about the limited democracy and the huge danger that would come from the German reactionaries (. . . which, unfortunately, I can see only half as clearly as the KPD does)—those arguments are the main trump cards that are supposed to justify the Russian concept of democracy and the unification.

Later, Lothar and Mischa had a heated argument about whether the German defense lawyers should be criticized by the German press during the Nuremberg trials. Lothar didn't share this view.

It was really, really nice, just like the old times and everyone sends their love.

Else Wolf
Letter to Zilya Voskresenskaya

August 20, 1946

Zilyenka, on the 15th Lothar came by and gave me a letter for you. Lothar called on the 17th. He was hardly able to speak. Erna has died. Zilyenka, there is no need to write about how much pain her death causes us. Her heart could not cope with everything that had happened. She died so unexpectedly. She wasn't at home but was visiting a sick acquaintance. I went to Lothar. He is in a dreadful state, but very brave as only people like he and Erna can be. Erna looked as if she was asleep and could open her mouth any minute and start speaking. It is unimaginable that she won't be here anymore. I'll go there once more and take the flowers that she loved so much. Lothar refuses any help. He wants to do everything for her by himself. I understand him. He cried a lot and said that she shouldn't have died so prematurely. How many plans they still had! We all knew that she was very sick, but we never thought that she would die so soon. Lothar got the news of her death on the 16th at 10:30 a.m., which is the very day and hour when, exactly six years ago, he was told his father had died. Both Lothar and Margochka are of course very independent, they will go on exactly in the same way as when they lived together with Erna. I will support them, of course, but can't replace Erna. There is too much sorrow at this time.

Warm regards, Zilyenka,

Yours, Else O.

August 31

Zilyenka, again warmest greetings. Lothar is very brave. When we were at the crematorium, he gave a speech about his mother himself. I don't see him often now. No time. Soya leaves in three days. Then I'll go and see them more often. Soya will tell you all about it.

Again, warmest greetings

Yours, E. O.

I believe that Koni will come to Moscow soon.

Markoosha Fischer
Letter to Else Wolf

July 31, 1947

Dear, dear Else,

I shall I try and explain why I haven't written? I don't know myself. Maybe now that I'm finished with the book my head is free again. I have been under great pressure while writing the book. It's also possible that, in general, I am too inward looking. I have "acquaintances" but no "friends," and I have rather forgotten how to pour my heart out to someone. But, whatever the reason, it is not that you are no longer close or dear to me, because you have always been. When I think of "friends" I always think of you.

I want to write a bit about my book. That has been and is a great event; and a huge manuscript, almost one thousand typewritten pages. I have cut it a lot, and it's now about 750 pages long. It's the story of a Moscow merchant's family between 1892 and 1942 (it ends in an occupied Russian village), three generations with people of all sorts of convictions and temperaments. My publisher (Harper, one of the oldest and best American publishing houses) praises the book as exceptional and has promised itself (and me) a huge success. I can't quite get used to the idea that I have written a novel. The book will be published in January or February.

And now I'm in the countryside with my flowers, trees (Vitya planted many young fruit trees and other trees last year), birds, mosquitoes, and so on, and enjoy nature with every fiber. You will understand what I mean. You asked me in one of your letters whether I remember Peredelkino. Very much so and every detail! I even often remember little remarks you made when planting vegetables or flowers. I often think of the big sunflower (every year I plant one here), of the radishes, and so on. There are no birches in our area, but Vitya planted one and that, too, reminds me of Peredelkino. There is very little hope that I will ever be near Peredelkino again. But I have high hopes that I will see you here; and in fact I have more than hope—it's absolutely certain that I will see you in Berlin in the spring of 1948.

I always enjoy reading that your little family has reunited again and also that you've got such a splendid addition. I don't see my family so often but I'm certainly not complaining. Everyone is alive, healthy, and hopeful for the future. Isn't that something that millions of people will envy one for? I will definitely do some work—writing or collecting material—when I come to Germany; that's one motivation, but the real reason for my journey is to see the Wolfs and Wlochs again. I have no doubt about that.

Maybe since I have now broken the ice and started writing, I will do it more often and slowly get used to keeping you up to date with our everyday life. For today it has to be enough. Please tell every single one of the Wolfs that I'm the old Markoosha who cherishes you all and that I'm thinking with great excitement about seeing you all next year.

And please, Else, don't follow my example, and write again.

Markoosha

CARE packages are on the way—food, cotton, woolens. Else, I never found out who got the packages I sent you last year. After Yura's departure everything got turned upside down, and the packages I sent for you and to the Wlochs went into "the general distribution," seeing as I had sent many there too. I just hope that someone who needed the things got them. When I'm back in the city in the autumn I can also send something other than CARE packages. What?

Konrad Wolf
Letter to Margot Wloch

Moscow, October 19, 1950

My dear girl,

It worked out wonderfully—the day before yesterday I received number 4, today number 5, so your good wishes and photograph arrived just in time, and I'm so happy and grateful for everything! Of course you'll be with me tomorrow and I'll be with you. It goes without saying that a thing like that doesn't often happen in life and the day should be only for the two of us. [. . .]

Tomorrow evening, as planned, I'll celebrate a little with Zilya. You will be there too of course—and I shall have to drink for the two of us . . . ?! On Sunday I might see Mischa. He has now finally received his furniture, his new apartment, and maybe he will be able to finish the move tomorrow or the day after; then we'll have two reasons to celebrate. We'll see . . .

I love the photograph very much, regardless of the bad paper. I can't wait for the gloves—it's so kind of you! You have a real flair for knowing what I need, because I really don't have any winter gloves, and I would wear them in any case even if I did have a pair. I'm glad that you're feeling well health-wise—stay that way, yes! [. . .]

With regard to Lothar—I did think of writing about it, but you have now touched on the subject yourself. You know my relationship with Lothar. Over the last years I still had hopes that he would learn to see things more clearly, tried my best to help him with this, but the result is the opposite. And if someone in the current time doesn't clearly show one's colors, or even chooses the wrong color, it seems almost unforgivable to me. And all this talk about "tolerance" and so on is merely a cover for one's own blindness, or even a malicious "don't want to see" position.

Lothar always talks about objectivity, but concerning his own viewpoints he's utterly subjective, the personal completely overshadows the general. When I met him briefly in Lehnitz this summer we only talked about very general things—the time was too short to "politicize" and, honestly, I wasn't convinced that it would serve any purpose (the latter remark is probably wrong, I can see this myself). So, this is in general.

But as for the two of us, and you personally, I think it's just right that he in particular finds out how it really is with us, because I think he's not convinced that we are committed to each other. And it would be unfair of you to push him completely aside now because, first of all, you are connected through a long life lived side by side, in which he has certainly tried to support you to the best of his abilities (if it didn't always have the right effect, that's is a different matter, but he meant it sincerely), and, second, you don't have to make him any concessions with regard to your points of view and political convictions. [. . .]

Else Wolf
Letter to Eva Siao

Warsaw, November 20, 1950

Dear Eva,

Finally we're in touch again! When Emi was in Prague last year, Wolf arrived just after Emi had left. But now it has worked out. I had the tiniest hope that you would accompany him, but it didn't happen since you had to take care of your son. Emi said that otherwise you would have come as well.

We only joined the Congress on the third day as we first had to go to Berlin, where W. actually should have stayed longer. However, he dragged himself away, as the Congress was undoubtedly much more important. I saw Emi straight away because he was part of the Presidium that day and therefore easy to spot. W. immediately arranged for him to visit us, and yesterday he came here. It wasn't easy for him to get away since he's involved in the Congress morning, noon, and night, but in the end, we had two hours to catch up on everything. He'll tell you all about it.

Unfortunately, I never got any news from you, otherwise I would have written much earlier. Once I tried to send you something via our friend Burgin, which proved to be the one and only opportunity. I will try sending something via the normal post; maybe it'll work. We're planning not to stay here much longer as W. hopes to do his actual work, the writing, again soon. Our permanent address is at the top of the letter.

Emi has told us a lot about you. Now you want to know what we were up to. Unfortunately I can't write in as much detail as I'd like, because there is so much going on during the Congress. The entire delegation, more than one hundred people, will come to us today. There is still much to prepare. And Emi will leave soon. But I will try to give you an update from all of us in brief. I hope that we will continue to stay in contact now.

We have now already been in Warsaw for nine months. W. has been restless in connection with his new work because we have very few people and he has to take care of everything. He has no time at all for his writing. He is compensated a little by the local theater life. Currently two Warsaw theaters are performing his plays. *Beaumarchais* has been performed more than fifty times, and at the Polish State Theatre they're showing *Tai Yang erwacht* [*Tai Yang Awakes*]. W. would have loved to go there with Emi but there was no time. The production would probably have been strange for Emi, because when Europeans play Chinese people, it's always a bit strange for a true Chinese person. But the content is the most important thing for the audience, and one has to say that the play is especially topical today, even though it was written twenty years ago. Many of W.'s plays achieve an exceptional relevance again after many years—sometimes, you have to say, unfortunately so, because nobody would have wished for the return of fascism in such blatant form.

Actually, we commute a lot between B. and here, because W. has a lot of things going on there. And it isn't really much of a distance. Our Hildchen, a very reliable girl, looks after our apartment, so that we always feel completely at home on our return. However, the commuting is tiresome, and W. especially wants to write again. He still has so many plans. On top of that he isn't young enough to waste time like that anymore. He also has a lot of sciatic pain, which makes that to-ing and fro-ing difficult for him. He wants to go to a sanatorium in February and probably afterward return to private life.

As you know my boys are in Moscow. Mischa's family is over there now as well, which makes me very sad, because in B. I at least had the possibility of seeing our grandchildren. It's impossible now. Mischenka is now over four years old and goes to kindergarten. Little Tanya turned one last June. The opposite of Mischenka, she is a dark type. She is a very energetic and lively little person. Emmi has enrolled at university and is studying Russian language and literature, *zaochno* [in absentia]. However, it is almost impossible to take care of everything, as they have a big apartment, an inefficient maid who only works eight hours, the children and so on, and on top of that all their social obligations. How she'll manage in the long run, I doubt it. Unfortunately what I regret the most is that she will also have less time to take care of the children, because they are always the ones who suffer the most. You know what I'm talking about.

I speak with Koni on the phone every week. He's in his second year at the Institute of Cinematography and enjoys it a lot. He and his dad dream that they'll make a film together when he has finished his studies. In the summer the entire Wolf family gathered by the Baltic Sea. It was completely unexpected and therefore all the more beautiful. Mischa's original plans were to go to the Black Sea, but the doctor dissuaded him. So, on the spur of the moment they joined us at the Baltic. Koni spent his whole vacation with us. He is determined to work with us once he has finished his course. We desperately need fresh minds, especially with such good training. We will have to wait a bit longer, though. His girlfriend Margot, Erna's daughter, is in Berlin, and they will probably get married. She studies biology at Humboldt University. I hear hardly anything from Lothar, because he lives on the other side and has little to do with us.

Lenochka lives self-sufficiently in Karaganda [in present-day Kazakhstan]. Last year she was sent to her mother but was recently thrown out again. She works as a draftswoman in a factory and finishes her general school education at the same time. She suddenly had a really hard time when she was pulled out of her far-too-comfortable life at the Lavrenovs, partly through her own doing, but I think she'll find her feet again and will turn into a useful human being. Koni corresponds with her; she absolutely adores him. We help her as much as we can.

So, there you have the whole family. I'm much better now too, after my serious illness. I had a bad nervous breakdown and it took me a long time to recuperate. But I'm feeling better now.

One ought to have a great deal more strength and be much younger to meet the demands of the new life. The developments here in our GDR happen at an unimaginable rate and our young people are coming along wonderfully so that soon a talented new generation will take over.

Who else of the old acquaintances is of interest to you?

Erich Weinert is still very ill. He is at home now and Li is looking after him wonderfully. I'm not in contact with many people in B. We live quite reclusively, it is far away from the city. It's wonderfully quiet there and perfect for W. to work. Hans Rodenberg manages a theater for young people. He is married. I like his wife very much and actually see her more often than Hans. Dagmar Horstmann is a teacher at the German-Soviet school. I never saw her again. If you want to know more, write to me, I'll gladly send you more information. However, I still hope that we will see each other again one day. When W. becomes a private man again, perhaps we could come and visit you. It's one of W.'s dreams to go to China.

I'm glad that the Weiskopfs are such good friends of yours. Now you are not alone any more. I'll have to go now, everyone wants something from me. Maybe I'll have time again to write before Emi's departure. If not, all the best to you! We should stay in contact now.

I gave Emi some photographs for you. Thank you for your photographs, and Emi also had some to show. My gosh, you have such grown-up boys! And now a little one as well!

Kindest regards and a big kiss,

Yours, Else

Also from me warmest wishes and all the best,

Your Wolf

Robert W. Hiatt[182]

President of the University of Alaska, Letter to Konrad Wolf, President of the Academy of Arts of the GDR

Fairbanks, December 18, 1974

Esteemed Mr. Wolf!

It is my pleasure to invite you as a guest lecturer for a visit to the University of Alaska in the forthcoming spring. Our Special Events Committee strongly recommended your visit to Alaska to share your experiences in

182. Although this letter was written in English, the original could not be located, and it has been translated here from the German edition of this volume.

the field of filmmaking and to show staff and students some of your films. We are especially interested in the films *Goya, Sterne,* and *Ich war neunzehn*.

We are certain that language will not present a problem. If necessary, several members of our staff are able to help with translation and numerous staff and students are able to speak German. While the University of Alaska cannot cover your travel expenses to Alaska, we are however able to take care of your accommodation and other expenses here. We hope that you will be able to visit not only Fairbanks but also the university campus in Anchorage and will have time to see other parts of Alaska, including the Arctic Slope region.

I do hope that you will accept our invitation. Your visit will be a great contribution to the enhancement of the understanding of art, and the time of your visit is especially favorable in light of our common national goals, which are to promote cultural cooperation.

We look forward to hearing from you soon and would be happy to accommodate your wishes with our plans and ideas.

Yours sincerely,

Robert W. Hiatt
President

Victor Fischer
Letter to Konrad Wolf and Lothar Wloch

Fairbanks, February 11, 1975

Dear Koni and Lothar!

It's wonderful!

As I have cabled Koni already, April is the perfect time for a visit. The university semester ends in mid-May, so that would be too late.

Around the 7th of April would be a great time to arrive in Alaska. We can arrange a number of screenings and discussions in Fairbanks. I will probably also arrange screenings in Anchorage. Furthermore, provided one or both of you are interested, we can fly to the Arctic coast or any other place you wish to see.

Koni—what would you like to do during your visit in Alaska?

Der geteilte Himmel [*Divided Heaven*] would be marvelous as a fourth film. As you wish.

I have written to the US Embassy in East Berlin and asked for help, if it becomes necessary. A copy of my letter is enclosed. I assume you will be able to get the films, preferably with English subtitles? If you need any kind of support from here in Alaska, please let me know and I will do my best. Should you incur any extra expenses for the mailing of or the insurance for the films, I'm sure we can figure out the money here somehow.

We are all very excited about your visit and hope that you'll bring Eva with you.

Let me know how things progress and if there are any problems with the films, visa, travel preparations, or anything else, I'm on standby and ready to help.

Love from all of us,

V.

George Fischer
Letter to Lothar Wloch

New York, February 17, 1975

Dear all, all my dears!

I hope you received my telegram last week that Koni's invitation is going to be sent this week by airmail from the City University of New York's Graduate Center (only for PhD students). I'm looking forward immensely and hope that everything works out. Because, as you know, one has to plan and arrange such things ahead of time, we have scheduled a program for Koni for the first week of April (Monday, March 31st). Every day of the week there will be one film or (on Thursday) lecture, discussion, 7 to 9 p.m. Films are being shown in chronological order of their production: *Sterne, Geteilter* [*Geteilte*] *Himmel, Ich war neunzehn,* and (on Friday) *Goya.* Sixteen-millimeter films would obviously be much better, but we'll also make something work in 35 mm format. The lecture is called "Film and Life in Communist Germany" . . . which is also the general title for Kon's visit. In our little program, which is supposed to be printed as soon as possible (hopefully this week), we provide English subtitles and the translation of Kon's lecture.

As the official invitation will state, the City University offers an honorarium of $1,000, which will cover everything.

Please reply officially to City University as soon as you can and also send me a copy so that I know where we are.

The screenings and the lecture will be advertised everywhere. How many people will hear about it and will come in the end, I don't know.

As you can imagine, in this Babylon-World there is so much going on here that people often simply don't know what is going on or at the most hear about it. I will also send Florian a copy of the actual program—I presume that it is desirable to inform him about such public details as well. If not, please call me.

I'll send our homemade program to you (Haag Street) as soon as it is printed.

Well, let's hope!!!

Yours, Yura

P.S. If you, Kon, or both, or all three of you will be in New York for March 31st, please consider arriving one or two days earlier if at all possible. Not just to have a bit of time off and so on, but also because my children will be here with me. On Sunday, March 30th, they go back to Boston, when the holidays are over.

P.S. KW film advertising texts and also the posters have safely arrived here.

Konrad Wolf
Notes from a journey through the US

1. 3rd to 30th April 1975—First impressions on the flight from Amsterdam to New York (11:30 a.m.–8 p.m. NY time):
   One feels like being in the belly of a tender boa snake
2. Relativity of the feeling of distance; the distance Berlin–New York today is like the distance between Moscow–Kaluga then;
3. Look out of the window at 10 km height and 950 km per h.—a piece of aluminum hangs in the air;
4. Descent at dark:
   "Kennedy-port" New York—disappointing.
   No sea of lights from the skyscrapers, rather more like the small garden pancakes before landing at Schönefeld.
   Planes are lining up in order to land like ducks in single file or nursery children crossing the street.
   Airport—one has to walk endlessly through a labyrinthine stronghold or bunker; will you be released from your prison into freedom or are you entering a fortress? The dreaded border control is no problem at all, only the customs officer wants to be informed about the nature of the "J-1" visa, shrugs her shoulders and smiling doesn't understand a word. Probably—as everywhere with inspectors—it was the luck of the draw.

Drive into the city, Manhattan—also very normal; highway, not too many cars; then finally a view of the city. Again somewhat disappointingly normal.

Alaska

Covers one-fifth of the USA—biggest state.

Was bought from Russia in the middle of the nineteenth century for $7.2 million—two cents per acre!

The capital then was SITKA.

Flight New York–Fairbanks: seven hours (five-hour time difference, eleven hours to Europe)

Plane flies over North Canada—a white endless area, forests, lakes. No signs of human life. And, before, over New York and its surrounding area, a crazy concentration of people. Manhattan seems small, the skyscrapers like toys. Still doesn't make an impression.

Fairbanks

It immediately feels like home—a small airport (Schönefeld, Varna). The houses here—mixture of dachas, Finnish country houses around Helsinki, and gold-digger cities from Westerns.

On a hill is a modern and smartly built university, situated outside the city.

About 5 km from there—in a forest of birches and aspens—Vitya's house. Self-designed, very practical.

Prudhoe Bay

On April 10 we fly with a little BP charter jet to where the pipeline starts, the source of the "black gold." North coast of Alaska, far above the Arctic Circle.

A beautiful jet airplane with eight seats. Below us the northern mountains, a white moon landscape.

Then a black crack, in a straight line through where the tundra starts—the new road from Fairbanks to the oil bay.

A small airport for the oil companies (there is also a large one for scheduled flights). Radiant sun and minus 30 to minus 35 degrees Celsius! A company car drives to the BP Operations Center. Shallow gravel roads connect the “points of work”—warehouse, drilling derricks, drilled boreholes, living quarters, port, and so on. Then follow strange buildings, like humongous great containers on massive steel legs—the BP Center.

One can’t believe one’s eyes, imagines being in a dream world, actor in a science fiction film—an icy, glistening snow desert only 1,500 miles from the pole; then you open a door, go up some stairs, and you’re in an Arctic Hilton hotel.

Pleasant music, warm, ultra-modern, extensive rooms with armchairs, aquarium, restaurant, swimming pool and sauna in the nicest range of colors. The living area—a corridor like in a feudalist hotel with fantastic play of color. The rooms—practical, beautiful, individual.

Everything has a calming effect, harmonious.

Damn you capitalist oil sheiks!

It was designed and built by Houston (space technology); it’s basically one of their castoffs! Long live space travel, if it benefits the ant people of the “old” Earth.

Then lunch: fantastic, and you can eat as much as you want of whatever you want, except for alcohol—*nyet*!—And all for free!

They work here about twelve to fourteen hours, seven days. After nine weeks you get two weeks off. Average salary: ten to twelve dollars per hour; according to Adam Riese that’s ca. $150 per day, $1,000 per week. $4,000–$5,000 dollars per month and free food and accommodation. *Vot svolochi amerikantsy* [Those Americans—those bastards]!

They work hard for the money, that’s for sure, but they also get something in return and not just money!

The films in Alaska (Fairbanks): shown on Saturday and Sunday, April 12th and 13th and the discussion on the 14th. Unfortunate: They can only run 16 mm films at the wonderful "Cultural Center" of the University; therefore they had to use a cinema ("Goldstream movie theater"—two auditoriums each with five hundred seats). The cinema has only a wide screen, that's why I had to explain to the audience that the "headless" film heroes are not an artistic feature, but due to the fact that the English subtitles had to be preserved. Because of the different venue considerably fewer (about 150) people, in particular fewer students than usual, came, because they only know their campus.

Saturday (April 12th) we show *Ich war neunzehn* and *Goya*. I'm terribly anxious since there are further surprises looming beside the heroes without heads—the reels have to be combined, they could get mixed up, even though I color-labeled them, foolproof . . . Everything works out.

The audience—about 150 to 200, probably mostly intellectuals, many speak German, not many students. I give a short explanation about the films in the intermission between the showings. A mammoth screening—almost five hours. I think the people are impressed and even more so on the next day, after *Sterne*. *Sterne* was the star of the program! Without doubt. Even so—it's the oldest film with many stylistic naiveties due to the time in which it was made. My assumption after checking the films in Berlin was confirmed: One shouldn't be arrogant toward older films and should watch them every now and then! Then followed *Goya*, then *Ich war neunzehn*.

Many people congratulated me from the heart. One has to however to distinguish between the German-Jewish emigrants whose own memories are stirred and the "Indigenous," who, at best, observe with curiosity the life of a different world. For them *Goya* is more interesting since the film appears beyond space and time.

Vic: "I never knew that you made such good films and that you are really a great artist."

Discussion: On Monday, April 14, from morning till evening. First a school: The German teacher has organized it, and seems to want to demonstrate their language abilities more than to discuss film art. The pupils are well "prepared" in German. Three pupils have a list of questions: How long it took to shoot the films, what it costs, what nationality are the Jews in the film (language), how do you make films, and so on. Nice young people—worlds away from real events in the world! Then three classes at the university follow: The liveliest (three hours) is with the art students; some have good individual interests (Brecht–GDR); the most reserved students are the political scientists! It's less about the films; only a few have seen them. The discussion is about factual issues and repeatedly the concept of freedom. They like the "critical view" of the capitalist system and are skeptical toward the "social path." Communism is simply and irrefutably the bogeyman. I think most of them would rather choose the lack of freedom that comes from their dependence on business and "personal-individual freedom" over the ideological "pressure," limited individual freedom within a safe material existence. Lots of speculation, stereotypes, and indeterminate ideas—you can't compare anything or just judge from tourism.

People are interested, correct, sometimes a bit too polite and reserved. Vic says that it will be different in New York—politically hotter. A pleasant tolerance is noticeable—actually everyone is free to do what he wants—the "only" limitation: You have to dance according to the law of the money. The only, but all-determining and iron law of life!

Victor Fischer
Letter to Lothar Wloch and Konrad Wolf

Fairbanks, May 3, 1975

Dear Lothar and Koni!

I'll be in Paris from June 2 to 6; that's now almost certain. I want to visit Paul in Grumbach and will come to see you in Berlin, unless you prefer to meet somewhere else. When I come depends on you and Paul. My plan is that I'll be in Berlin from May 26 to 28 or June 9 to 11, whereas the earlier date would be more convenient. If Paul isn't there I could come to Berlin from May 28 to 30. Write back soon and let me know what suits you best.

Your visit to Alaska was wonderful. Lotka—Koni must have told you about our warm and intimate conversation at the Anchorage airport. We particularly noted that the important bond between us still exists and that was, as Koni wrote, a highlight of the visit. I'm very sorry we could not establish this level of relationship from the very beginning, but maybe we simply needed more time, or needed to be alone more. In any case, it is very important to continue our friendship, to keep it alive. I am very excited at the prospect of seeing you both again and also Ev and Kristl and Holger and Koni's children.

See you soon.

Vit

Konrad Wolf
Statement upon the Withdrawal of Citizenship for Wolf Biermann

November 22, 1976

Wolf Biermann's citizenship has been withdrawn. There is an open letter concerning this action, significant because of the names and the number of signatories, that requests a reconsideration of the measures taken. I, and certainly many friends, colleagues, and comrades, whether signatories or non-signatories to this letter, are concerned about this decision.

However, as I am aware of Biermann's performance in Cologne, I cannot accept the wording in the letter that describes Biermann as an "inconvenient poet." From now on Biermann is a different person for me: not the inconvenient one, the one that sometimes goes too far (those are his words), and—as I sometimes thought—perhaps the unfairly suspected songwriter; but a man who treads a different political path from us.

I don't know how he sees himself today.—In fact, and this is my conviction, he is supporting the actions of those for whom the destruction of the socialist society is postponed but not canceled. Is there even the smallest sign that Biermann would be ready to rethink this aspect, in which lies the decisive question of life and death for every revolution?

It is about our joint cause, and I know no better answer than the one that we would find together. In this current situation, in which our enemies are trying to inflate differences of opinions into battlefronts, we should recognize our joint responsibility and not weigh one signature against another.

It wouldn't be an honest reconsideration if we—the artists and politicians—did not decide to ask ourselves, everyone in his own way, with full awareness of our political responsibility, what we are doing right and what we are doing wrong, what we can achieve and where we still have room to improve.

However, one revolutionary experience applies: We will only have the time and opportunity to work, argue with each other, and grow wiser together when the counterrevolution cannot succeed.

Konrad Wolf
Letter to Ule Lammert

November 17, 1979

Dear Ule!

I have just heard it from Lore that our Hette is no longer with us. I understand completely why I didn't get this news directly from you—I'd have done the same, because first of all one wants to be alone. At least that is how I feel . . .

Now they are not among us anymore—the three most magnificent women I ever knew: Meni, Markoosha, and Hette. As different as they all were, they did possess the gift—rare in this world—of being completely selfless, with courage and imperceptibly discreet devotion for other people. It is truly difficult to find suitable words or expressions to describe the uniqueness and determination of such persons—I'm sure you, dear Ule, will understand what I mean and how I feel at the moment. That some women almost became saints is due to this crazy time, its pain and sorrow, its beauty in battle and happiness, but also due to the brutality and injustice and greatness of men.

I loved and adored Hette, especially because she was so closely connected to Meni. My God, if only we could just keep a little of that in us which made our mothers carry themselves with so much dignity throughout their lives.

Meni suffered a great deal in her last days. Hette at least was largely spared this ordeal—not a cheap, banal consolation, but at least that way it was better for her.

Ule—I can't share your inner feelings, nobody can, but I believe I belong among those who have the right to shake you firmly by the hand! Marlis, Maja, and Mark too.

Yours Koni

Konrad Wolf
Letter to Ruth Werner

November 25, 1979

Dear Ruth Werner!

Coincidences are a funny thing: They are appealing, dangerous, stimulating, disturbing; in any case, without them life would be less worthwhile. So—as coincidence would have it—I got hold of your book only recently (it's not entirely a coincidence, since the bookseller played a part in it too, and I was only able to purchase it in a "military bookstore" on the occasion of the swearing-in of a young soldier a short while ago), and I had just been in Japan before that to seek out Richard Sorge's grave, and so on. And now I'm probably rather at the end of the line of letter writers . . . Writing a letter is something I do relatively seldom (about which my mother has complained, unsuccessfully, every now and then), since I'm rather inhibited using my mother tongue and am to this day much better at expressing my thoughts and feelings in Russian. Which is, of course, a barefaced shame for the son of a writer—but that's how it is!

To be honest, it was not without fear and prejudice that I took your book into my hands. You will probably know or suspect why. Autobiographies, memoirs, and this whole flood of—please excuse me—egocentric diarrhea brings me more pain than joy in recent times. And even more so if they are so-called authentic descriptions of the work of a spy. I need time to shake off this defensive attitude. But then I was drawn all the more into your world, your life, your thoughts, and I was relieved, really happy: It can work! It can be described when you have the skills! Because of the things we have lived through, our nerves are so easily jangled and far too deeply hidden by us, but we are not at the mercy of apathy, callous doubts, or the contemporary false bustle. Is it too pretentious if I tell you which agonizing doubts almost paralyzed me when unsuspecting friends urged me to make *Ich war neunzehn*? Nobody these days would believe how I fought against it tooth and nail! And then I couldn't stop writing, was downright taken by surprise by the response I got, how young people especially were receptive. Therefore it is up to us, and only us, whether we find the way to a new generation or not . . .

Please excuse, dear Ruth Werner, that I write about God and the world, but not about your book and its particularities. It's not easy for me and I will certainly not be able to add anything new to the numerous opinions, analyses, and finely dissecting "dismantlings" . . . You have simply written it down as you just had to write it, that is my impression. Saying that, however, is not the most unique or valuable comment. Yes—it is honest, yes—it is humble, yes—it is authentic, yes—it is courageous and so on. Yet—there is so much more in this book, and I can only express it foolishly and simply: IT IS MINE! And there is something else (which, by the way, shook me to the core about Max Clausen when I met him immediately after he stepped "into the public eye"): People can live beside you, with you, who did what they did, out of deepest conviction, and who did what they thought was correct and necessary and thereby lived through it and suffered without complaint without being, day by day, caressed and praised—and one doesn't have the slightest idea about them. You even might dismiss them; put them on a par with the gray average, and overlook, in the pile of rubbish and rubble, the little piece of gold that is a thousand times more valuable than the highly polished sheet metal that constantly thunders into your ear . . . And by that I mean so many fellow human beings, contemporaries with completely different fates from yours. So many things touched me deeply—the children (!!), the men, the nanny, of course—Moscow, the "incident" at the office with the supposed "violation of vigilance" and many more other details, the ones that are so inconspicuous yet IMPORTANT . . .

I'll stop now! And please don't take offense at my banal, vain statement that I, just in terms of subordination, as a former lieutenant, have to stand at attention before you (I too had my problems in this matter, when for example in the summer of '45 in Moscow near the Voentorg because of my shortsightedness and without my glasses, I saluted a lieutenant, but not the general, and had to do drills for five hours . . .). I stand to attention before you, but not because of rank!

Warmest regards to you and your loved ones

Koni Wolf

P.S. I'm enclosing a photograph—from Tokyo when I was there in October.

George Fischer
In conversation with Wolfgang Kohlhaase

Woodstock, New York, July 1984

[. . .] In recent years I've been writing my autobiography and for that I have made a list of my heroes. I have divided my own life into nine stages, starting with the first, the red phase, as a boy, then as a Komsomol in Moscow. Then followed a kind of pink period, which wasn't yet anti-Communist, but not full Communist any longer in the time of the cold war. Later, in the 1960s a renewed convergence with many journeys and visits to Moscow, which were for me personally exceptionally important, emotionally exciting, sympathetic but also very difficult, because I had returned to my home city and felt partially at home there, where I found old intimate friends of the family and, yet again, I wasn't at home because I was an American. Only at the end of the 1960s, when I had my inner conflict because of the Vietnam war—but not only because of that—but because deep conflicts shook the whole of America in the battle for civil rights and the so-called New Left came into existence and so I found the way to my current opinions via a kind of pedagogical reformer at the university.

The list of my chosen heroes is connected to these stages of my life. There is Eleanor Roosevelt, who was a wonderful American democrat and liberal. There is Mahatma Gandhi, a magnificent pacifist, a man of soul and fight. And because I was such an enthusiastic, deeply believing pioneer and later young Communist in the first long years in Moscow, the red years, there was of course at the top of the list Karl Marx. A great figure, somehow an almost biblical prophet and a genius theoretician of the whole modern world. Yes, he still excites me hugely, although I don't follow some of his axioms anymore. But he remains for me still a huge, rich, heroic figure. And then there is Paul Massing, the very close friend of the Berlin years, the Hitler period, from the German communist movement; then in America, with whom I shared the red and part of the pink period, the doubts and disappointments, which, however, did not lead to a complete rejection of my former beliefs. And then I needed someone for my current feelings, after I denounced the cold war and still felt very strongly for the time of my youth.

And so Koni joined my list of heroes. Koni is closest to me, a contemporary, and I have thought about him a lot. For me he is symbolic, for the great things in my own life, my aims or my hopes or the things that I don't do but that others do, and I envy and respect them for that. I never felt that so intensely as now during his visit to America. He has a love for people, a belief in people, a deep and such a warm hope. He had such a spiritual, such a holy depth or strength, which I call goodness.

This closeness to Koni showed itself during the evening at the White Horse Pub, when Koni and Lothar were in New York. We sat there for hours, talking about the whole world and its history, about our history and we felt very close to each other. Partly because we shared the Moscow past and the friendship in Berlin, partly because all three of us are some kind of world seekers; we always wanted to try and change it for the better and to be involved. And then Lothar's outburst happened because of Vietnam; he simply couldn't comprehend and share my recently changed political position. It became very dramatic and it came to an explosion. We yelled at each other, it was one of the most unusual and severest moments of my entire life and I think it was that for Koni, too, and especially for Lothar who died soon after. This moment played a great, very tragic role in his own end. Now I think a lot about my life, about the world's life, how it will continue after the cold war, where those crazy, fantastical and dangerous conflicts of the super powers will lead us to. Through my relationship with Koni, during his two very short visits, I gained new ideas, partially directly through him. What we also both shared with Lothar was a worry about the whole world, about human society. But Koni had something else and spoke about it a lot. He wanted to reach not only a small audience but the simple people, especially the young through his work and his art and to share his ideas with them. He wanted to impart his experiences, his ideals, his convictions to many people and not through slogans or dogmas. There are many wonderful decent simple people in America, with whom many critical left-wing intellectuals can hardly communicate because for them we are too complicated and isolated. I had the feeling with Koni, that he somehow understood this very well and, yes, dedicated his whole life to this cause.

Koni believed deeply in the goodness within people. And because so many people currently have the feeling that they have lost their way, and I sometimes think I'm the same, it is my hope to find a way to the hearts of people, of many people. I believe you don't have to turn the world completely upside down and rebuild it from scratch, but you do have to reach people, and I think Koni and I shared this feeling although we had different ideas on how to do it and where we could do it. This hope in the goodness in people and that you can reach people, that you have to get deeply involved in this, yes, this is my hope. [. . .]

Victor Fischer
In conversation with Wolfgang Kohlhaase

Anchorage, Alaska, July 1984

[. . .] When we were young, we were very close, happy and in high spirits. We were patriots and we cared about people, about the social order, socialism, about a fulfilling life; and we always thought: What can I do to make life the best it can be? And then we went our individual ways. When we met up again, we discovered that we actually went the same way, because: Here was Koni, who had become a filmmaker, who worked with people and who communicated through his films; he spoke in his own way about a fulfilled life.

I worked as a professor—a non-political—as a city planning researcher. I also worked to build a fulfilled country, a fulfilled city, a fulfilled society. And so we were actually the same people that we used to be. Certainly, we were then very young, never thought about where we would end up, but the ideas that we had—Koni was able to realize them and I realized them too, and we respected each other.

From the time when I arrived in Alaska, 1950, I was always interested in how close Alaska and Siberia were to each other. I read many books, professional journals—articles in English and Russian—about the development in Siberia, and I thought that the conditions and the problems there were very similar to those in Alaska. When I was in the Soviet Union I spoke with many Soviet colleagues about these problems. At that time there weren't as many professional or academic relationships as there were later. I made links with research colleagues, was invited to visit the Soviet Academy, went to the Institute for Geography in Moscow, spoke with the director of the Academic Institute, Gerasimov, went to Novosibirsk and met people from the Institute of Economic Development in Siberia, visited Irkutsk and met up with the people from the Far East Department of the Academy's Institute for Geography and I found a wonderful atmosphere of cooperation on an academic level. The other important element was the personal contact, because it gave me the opportunity to come back and work with people from a country that was an important part of my own life. And that was very good. Some Soviet colleagues have been visiting here, and they were very keen for me to return to the Soviet Union because they recognize that I can influence further cooperation. It is vital to keep such relationships alive.

Koni and I talked a lot about building a bridge, metaphorically, not a real bridge, to link people together; let's say the people of Siberia and Alaska. And in this way we would be able to tear down some of the political and bureaucratic barriers which now divide people.

I've put in my personal veto for that and have initiated in the Senate of Alaska a resolution for a nuclear free Arctic. The Senate accepted this resolution and forwarded it to the US Government. For me it would have been an important step towards peace. There are regions in the USA and other countries who have declared themselves to be nuclear free zones. Such a declaration for the Arctic, however, is still a long way off. I'm an optimist with regard to the future, because I remember 1950 when the cold war was proclaimed, when an iron curtain divided East and West. The people were then in despair and talked about a third World War. I think that everyone knows that the world can't afford an atomic war where everyone would be affected, and I think it won't happen. And so I see a better future. Someone who has experienced what the Russians experienced in the Second World War would never want to enter into a global conflict. The Americans don't have these war experiences, but in principle, the Americans don't want war. It is certain that no one in the world wants war. [. . .]

Konrad Wolf

Keynote speech given at the plenary session of the Academy of Arts of the GDR on the topic "Art and Society in the Year 2000"

Rostock, March 12, 1981

What can an artist do? I think in his work an artist can reflect the present time and contemporary history. The arts and the artists contribute to the distribution of the truth. They are involved in the communication network of human society with their creativity. They don't simply react; they create and also bring influence to bear.

But is it correct to believe that art has a monopoly on creativity and humanity, on morality and imagination? Has science no part in it? And, on the other hand, doesn't the work of an artist also demand knowledge of facts, data, and details in order to make contexts transparent? Does it not also demand discipline and rigor? Do art and science really stand on parallel tracks? In short: Isn't it a fact that the level of our ability to understand the world is in direct proportion to the individual character and the irreplaceability of both of these forms of human productivity?

From childhood, man tries to understand himself and the world in which he lives. This process of learning is linked with achievements in science and art. The most impressive evidence for this is provided by the Renaissance. The unity of art and science was later destroyed by capitalism. What besides socialism will be able to restore it?

Man must understand today who threatens peace. He must understand that even those warmongers in their own subjective self-concept are not suicidal, but that the objective processes that lead to war come from the laws governing capitalist production. And in the same way a scientist must realize into whose hands the results of his research might fall, and has to take responsibility to ensure those results serve humanity rather than destroying it, so the artist must take responsibility for his talent and his skills to make transparent the possibilities of the use and misuse of human inventions.

The increasing confrontation between political systems, which comes as no surprise considering what's at stake both for imperialism and for the future of humanity, forces the artist to question ruthlessly and unceasingly his role and position in our time. He must keep up to date with what's going on and know what there is to do. Therefore, he has to have political beliefs, and must be committed to them!

Given the growth in systems of worldwide communication, the international importance of the arts will increase. In art, man will recognize his part in world history and the social consequences of his individual actions.

The times when one didn't have to be interested in what "is going on over in Turkey" are over. Even Goethe had undermined that attitude with ironic sarcasm. Today everyone can inform themselves about what fascism looks like in Chile, about the war in El Salvador, and about the hunger in the Sahel. Information about the events, however, is one thing. The potential of art to make each individual understand that it is his own cause that's relevant in those places, and that therefore his commitment is also required, is another. [. . .]

Perhaps it's possible to imagine human life without art, but only in a Neanderthal vegetative state! For me art is the freedom to speak, write, and put into images what a humane world should look like.

The forces of peace must prevent a third world war. We artists are such forces. This is what we have in common and what forms the basis on which we can begin our discussions.

I return to my original question: Are optimism, confidence, and hope still at all justifiable today? The medium and long-term thoughts and tangible specifications of the communists in the world demand a positive answer.

This is how I understand the great political-social optimism that gives an artist the ability, today and twenty years from now, to be accountable both to history and to people. Alongside that, I want to present a much more modest, personal voice. For me she possesses considerable human greatness, since in her own way she's full of optimism. A terminally ill woman writes to a pen pal who's complaining in a letter about lamentable conditions: "You are right to complain, but the fact that you can complain and have the necessary awareness speaks to your privileged position within a global context. The older I get, the more deeply I perceive life under our conditions as a continuous struggle! What your outlook on this life is remains a question of strength. Certainly, if you don't have the feeling that changes are at least happening in small steps, that you yourself can improve things, you might as well just hang yourself! I have, no doubt, made profound mistakes, but one thing I'm almost proud of is that I never lose hope, I always get up again and tell myself: People will do it; they will learn to take control of their lives. Who gives me this hope? Shukshin, my father, Peter, Fred, your Jule, Lenin, Jesus, Christa Wolf, Tilman Fürniß from West Berlin, Ingmar Bergman, David Oistrakh, our potter, Evi and her Harry, Lao-tzu, Romain Rolland, Chagall, Heinrich Böll, Albert Schweitzer, sister Doris from my ward, our friends the Draers in Paris, Michelangelo, Aitmatov . . . I could fill seven pages with names!" And then Maxie Wander, who died in 1977, concludes her letter by saying: "To live would be a great alternative!" That says it all!

The Troika Notes

January 6, 1977

Konrad Wolf

A short description of the material, first rough ideas for a possible story. It could be called *The Troika*.

Three people at the middle of this century, three stages of their life—childhood, youth, and maturity, before and after the war, and today. "Troika," Russian for a set of three—three horses running freely, inseparably connected with each other, pulling their heavy load, or as in the encyclopedia: "way of harnessing three horses side by side. The middle horse walks at a trot, the side horses gallop."

The Photograph

It's small, intended for a breast pocket or a wallet; was taken in 1945 in Berlin-Dahlem and shows three young men: the outer ones are wearing officers' uniforms, one Soviet, one American. Between them—a man in civilian clothing. The Soviet officer wears a gala jacket with golden buttons, awards and medals, long blue pants; the American wears a comfortable everyday uniform, a sort of sporty windbreaker with long pants in the same color. The civilian wears a light leisure suit and an open-necked shirt. They stand close to each other, arms around the civilian's shoulder, who in turn has his arms around the soldiers' waists.

The "middle man" (by the way, in a troika the "middle horse" has to guide and lead the outer horses . . .) looks openly into the camera; he is of stocky build, but a bit haggard, nearly falls out of his suit. It seems as if he would attach himself to the two taller and more stable men at his side as if they were columns.

The American standing on the right is a bit too plump for his age, seems clumsy, not very military, looks to the right of the lens. The Russian on the left—tall, slim, stiff; his posture expresses something military and magnificent. He looks to the left of the camera.

Not a very meaningful photograph, perhaps just a suggestion that there was a short time in which the events of the war that they had in common connected young Germans, Russians, and Americans in friendship . . . Maybe also just some coincidental, short-lived companionship after a carousing night . . . In other words—*nothing special*, a quick glance, immediately obvious, one impression is enough . . .

But what if now there was a hint of the real authentic story of these three, the Troika? What then?

Childhood

They grew up together *in Moscow* in the 1930s, were inseparable friends, went to the same school, the same class; tested their courage in Moscow's suburban dacha colony—jump from the bridge railing into the shallow lake, jump over a self-made ski jump in the winter . . . They played dodgeball against hooligans, the Austrian Schutzbund children. They went as a group to the demonstration in Red Square, cheering for Stalin, as well as to Gorky Street for the first conqueror of the North Pole, the Soviet Union–USA North Pole route: Valerii Chkalov. One of them played in the school's marching band, a German school with the name Karl Liebknecht; he played the flute, the other two are in the choir, also songs by Ernst Busch. Once, at the Hall of Columns, together with Busch. In the tiny apartments they played the most wonderful battle games—Spain, with real "*madridkas*," a military cap from the Republicans. And then came the *separation*—incidental, inconspicuous, incomprehensible, oppressive. First their "leader" vanished, the "pilot," or, as they called him, "Chkalov"—the heart of the inseparables. Where to wasn't said—on a journey for some time . . . Then the second said goodbye, he was going to America, his *Heimat*, which he had never seen before . . . (Yes, by the way, his father was an American, a journalist in Moscow.) And the third stayed in Moscow, first a little sad, a few letters were exchanged between Moscow and New York, then—new friends, new favorite films, and . . . the war!

Youth

They met up again in the *postwar Berlin* in '45; surprising, today unbelievable, then *normal*. First the "Russian" and the "American"; they were translating for the Allied Headquarters, then suddenly they found each other at a buffet for lower ranks, the "Captain" and the "Lieutenant." There was less talking but more drinking. Then they ended up in an American jeep, roaring north through the landscape of ruins. "Abduction?" asked the Russian. "Surprise," replied the American.

Courtyards in Wedding, a damp subterranean apartment with "Hindenburg light," an emaciated figure hard to recognize—"Chkalov," their "leading horse"! Just returned from a British prison camp. He really became a pilot—on a "Focke-Wulf," Hitler's pilot . . . That has to become a "historical photograph"!

Maturity

And this is how they live *today* . . . One in Berlin, the capital of the GDR; the other one in West Berlin; the third in New York. They are about fifty years old.

It would be more correct to say: "This is how they *lived* today," because the above took place about four or five months ago, about the middle of 1976. The three lived, as said, in East Berlin, West Berlin, and New York . . . Now there are only two left, since, as of June '76, one of the three lies in a so-called anonymous grave in West Berlin!

And so the story has been brought to its natural end . . . Ten years ago, when the first idea came to assemble material from the past for a story, the "third part," maturity, i.e., the present day, was the weakest. There was little concrete material, and everything was vague. Then came the meetings, the get-togethers after many years of separation, the journey to the US, and then the strange death of the "middle man" from the photograph, the leading horse of the Troika! This death is maybe the key; it has a prequel, and no one will be able to explain it completely. But many things point to the fact that at the end of one of the lives, the inevitable and consequent tragedy of that life is wedged between the fronts. Or is this explanation too simple, too apt, and too expedient, too forced? One thing, however, is clear—from now on there is no going back, no putting it off . . . This story has to be told now; now or never! The fear is great, the fear of timidly gambling away a great opportunity, the fear of moral responsibility, even of the ethical guilt toward the one who died. Should one not wait a bit longer, especially in the current time?! Or will the fire die forever then?! If only one knew . . .

Nearly thirty years passed, half a lifetime, and everything was normal—as it should be, according to the indisputable rules of this world. Everyone just lived his life in familiar surroundings among people he knew. The emotional bonds between the Troika frayed even though the two Berliners met regularly, more often in the East and less frequently in the West. Through their meetings they continued to sustain not only the fading friendship, but also the friendship's growing disagreements and contradictions. And the Troika no longer existed anyway. Our third man, the "Yank," was far away, and not only geographically. How could it have been otherwise? It was simply the way things were!

And then came the meeting. Actually, that was very normal, too. It was only for one day, on a return flight from Moscow to New York—a stop-over at Berlin's Schönefeld airport; a day with "the Russian" in East Berlin; the middle man of the Troika joining, then taking the American with him to West Berlin; and finally, a flight out of Tempelhof the next day, back to New York. Really, it was nothing out of the ordinary.

But then came the invitation to travel to the US—an official invitation, of course, from his university. There were complications, but the West Berliner took matters into his own hands. He was determined, and applied himself as if his life depended on it. And it worked! The adventure was on again—dynamic, tangible, and ready to be experienced. The West and East Berliners flew together from Schönefeld, via Amsterdam, to New York. They spent ten days there and the memories flooded back: the years in Moscow, the postwar years in Berlin. It was all there, but it was also so far away; further away than ever . . . Everything is coming thick and fast (internally; externally, everything is as it should be: normal; tourists in New York, friends from long ago meet up again, so what . . .). However: The war in Vietnam ends; the American's mother, a living memory of that time; Manhattan—melting pot of political, social, and ethnographic contradictions—a new, a fantastic image, a shocking, stimulating version of life on this planet; a half brother appears, an old acquaintance from Moscow, a girl—of German-Jewish origin, perfect in Russian, German, with a leftist political position, and so on, and so forth. *And then the explosion happens*: The one who seeks harmony and tolerance, the one who has made mediation his motto, cannot deal with the stark contrasts and the agreement of the "outsiders," *and he erupts*. An internal rupture takes place, exposed like never before. This world of youthful dreams and desires was back again; however, this world as it used to be could not be brought into the world today. He can no longer cope. Coldness sets in between the middle man, who always stood in the center, and the wingmen, who up till now were followers. He broke off from the carriage, turned everyone away (except for one, who seems to be like a savior, in the recent past—a woman . . .). And then—death, also normal, as it should be—in the hospital, and nothing should remain of all the illusions and dreams from youth: The ash disappears into the anonymity of a common grave. The Troika has ceased to exist—without the middle man, the leading horse, there is no point to it!

Or is there . . . ?

Notes

Markus Wolf

The documents published in this book have been cautiously adapted to conform with present applicable linguistic norms. Omissions, when the content was too private or deviated too much from the topic of the book, are marked with [. . .].

The author thanks for their help while working on this book: George Uri Fischer, Elisabeth Gebauer, Margot Goldstein, Rudolf G. Greulich, Wolfgang Kohlhaase, Ule Lammert, Aune Renk, Günther Rücker, Eva Siao, Erika Tlusteck, Angel Wagenstein, and Cecilia (Zilya) Voskresenskaya. Thanks too for the documents and photographs forwarded from the Central Party Archives of the Institute for Marxism/Leninism at the Central Committee of the CPSU and the SED, the Friedrich Wolf Archive and the Konrad Wolf Archive at the Academy of Arts of the GDR, and the Princeton University Library in New Jersey.

Appendix

Curricula Vitae

Louis Fischer

1896	Born in Philadelphia, United States.
1914–16	Beginning of teacher training in Philadelphia.
1916–17	Work as teacher of English and journalism at a state school.
1917–20	Military service in a Jewish legion of the British Army. Deployment in Europe and Palestine.
1921–22	Foreign correspondent of *The New York Evening Post* in Berlin.
1922	Foreign correspondent of the US periodicals *The Nation* and *The Baltimore Sun* in Berlin and Moscow. Marries Bertha Mark. Annual travels to the US with lectures about the Soviet Union. Travel to West European countries to conduct research for reports.
1927	Publication of the book *Oil Imperialism: The International Struggle for Petroleum.*

Bertha Fischer, née Mark

1896	Born in Libava (also known as Libau, now Liepaja, Latvian SSR; modern-day Latvia).
1904–13	Studies music in St. Petersburg. Language studies at the University of Lausanne.
1915	Pianist in the United States. Meets Louis Fischer in New York.
1922	Moves to Berlin. Works at the Soviet Railroad Mission. Marries Louis Fischer.
1923–24	Birth of sons George and Victor, in Berlin.

1927 Together with her sons, she follows her husband to Moscow. Housewife as well as an interpreter for Chicherin and Litvinov at diplomatic conferences with Western countries.

1931–33 George and Victor in Berlin, then Moscow again.

Friedrich Wolf

1888 Born in Neuwied, Rhineland (Germany).

1907–14 Medical studies in Heidelberg, Tübingen, Bonn, and Berlin. Doctorate in Medicine.

1914–18 Medical officer in the Imperial Army on the Western and Eastern Fronts; member of the first Soldiers' Committee in Dresden; later, member of the Central Workers-and-Soldiers Committee, Saxony. Joins the USPD.[1]

1920–22 Elected city doctor in Remscheid, arrest because of participation in the fight against the Kapp Putsch. Lives with Else Dreibholz at the artists' colony in Worpswede, later marries her—his second marriage.

1923–28 Doctor and writer in Hechingen, Höllsteig at Bodensee, and in Stuttgart. Joins the KPD.

1931 First journey to the Soviet Union at the invitation of the Union of Soviet Writers.

1933 Emigration via Switzerland and France to the Soviet Union.

Else Wolf, née Dreibholz

1898 Born in Remscheid (Germany).

1917–18 Works at a nursery in Remscheid.

1920–22 Meets Friedrich Wolf and follows him to Worpswede. Then, marriage.

1923–25 Birth of her sons Markus and Konrad in Hechingen.

1927–28 Moves to Stuttgart. Joins the KPD.

1933 Emigrates with her sons via Switzerland and France to the Soviet Union.

1. The USPD (Unabhängige Sozialdemokratische Partei Deutschlands, known better in English as the Independent Social Democratic Party of Germany), split off from the SPD during World War I. By 1931 its membership had been absorbed into a variety of other parties.

Wilhelm Wloch

1897	Born in Berlin.
1911–14	Apprenticeship as an engraver.
1914–16	Works as molding cutter and turner at S. Bergmann Co.
1915	Joins the SPD.
1916	Military service. Serves at the Western Front.
1916–17	Works as turner at the Rumpler Company in Johannisthal, Berlin. Joins the USPD.
1917–18	Machine-gun training. Service in the Landwehr Regiment on the Eastern Front. Elected to the regiment's soldiers' committee.
1919	Participates in the revolutionary struggles in Berlin.
1919–25	Construction worker. Joins the KPD in 1920. Works for the party in the Comintern in 1925.
1933	Leaves Germany following the party's directive.

Erna Wloch, née Falkenberg

1896	Born in Berlin.
1911–18	Training as a shop assistant, afterward works in this profession for Die Konsumgenossenschaft Berlin und Umgegend (Konsum Cooperative Berlin and Vicinity).[2]
1918–21	Clerk at S. Bergmann Co. Member of the Spartacus Federation.
1921–28	Works on and off for Konsumgenossenschaft Berlin und Umgegend. As of 1924, a member of the KPD.
1923	Her son, Lothar, is born.
1928	Adopts Margot (also b. 1923) into the family as a foster child.
1928–33	Housewife. Political activities in Bohnsdorf, Berlin.
1933	Leaves Germany together with Wilhelm Wloch.

2. Die Konsumgenossenschaft Berlin und Umgegend was originally founded in 1899. After the war, the Konsum Berlin, as it was known, was the largest consumer cooperative in the GDR.

About the Contributors

Katharina Friedla is a research fellow and the Taube Family Curator for European Collections at the Hoover Institution Library & Archives at Stanford University. She has studied history and East European and Jewish studies at the Free University in Berlin and at the Hebrew University in Jerusalem, and received her PhD from the Department of History, Institute of Eastern European and Jewish History, University of Basel, Switzerland.

Before her appointment to Hoover's Library & Archives, Dr. Friedla worked as a researcher, lecturer, translator, and advisor for institutions and universities in Germany, Israel, and Poland. She has published several books and dozens of articles on nationalism, identity politics, state ideology, and forced migration in twentieth-century Europe. Most recently, she edited the book *Polish Jews in the Soviet Union (1939–1959): History and Memory of Deportation, Exile, and Survival* (Academic Studies Press, 2021).

Christian F. Ostermann is the Peter J. and Frances Duignan Distinguished Visiting Fellow at the Hoover Institution. He has served as the director of the History and Public Policy Program of the Woodrow Wilson International Center for Scholars, which has been a global leader in making public the primary-source records of twentieth- and twenty-first-century international relations from repositories around the world; training interdisciplinary groups of next-generation scholar-practitioners in archival, qualitative, and collaborative research methods; and applying new sources and history to inform public policy debates and decisions.

He directs the National Cold War Center in Blytheville, Arkansas, the future site of the National Museum of the Cold War. A specialist in Cold War archives, contemporary German history, and intelligence studies, Ostermann led the Cold War International History Project, codirected the Nuclear Proliferation International History Project, and founded the North Korea International Documentation Project. He is the author of *Between Containment and Rollback: The United States and the Cold War in Germany* (Stanford University Press, 2021), which won the Organization of American Historians 2022 Richard W. Leopold Prize and the 2022 Harry S. Truman Book Award. He is currently working on a biography of Markus Wolf. He received his PhD from the University of Cologne, Germany.

Markus Wolf was born on January 19, 1923, in Hechingen, Baden-Württemberg, Germany. In 1933, his family fled Nazi Germany, living in Switzerland and France before settling in the Soviet Union, where Wolf studied aircraft construction. After the outbreak of war between Germany and the USSR, he trained at the Comintern School in preparation for future deployment in Germany.

Following World War II, Wolf returned to Germany and worked for Berliner Rundfunk radio station. In 1945–46, he served as a reporter at the Nuremberg war crimes trials. With the founding of the German Democratic Republic (GDR) in 1949, he was appointed first counselor at the East German embassy in Moscow before being recalled to East Berlin in 1951 to help build the state's foreign intelligence service. In 1952, at just twenty-nine, he became its head. When the service was integrated into the Ministry for State Security (the "Stasi"), he oversaw its foreign intelligence division, the HVA (Hauptverwaltung Aufklärung), developing an extensive network of agents and informants.

Long known in the West as "the man without a face," Wolf's identity was publicly revealed in 1979. He retired in 1986 and later published *Die Troika*, reflecting critically on the GDR. After German reunification, he faced several trials, receiving a suspended sentence in 1997. Wolf died in Berlin on November 9, 2006.

Index